THE CULTURE
OF CLASSICISM

ANCIENT GREECE AND ROME
IN AMERICAN INTELLECTUAL LIFE,
1780-1910

CAROLINE WINTERER

THE JOHNS HOPKINS UNIVERSITY PRESS
Baltimore & London

© 2002 The Johns Hopkins University Press
All rights reserved. Published 2002
Printed in the United States of America on acid-free paper

Johns Hopkins Paperbacks edition, 2004
2 4 6 8 9 7 5 3 1

The Johns Hopkins University Press
2715 North Charles Street
Baltimore, Maryland 21218-4363
www.press.jhu.edu

The Library of Congress has cataloged the hardcover edition of this book as follows:

Winterer, Caroline, 1966–
The culture of classicism : ancient Greece and Rome in American intellectual life,
1780–1910 / Caroline Winterer.
p. cm.
Includes bibliographical references and index.
ISBN 0-8018-6799-1 (hardcover : alk. paper)
1. Universities and colleges—United States—History—19th century.
2. Classical education—United States. 3. Classicism—United States.
4. United States—Intellectual life. I. Title.
LA227.1.W56 2001
378.73'09—dc21
2001000968

ISBN 0-8018-7889-6 (pbk.)

A catalog record for this book is available from the British Library.

FOR KURT

CONTENTS

ACKNOWLEDGMENTS

It is a pleasure to acknowledge all those who have helped to shape this book. I have benefited over the years from a number of grants and fellowships. At the University of Michigan an Andrew W. Mellon Predoctoral Fellowship (1993), a Horace Rackham Predoctoral Fellowship (1994–95), an Andrew W. Mellon Dissertation Fellowship (1995–96), and a number of small travel and research grants speeded progress toward completion of my dissertation. A Spencer Postdoctoral Fellowship (1998–99) provided a year's leave for research and writing, and a faculty affiliate position and research grant from the Alice Berline Kaplan Center for the Humanities at Northwestern University (1998–99) enabled collegial interaction with other scholars in the humanities. In addition, I would like to thank my department chair at San Jose State University, David McNeil, for his support of my research endeavors over the last two years.

Archivists and librarians at the following institutions were helpful in obtaining manuscripts and printed sources: the Archaeological Institute of America, Bowdoin College, Brown University, the University of Chicago, Dartmouth College, Dickinson College, Hamilton College, Harvard University, Middlebury College, the University of Michigan, Northwestern University, Princeton University, South Carolina College, Stanford University, and Yale University.

A number of scholars generously provided me with helpful comments and criticisms of some or all of the book manuscript. I am very grateful to Anthony Grafton, Kathleen Mahoney (who heroically raked through several later drafts), Michael O'Brien, Louise Stevenson (whom I thank for suggesting the phrase "from words to worlds"), Christopher Stray, Robert Todd, James Turner, Robert Wiebe, and the two referees for the

Johns Hopkins University Press, both of whom improved the manuscript immeasurably with detailed and thoughtful evaluations. My colleague Jonathan Roth regularly demystified the world of classicists for me and was also a source of wisdom and good humor. My most effusive thanks go to James Turner, with whom I studied at the University of Michigan. Since I became his student he has been a model of intellectual generosity and personal kindness, and I am pleased, as always, to call him both mentor and friend.

A family of scholars is uniquely sensitive to the vagaries of academic life, and my own has been boundlessly encouraging over the years. I especially thank my mother, Jacqueline Mammerickx Winterer, without whose help in every respect this book could not have been completed.

THE CULTURE
OF CLASSICISM

INTRODUCTION

Next to Christianity, the central intellectual project in America before the late nineteenth century was classicism. Given our devotion to more modern concerns today, it is difficult for us to grasp how dazzled Americans were by the ancient Greeks and Romans, how enthusiastically they quarried the classical past for more than two and a half centuries. From the time of the first European settlements in Virginia and Massachusetts to the era of the Civil War, reverence for ancient models helped to structure ethical, political, oratorical, artistic, and educational ideals, sometimes overtly, sometimes subtly. Then, in the last third of the nineteenth century the classical world quite rapidly receded from its important position in American intellectual and civic life, pooling instead in the esoteric byways of elite, high culture, where it remains today. This book tells the story of how and why that happened. It is less a story of decline than one of transformation, charting how Americans over the course of the nineteenth century fundamentally changed their relationship with classical antiquity, seeking in the remote past new guides for modern life.

Curiously, for all the debates about the degree to which classical ideals shaped the ideology of the American Revolution, no one has systematically investigated the group of Americans who knew the most about the classical world: classical scholars.[1] This study focuses on those scholars and on the intellectual world they helped to create in the late eighteenth and nineteenth centuries. It focuses especially on the colleges, which were the most classically saturated venues in America for more than 250 years. From the founding of Harvard College in 1636 to the 1880s, when colleges across the nation began to drop their Greek and Latin requirements, classical learning formed the core of college education in America. While other subjects, such as mathematics, rhetoric, and moral philosophy, figured importantly in the curriculum, higher education in America through the antebellum period became synonymous with the term *classical college*. In fact, until the late nineteenth century American college students spent roughly half their time in classical studies, a program that rested on a similarly concentrated classical preparation in the grammar schools. Regardless of the classical reading that many educated Americans pursued in their adult lives, a good portion of their classical orientation rested upon the education they had received as youths. The study of Greek and Latin dominated the American college curriculum during this period, an example of extraordinary intellectual continuity during a time of wrenching ideological change. Moreover, classical scholars, who might easily make up half the faculty in the days of small colleges, formed an influential corps for the dissemination of ideas about antiquity. During a lifetime of teaching, a single professor of classical languages trained hundreds of boys and also broadcast his erudition in lectures, pamphlets, journal articles, and books directed to a broadly learned public. The schools and colleges were the nurseries of classicism until the late nineteenth century; they therefore stand as the obvious place to begin to examine the American imagination of ancient Greece and Rome during that time.

Werner Jaeger has called the educational ideal among the ancient Greeks *paideia*, defining it as the process of realizing the full potential in human nature through education.[2] His definition reminds us that classical education was at no time a narrow concept, however crabbed and deadly a curriculum might look on paper, but instead a process of molding that touched on ideals of selfhood, morality, and intellect. Since the Renaissance, Europeans had imagined the study of Greek and Latin in broad terms, as fundamental to forming ethical human beings and upright citizens. European education positioned the study of the ancient languages at the center of the curriculum because the example of antiquity was the primary path to forming individuals, a goal implicit within any pedagogy. Anyone who aspired to be truly educated in the republic of letters had to be steeped in the tradition of character formation through the study of ancient letters. This classical educational tradition resonated powerfully in America, running through the thought of ministers, statesmen, lawyers, artists, and other educated citizens. Nor was this classical influence confined only to men. American women were denied access to higher education until the second half of the nineteenth century, and only a small proportion in the antebellum era learned the ancient languages in seminaries or academies or from private tutors at home. Yet so pervasive was the habit of looking to antiquity that we find classical motifs and images forming a part of the ideological vocabulary of educated American women even in the eighteenth century. Finally, much art and civic iconography drew from a rich fund of classical imagery, part of a convention of looking to the Greeks and Romans to make sense of the present.

Within this broadly disseminated culture of classicism stood classical scholars, who arguably thought more deeply about the place of antiquity in American life than any other Americans during the nineteenth century. Classicists are routinely cast as the great villains of nineteenth-century higher education—as shuffling pedants, dull pedagogues, quixotic defenders of arid traditionalism.[3] Their apparent deficiencies have helped to banish them to the fringe of American intellectual history, although their counterparts in England and Germany are receiving ample attention.[4] We can find dreadful teachers and shoddy scholars in any sample, of course, and American classicists are no exception. But far from being bastions of intellectual conservatism, nineteenth-century American classicists were among the most innovative of American scholars during that century of change. First, they were among the earliest Americans to popularize the new historical scholarship from German universities between 1820 and 1860, when that scholarship was truly avant-garde, and to embed the new historicism into American colleges, where it helped to shape the modern ideal of a liberal education so familiar to us today. Second, as early as the 1830s they created some of the first postcollegiate training programs in America. Finally, and most importantly, they confronted some of the wrenching transformations of the nineteenth century—industrialization, materialism, democracy, specialization—and fundamentally reimagined how classical antiquity might mitigate the worst effects of those changes. I have tried to recapture the centrality of their concerns for our understanding of the nineteenth century, positioning classicists both as scholars and as Americans grappling with the momentous and troubling developments of that era.

The major argument of the book is as follows. During the antebellum era, classical scholars and other educated Americans turned from a love of Rome and a focus on classical grammar to a new focus on ancient Greece and the totality of its society, art, and literature. This shift from Rome to Greece and from words to worlds was at the most basic level a pivotal transformation in the American college curriculum. For the first time a recognizably modern canon—with new texts of old authors and a new way of reading them—appeared in higher education, gradually changing the old college of mental discipline into the post–Civil War college of liberal culture that we retain, in more or less its original form, today. More broadly, the infatuation with ancient Greece marked a change in American concepts of the formation of self and citizen. Ancient Greece, and more specifically, fifth-century B.C. Athens, grew in appeal as democracy itself became more palatable during the first half of the nineteenth century. Yet just as they embraced Greek democracy, Americans recruited classicism for a radically new purpose: antimodernism. Rather than looking to antiquity as a guide to the present, they now looked to the remote past as a way to combat such cancers of modernity as materialism, civic decay, industrialization, and anti-intellectualism. The new way of reading texts in the classical classroom was a way for students to enter fully into the classical past, to shed their modernity and imbibe the purifying, ennobling spirit of antiquity. The creation of classicism as antimodernism during the antebellum era likewise brought into sharper relief the class tensions inherent within classical study. Long viewed as the critical ingredient in the creation of the Christian gentleman, classicism by the Jacksonian era appeared especially unsuited to a flourishing market economy with an increasingly populist ethos, a dilemma that classicism's new focus on Greek democracy failed to resolve.

These trends continued in the decades after the Civil War as the small religious colleges of the antebellum era yielded influence to the great universities of the Gilded Age, with their large faculties and student bodies, their graduate programs, their scientific, quasi-secular, and cosmopolitan outlook. As the natural and social sciences gathered adherents and ideological force in the late-nineteenth-century universities, classicists were the first to propose a major critique of the ideal of social utility that many scientists advocated. Arguing that scientism and utilitarianism in education could devolve into crass materialism and an aloofness from civic concerns, classicists proposed a new ideal of culture as a form of secular perfection, a kind of truth higher and therefore more valuable than the mere getting and spending encouraged by the industrial age or the pragmatic concerns of science. Many classicists remained deeply and openly ambivalent about the business culture of the day and about intellectual specialization; they favored older conceptions of civic duty and a generally educated citizenry and promoted classicism as a cure for the cancers of modernity. Yet it was precisely these modern trends that helped classicism to weather the Gilded Age. New museums housing classical artifacts depended in part on opulent new industrial fortunes, while machinery enabled large numbers of classical artifacts to be manufactured for a growing middle class eager to acquire the patina of high culture it associated with a vanished, classically educated aristocracy. Likewise, the democratization of higher education in the late nineteenth century at once helped to consign classical study to a small province of the ever-growing curriculum while also opening it to a larger, more diverse spectrum of students than ever before. Women and blacks, for example, long denied the benefits of a gentlemanly education, turned now to classicism both as self-perfection and as social ladder.

Classicists' invocation of high culture in the last third of the nineteenth century was partly an exercise in self-preservation, a way of arguing for the ongoing inclusion of Latin and Greek in a curriculum increasingly crowded with new disciplines. In this, classicists failed: they lost their once central place in the academy, and year after year (with some exceptions) the percentage of students enrolling in Latin and Greek dropped off. Hardly anyone studies Latin or Greek anymore, and even on college campuses classical scholars are regarded as purveyors of the most truly arcane knowledge. What is more, the new historical spirit of classical inquiry that took root in the early nineteenth century ultimately helped to erode the place of the ancients in the American imagination by the end of the century. By emphasizing the cultural and chronological remoteness of antiquity—the very traits demanded by modern historicism—nineteenth-century classical scholars paradoxically enabled the abandonment of antiquity. No longer the mirror of modernity, antiquity became its antidote, a refuge from the present rather than a fund of immediately relevant political instruction. Classicism simply could not win a battle for utility and relevance anymore, for historicism and the ideal of high culture had now made classicism valuable precisely for its uselessness.

But classicists' idea of the cultured person, fluent in the humanities, represented nothing if not a huge ideological victory. The rationale for studying antiquity adopted by nineteenth-century classicists, that it ennobled the self and formed the conscientious citizen, was adopted by the other disciplines in the newly constituted humanities—modern literature, history, music, philosophy, art history—becoming central to the ideal of liberal learning we articulate today. Rather than casting classicists, the purveyors of dead languages, as the defeated armies of the nineteenth century, we should see them as the scholars who bequeathed an enduring legacy to American intellectual life: the use of classicism as a critique of modern materialism and civic degeneracy, an idea embedded in higher education through the new humanities.

This study requires us to chart a few of the more remote byways in American intellectual life. First of these is that most neglected backwater, the classical classroom. The disregard for pedagogy as a window onto the scholarly life of the past is a result of our own preoccupations with scholarship rather than teaching, our concern for the publications of professors rather than the ideas they convey to their students. These concerns, however, are anachronistic. Until the late nineteenth century, American professors would not have made such distinctions between scholarship and teaching. Their chief avenues for scholarly output were college textbooks, articles in literary and popular journals, and lectures directed at the learned public. In these venues they did not display the results of their own new research; rather, they distilled the fruits of German and English scholarship for a broadly educated American readership. Sometimes they just copied books or passages outright, with little or no attribution. It is tempting to dismiss this practice as shoddy or incipient scholarship, but this ignores the broad function of much nineteenth-century classicism. Classicists considered their output to be legitimate scholarship because it raised the level of general knowledge among students and the public.

It is thus to the archaeology of the classroom—students' marked-up textbooks, their lecture notes, and memoirs and obituaries by students and scholars—that we must look to recapture the flavor of the textual study of antiquity in eighteenth- and nineteenth-century America. But classroom learning is difficult to recover. What professors say they teach is often different from what students hear, or what they write in their notebooks, or what they say they remember learning through the rosy haze of alumni nostalgia. What is more, the classroom represents only a portion of the student's experience in college, and not always the most important part, at least by students' reckoning.[5] It is far easier, of course, to ascertain what professors hoped to teach students, and so my efforts have largely been focused here. My sources include published college curricula, lectures and journal articles on classical learning and the classical past, histories and grammars, and finally, archival materials such as faculty diaries and internal college correspondence. Among classicists, the expectation that the study of the classics would mold ethical, knowledgeable, and eloquent future citizens always loomed large. Why should students study the texts of the classical world? How should they read them? The justifications for classics teaching changed significantly between 1780 and 1910 in a way that reveals the study of antiquity to have been of momentous concern to many American scholars throughout the nineteenth century.

Besides teaching, another major branch of the classical tradition in America was classical scholarship. In Renaissance and early modern Europe some of the greatest scholars had been classicists because knowledge of Rome and Greece was believed to lie at the core of true erudition. The ancients attracted the attention of Europeans like a magnet. Anthony Grafton, Joseph Levine, and Francis Haskell, among others, have shown the passion with which topics from antique coins to pots and vases were discussed in Europe.[6] Among the most compelling aspects of the study of antiquity was classical philology, the critical study of ancient texts. Newly attentive to the texts inherited from the ancient world, scholars in Renaissance and early modern Europe attempted to reconstruct them in their ancient authenticity by paying attention to textual clues and linguistic guides. Some of these scholars came to embody erudition in the early modern world. Joseph Scaliger, Isaac Casaubon, and Richard Bentley, for example, stand out as giants of early modern scholarship.

The practice of classical scholarship was inseparable from the debate over the nature of erudition and knowledge. Such debates among classicists and other scholars illuminate the contours of scholarship in this formative era. Americans knew that erudition was a two-edged sword, for it was easy to cross the boundary between learning and pedantry. The faults of classical scholars—their vanity, their aridity, their swollen and forbidding tomes on remote subjects—were legendary in the republic of letters.[7] It is no surprise that George Eliot chose the name Casaubon for the passionless, pedantic classicist in her novel *Middlemarch* (1871–72). But what was the nature of the good scholar? Should he confine himself to a narrow field of learning or cast generously about? What was the correct way to present erudition to others, and which ways were insulting? What was the function of the scholar in his narrow coterie of colleagues, and what were his duties to himself and to the larger society? These questions engaged the learned community in Europe and America for centuries and frequently found expression in discussions of classical scholarship. The content of scholarship and the duty of scholars were overlapping discourses, and they can reveal the transformation of American ideals of scholarship from the general learning valued in the eighteenth century to the specialization so prized in the twentieth.

For classical scholars, these were especially critical decisions because knowledge of Greek and Roman antiquity had stood for so long at the center of learned European and American discourse. When the example of antiquity began to recede in the popular and scholarly imagination during the late nineteenth century, classical scholars struggled with the implications of the retreat from generalism and the classical learning that had been so integral to the ideal of the citizen. Yet they did not snub specialization, for they recognized its benefits for the study of antiquity. The fate of classical antiquity in the late nineteenth century, then, complicates our understanding of the shift toward modern scholarship, where classicism is so often painted as a dinosaur lumbering inevitably toward extinction. For a while in the late nineteenth century a number of classicists advocated models of advanced training in higher education that blended specialization and generalism in a way that they hoped would preserve older models of learning while also welcoming the exciting new results of modern scholarship. These models failed, but they represented a compelling alternative to the specialization advocated by many of the other university builders and point to a critical moment in the renegotiation of models of scholarship.

Finally, Americans' changing approach to the classical world can illuminate another important shift, from the religious colleges of the eighteenth century to the secular universities of the twentieth century. Christianity had emerged in the classical world of late antiquity, and thereafter erudition had combined, albeit uneasily, reverence for Greek and Roman pagans with Christian ends in a synthesis known as Christian humanism. This complex was transferred to American higher education in the seventeenth century and remained integral to it until the late nineteenth. However zestfully they might read the ancients, the majority of American Protestants until the late nineteenth century were committed to the literal truth of the Bible and the superiority of Christian revelation to the paganism that had preceded it. These two traditions, the Christian and the pagan, the biblical and the classical, nevertheless coexisted in American higher learning throughout the century. Athens and Jerusalem had everything to do with one another, although they occasionally conflicted. In the pages that follow I examine some of the encounters between religion and classicism in higher education. Significantly, there was a change in the approach to both classicism and religion in American higher education in the mid-nineteenth century. The secularization of the academy resulted from a number of forces that also altered the way Americans viewed classical antiquity. Modern historical scholarship undermined both the idea of biblical literalism and the insuperable authority of classical texts, lessening the immediate relevance of the biblical and classical traditions by the beginning of the twentieth century.

We no longer live in a classical world as Americans did until the late nineteenth century. Our concerns now lie elsewhere, even though the remains of the Greeks and Romans are more abundant and accessible than ever. The ancients have stayed with us in more subtle ways, however, most especially in the modern ideal of the cultured citizen. If we no longer gaze into the mirror of antiquity as earlier generations did, we remain nonetheless illuminated by its example.

1

ANTIQUITY IN
THE NEW NATION

A LITERATE MINISTRY

Classical antiquity arrived in the New World with the Europeans. Though removed from the ancient Greeks and Romans by about two thousand years, Europeans of the sixteenth and seventeenth centuries conveyed across the Atlantic a habit of venerating the glories of the classical world, of viewing the exoticism of the new within the framework of the old. When sixteenth-century Spaniards beheld the Inca capital of Cuzco, they thought of ancient Rome and embellished the New World city accordingly in sketches and descriptions. The British settlement of North America was equally indebted to the example of the ancient Mediterranean. Convinced that the Renaissance revival of classical learning had prepared the world for the Protestant Reformation, British colonists placed the ancient authors at the core of their ideals of civility, learning, and piety. The examples of Plato, Aristotle, Cicero, Virgil, Ovid, and others filled seventeenth-century courtesy manuals, sermons, and rhetorical and educational ideals, imbuing the new colonies with the classical outlook of their European origins. "In crossing the Atlantic Ocean," a colonist paraphrasing Horace wrote, "we have only changed our climate, not our minds, our natures and dispositions remain unaltered."[1]

Education in the colonies reflected this preoccupation with antiquity, making the education of Christian gentlemen essentially synonymous with classical learning. "Us from Virgil did to David train," wrote the Puritan divine Cotton Mather (1662–1727) of his teacher's program of study.[2] In the settlements of early Virginia and Maryland primary education remained necessarily scattered, but it flourished in New England, where towns immediately moved to open schools. By 1647 there were nine grammar schools in Massachusetts alone.[3] The curriculum used by schools and private tutors was fairly standard, modeled on the progression of studies in contemporary English schools. It emphasized Latin, with more modest offerings in Greek and Hebrew, usually with an eye to the language-intensive entrance requirements of Harvard, the only college in America until the end of the seventeenth century. Boston's two public grammar schools were the most rigorous. Boys beginning to learn Latin used an *accidence*, a book that explained how to decline nouns and adjectives, conjugate verbs, and the like; the *nomenclature*, essentially a Latin-English dictionary, helped with vocabulary. Next, students began to study short phrases and dialogues, which they orally construed and parsed. The fragments and conversations in books like the *Sententiae Pueriles* (Sentences for boys), the *Disticha Catonis* (Sayings of Cato), the colloquies of the sixteenth-century Protestant schoolmaster Corderius, and Aesop's fables were baldly moralizing, befitting a study that was intended to encourage ethical behavior and to teach grammar. Greek was studied far less, though in a similar way. By the fourth year of grammar school, boys were beginning to read simple classical texts, usually Ovid's *Tristia* and *Metamorphoses* and Cicero's epistles, in later years progressing to Cicero's *Orations* and Hesiod. They practiced writing dialogues, scanning verse, making verse, writing themes, and turning themes into declamations. They translated, turning Latin into English and then English back into Latin. Grammar schools and private tutors throughout the northern and southern colonies followed a similar if sometimes less rigorous program.[4]

Like the grammar schools, institutions of higher education in America grew from English models, a product of the impressive concentration of university men among the original migrants to North America. By 1646 the Puritan migration had brought 130 men educated at Cambridge and Oxford.[5] More than one hundred of the clergymen in Virginia between 1607 and 1685 had been educated at one of the two British universities (and sometimes at both).[6] By the seventeenth century Oxford and Cambridge had absorbed the new learning of classical humanism, which sought in the original writings of the ancients, especially the Greeks, new authority in philosophy and science to challenge the medieval curriculum.[7] The first American college, and the only one for more than half a century, was Harvard College, founded in 1636. Its curriculum, like that of Oxford and Cambridge, stressed the three learned tongues, Latin, Greek, and Hebrew, and it was staffed entirely by clerics. Other subjects of study were logic, mathematics, rhetoric, politics, divinity, and natural philosophy. Entering students had to demonstrate their ability to "read Tully [Cicero], or such like classicall Latine Author ex tempore & make & speak true lattin in verse & prose, suo (ut aiunt) Marte [by his own exertions]; & decline perfectly the Paradigmes of Nouns & Verbs in the Greek Tongue."[8] In the mid-seventeenth century the course of study continued this emphasis on ancient languages: each year students studied Latin, Greek, and Hebrew.[9] Academic exercises, such as the lecture, the declamation, and the disputation, reinforced the classical message. In the declamation, for example, in which they formally and systematically argued a position, students deployed classical authors not only for the substance of the argument but to pepper the delivery with apt or witty quotations.[10]

A century later the language curriculum had hardly changed, an example of the intellectual constancy that characterized American college education into the mid-nineteenth century. By 1746 three new colleges had been founded in the American colonies—William and Mary (1692), Yale College (1701), and the College of New Jersey (Princeton, 1746); the number increased to nine in 1776 and to twenty-five in 1800.[11] Geographically and religiously diverse, they were remarkably uniform in their classical curriculum and their classically based admission requirements. Between 1790 and 1800 the admission requirements at Williams, Brown, King's College (Columbia), Yale, and Harvard remained nearly identical; all required that students be able to read Cicero, Virgil, and the New Testament in Greek.[12] The curriculum that students pursued over the next four years mirrored this classical focus. At Princeton in 1753 freshmen studied Xenophon, Cicero's *De Oratore*, and Hebrew grammar; more advanced work included Cicero's orations, Horace, and Homer; and graduating seniors took examinations in Hebrew, the New Testament (which they referred to as the "Greek Testament"), Homer, Cicero, and Horace.[13]

This resembled the curriculum at South Carolina College half a century later, where in 1801 freshmen read the Greek Testament, Virgil's *Aeneid*, Cicero's political orations, and Xenophon's *Cyropaedia*, sophomores read Homer's *Iliad*, juniors read Longinus's *On the Sublime* and Cicero's *De Oratore*, and seniors read works by Demosthenes.[14] Given the limited range of other college offerings even by the mid- to late eighteenth century—mathematics, natural and moral philosophy, and rhetoric—classics occupied proportionally a large amount of students' time. Moreover, the small number of total faculty, often just one or two, plus a few tutors at most, meant that those teaching classical languages formed a proportionally large constituency on the campus.

The curriculum built on classics, logic, theology, philosophy, and moral training reflected the prevailing function of colleges in the colonial era, which was chiefly to train a learned ministry. Although the preparation of gentlemen for responsible governance was also a goal, in terms of sheer numbers ministerial schooling remained the primary function of colleges until the mid-eighteenth century. Of the 130 original university men who settled in New England, 98 were ministers; just under half the alumni of Harvard through the seventeenth century became clergymen.[15] Even in 1750 around 40 percent of Harvard, Yale, and Princeton alumni went on to the ministry.[16] The founders of Harvard had declared their ambition to advance learning in general and more especially to train a ministerial class: "After God had carried us safe to *New England* . . . One of the next things we longed for, and looked after was to advance *Learning* and perpetuate it to Posterity; dreading to leave an illiterate Ministery [*sic*] to the Churches, when our present Ministers shall lie in the Dust."[17] The whole course of study and of campus exercises pointed to godliness as the chief goal of education. According to an early Harvard pamphlet, the main end of study was for a student "to know God and Jesus Christ which is eternal life, . . . and therefore to lay Christ in the bottom, as the only foundation of all sound knowledge and learning."[18] Students read Scripture twice a day and were exhorted to behave soberly on campus.

The focus on ministerial training influenced the choice of Greek texts used in American colleges into the early nineteenth century, in which Hellenistic rather than classical ("heathen") Greek occupied the bulk of students' time in Greek language education. Classical Greek had three major dialects: Ionic, Aeolic, and Doric. Ionic (or Attic) Greek became the literary dialect used by the philosophers, playwrights, and orators of Athens during the fifth and fourth centuries B.C., the so-called Golden or Periclean Age. From the end of the fourth century Ionic Greek absorbed parts from other Greek dialects as Greek became the language of trade in the Mediterranean. This Greek dialect, called koine (the Greek word *koinos* means "common"), together with some Semitic elements, formed the Greek used in the New Testament.[19] The Greek Testament remained a staple of American college admission requirements and of collegiate study for more than two hundred years, and the time devoted to it far surpassed that devoted to other Greek texts, usually portions of Homer, Hesiod, Demosthenes, and Isocrates. This is not to say that students could not read classical Greek texts on their own. A number of seventeenth-century Harvard students owned Jean Crespin's fat, annotated collection of Greek poets, which included Hesiod, Theognis of Megara, Phocylides, Pythagoras, Theocritus, Bion, and Moschus, all with a Latin translation on the facing page.[20] The college library owned works by Demosthenes and Herodotus by 1682; one freshman purchased an edition of the tragedies of Sophocles in 1676; another student owned Homer's *Iliad;* Euripides and Aristophanes appear in the library catalog of 1723.[21] But from the evidence in college catalogs, it appears unlikely that these works were studied in the classroom, where Greek lessons remained devoted to churchly purposes.

So indebted to classicism was this godly education that many Protestant ministers happily reconciled the ethics of the heathens with the morality of Christianity. Their general attitude was that the great Greek and Roman philosophers and moralists had groped near enough to Christian truth that their message could be profitably adopted by modern Protestants. The Greek and Roman authors yielded up such a rich store of learning as to be irresistible, and their wisdom seemed to carry examples of timeless, universal truth. American ministers remained vigilant, however, aware that even the best of the ancients fell short of the Christians. Like Dante, who stowed virtuous pagans like Socrates and Cicero in the first circle of hell, they were loathe to imagine heathens ascending to the Christian paradise. In 1655 Harvard president Charles Chauncey (1592–1671) defended the classics as sources of Christian ethics against those who had argued for an exclusively scriptural education for ministers. There were "certain principles of trueth written," argued Chauncey, "even in corrupt nature, which heathen authors have delivered unto us, that doe not cross the holy writ."[22] Colonial sermons were filled with classical citations and examples of classical philosophy.

This embrace of heathen wisdom was not universal, however, and fears for the corrupting influence of the Greeks and Romans on tender minds persisted well into the nineteenth century. In the late seventeenth century the Massachusetts merchant Robert Calef deplored "the pernicious works of pagan learning" in Virgil, Ovid, and Homer. "If I err, I may be shewed it from Scripture or sound reasoning, and not by quotations out of Virgil."[23] Some pious students concurred. Appalled that the heathen poets ascribed "those Things unto the *False Gods* of the *Gentiles,* that could not without *Blasphemy* be ascribed unto any, but the *Holy One of Israel,*" some students amended objectionable passages in oral recitations to their tutors.[24] Such fears remained pronounced in the late eighteenth century. In 1769 John Wilson, a teacher in the Friends' Latin School in Philadelphia, called classical learning "the grossest absurdity that ever was practiced," charging that it "contributed more to promote Ignorance, Lewdness & Profanity in our Youth than anything I know besides."[25] The Congregational minister Timothy Dwight (1752–1817) waged a long battle against the authority of Homer in American schools and intellectual life, publishing his epic *The Conquest of Canaan* (1785) to displace the *Iliad* as America's ideal epic. Later, as president of Yale, he discouraged Homer from being taught on Mondays lest students turn to the bard rather than the Bible on Sundays.[26]

THE CULTURE OF CLASSICISM

Perhaps the most important feature of classical education in America, especially after the mid-eighteenth century, was that it formed part of a culture of classicism that permeated not only the college curriculum and campus rituals but also numerous areas of American life, blending seamlessly with politics, literature, and art. Classicism was an important part of what Thomas Bender has called the "civic culture" of the eighteenth century, in which Americans participated in a decentralized, cosmopolitan republic of letters. Educated Americans in the late eighteenth century promoted not only institutions like colleges but also numerous organizations for civic improvement, such as libraries and societies for the promotion of "useful knowledge." These organizations depended not on disciplinary specialization but on an ideal of a generally learned citizenry.[27] Central to the culture of classicism was the mid-eighteenth-century proliferation of print, which helped to disseminate the number of classical allusions, images, and motifs available to Americans, whether those Americans had attended college or not. Whereas in 1720 there had been only nine master printers in the colonies, by 1760 forty-two flourished. More newspapers were founded in the 1790s than had been established in the entire preceding century.[28] With the expansion of print came the expansion of the public sphere, an arena of newly impersonal political discussion. Implicit and explicit classical images and motifs, such as in the title of Noah Webster's short-lived newspaper, *American Minerva* (1793–97), poured into these debates and were thereby disseminated to a growing reading public. But print was far from the only medium through which Americans could acquire a knowledge of antiquity. Let us look at the various manifestations of the culture of classicism in Revolutionary and early national America to see how it could resonate in a number of arenas.

The cradle of classicism in America had always been the colleges, with their classically saturated curricula, but in the mid-eighteenth century graduates slowly began to change the function to which they put their classical learning, making it more overtly political. This shift had something to do with the career trajectories of college graduates. By the mid-eighteenth century colleges has ceased to be primarily training centers for future ministers and instead served as what James McLachlan has called "pre-professional schools" for the emerging professions. In mid-eighteenth-century Princeton, for example, 75 percent of the students in twenty-one graduating classes went on to become lawyers, ministers, or doctors.[29] The colleges likewise served as training grounds for the ideological architects of the American Revolution and its aftermath. Although there were only about three thousand college graduates in America at the beginning of the Revolution (in a population of 2.5 million), these alumni formed an absolute majority in important arenas like the Constitutional

Convention of 1787. Of the fifty-five men who attended, thirty-one were college graduates.[30] College-educated men continued to be well represented in politics during the years of the early republic. Sixty-three percent of the higher civil service appointees of President John Adams (1735–1826) had attended college, as had 52 percent of those appointed by Jefferson. Both felt strongly that a college education was indispensable for government officers.[31]

It was especially among classically educated lawyers that the newly political ends of classicism became obvious. The great literary and ideological ferment of the late eighteenth century arose disproportionately among American lawyers, whose education was firmly rooted in the classical tradition. Their contributions to an increasingly secular political, oratorical, and literary culture after 1750 challenged the clergy's dominance in American intellectual life and allowed classical erudition to be deployed for political as well as religious ends.[32] They used their classical learning in a number of ways. Most importantly, they hitched literature to politics, words to action, knowledge to liberty. "Let us tenderly and kindly cherish, therefore, the means of knowledge," wrote the lawyer John Adams in 1765. "Let us dare to read, think, speak, write."[33] The lawyer James Kent in 1794 urged lawyers to turn to the Greek and Latin classics to master "the whole circle of the arts and sciences" as well as "the general principles of Universal Law." Books used for training lawyers deployed the ancients to teach legal theory. Law students into the 1830s used David Hoffman's *Course of Legal Study* (1817), which referred to Cicero, Seneca, Xenophon, and Aristotle to help give budding lawyers "every species of knowledge" that they might need. Lawyers depended not only on Ciceronian oratorical skills but also, more broadly, on the early republican ideal of Ciceronian eloquence as the guarantor of liberty. The model lawyer-citizen joined political themes to public eloquence. The classics, affirmed the lawyer Rufus Choate in 1844, formed "'a library of eloquence and reason,' to form the sentiments and polish the tastes, and fertilize and enlarge the mind of a young man aspiring to be a lawyer and statesman."[34] Moreover, the finest Greek philologist in the early republic by many counts was not a college professor but the Boston lawyer John Pickering (1777–1846), author of the *Comprehensive Lexicon of the Greek Language* (1826).

Just as a classical education had buttressed ministerial training in the seventeenth century, so after the mid-eighteenth century it increasingly supported the political ideology of classical republicanism. Above all else, eighteenth-century classical learning was intended to be useful; it provided, in the famous words of Patrick Henry (1736–99), the "lamp of experience" for the Revolutionary generation. Central to this conception of the function of the classical past was the Enlightenment theory of history, which suggested to eighteenth-century Americans the immediate relevance of antiquity to their own lives.[35] Americans of the Revolutionary generation believed they shared with the ancients what Joseph Levine has termed an "imagined affinity," which made classical example crucial for anyone devoted to public affairs.[36] Indeed, it made the classical past appear almost timeless: what mattered to eighteenth-century moderns was not the gap of time that separated them from the ancients but the proximity of example that united them. This philosophy of history was most neatly encapsulated by Lord Bolingbroke's *Letters on the Study and Use of History* (1752), often quoted by Americans, in which he asserted history's use as a guide to the present. "To teach and to inculcate the general principles of virtue, and the general rules of wisdom and good policy . . . always should come, expressly and directly into the design of those who are capable of giving such details: and therefore whilst they narrate as historians, they hint often as philosophers."[37] The classical past shaped the cyclical narrative arc of the present time, suggesting to moderns the path of vice as well as the road of virtue. "Accurate information of every thing appertaining to the ancient nations of Greece; to the Romans; and the Carthaginians . . . would be of inestimable value to us in the administration of our republic," argued a contributor to the *Port Folio* in 1816, "by teaching us what it would be safe to imitate, and what it would be prudent to avoid."[38]

College textbooks reinforced the lessons of classical history, urging students to study the past "as in a faithful mirror."[39] One commonly used college textbook in the late eighteenth and early nineteenth centuries was *Roman Antiquities*, by the Scottish schoolmaster Alexander Adam (1741–1809), who hoped "to impress on the minds of youth just sentiments of government in general, by showing on the one hand the pernicious effects of aristocratic domination; and on the other, the still more hurtful consequences of democratical licentiousness, and oligarchic tyranny."[40] Adam's dire warning showed that classical history especially supplied Americans of the early republic with the cautionary tales central to classical republican political theory: that republics were fragile entities suspended perilously in time and that balanced governments depended upon the civic virtue of their citizenry to withstand corruption, private ambition, and dependence, the relentless forces of decay. Caleb Strong (1745–1819), the Federalist governor of Massachusetts during the presidency of Thomas Jefferson, recruited classical antiquity to illustrate the precariousness of modern felicity. "In modern republicks of Europe, the scenes, which were formerly displayed in those of Greece and Rome, have been repeated. . . . Let us take warning from their errours and misfortunes; and may Heaven preserve us from a similar destiny."[41]

The overwhelming preference for Rome over Greece in the American imagination of the eighteenth and early nineteenth centuries rested on this imagined affinity between antiquity and modernity. Americans found a number of interlocking features in republican Rome congenial: the Senate as guarantor of liberty and stability; the ideal of the cultivated, virtuous Ciceronian orator; and agriculture as safeguard to civic virtue. William Smith (1727–1803), the immigrant Scottish clergyman best known for his pamphlet *A General Idea of the College of Mirania* (1753), noted that in American studies of ancient history "everything between Augustus and the beginning of the sixteenth century is past over."[42] Educated Americans turned to didactic historical works that reinforced such views of the applicability of republican Rome to modern America: the French Jansenist Charles Rollin's *Ancient History* (1730–38) and *Roman History* (1738–41) and the Englishman Oliver Goldsmith's *Roman History* (1769), all reprinted a number of times in eighteenth-century America.[43] Moreover, Rome's descent into corrupted empire supplied Americans with cautionary tales about the fragility of civic virtue. "But of all the ancient Republicks," wrote Edward Wortley Montagu, in his widely read *Reflections on the Rise and Fall of the Antient Republicks* (1757), "Rome in the last period of her freedom was the scene where all the inordinate passions of mankind operated most powerfully and with the greatest latitude. There we see luxury, ambition, faction, pride, revenge, selfishness, a total disregard to the publick good, and an universal dissoluteness of manners, first make them ripe for, and then compleat their destruction. Consequently that period, by shewing us more striking examples, will afford us more useful lessons than any other part of their history."[44]

Americans similarly used the history of the ancient Greek republics as counterexamples, viewing them as sites of a giddy, fluctuating mobocracy and dangerously destructive interstate war. Such views emanated from the English histories of ancient Greece commonly read by Americans in the colonies and early republic: Temple Stanyan's *Grecian History* (1739), Oliver Goldsmith's *Grecian History* (1774), John Gillies' *History of Greece* (1786), and William Mitford's *History of Greece* (1810). Sparta was partially immune from these negative assessments, for its disciplined soldier-farmers seemed to be suitable exemplars for America's young agrarian republicans.[45]

In addition to instructing statesmen and professionals, a formal classical education formed an essential ingredient in the alchemy of the gentleman, supplying the indefinable acquisition that distinguished him from the masses. As in Renaissance Europe, it was widely believed that only the liberally educated man possessed the apparently effortless command of classical style and allusion, the eloquent prose and diction that marked the bearer of gentlemanly status. One favorite book in boys' gentlemanly education, for example, was the *Colloquies* of Erasmus (1466?–1536), a collection of "prompte, quicke, wittie, and sentencious" classical phrases that they could brandish insouciantly at the appropriate moment in writing or conversation.[46] An anonymous writer in Philadelphia's *Port Folio* distinguished in 1815 between the rabble of the commercial classes and the gentleman: "It is not the ordinary accomplishments of the counting-house that qualify a man to appear with becoming dignity in that exalted station [the statehouse]."[47] Indeed, a classical education distinguished the true gentleman from the impostor or the arriviste. The benefits of a classical education were especially obvious in oratory. Aristotle, Quintilian, and Cicero all had insisted on the link between rhetoric and moral wisdom, and such sentiments were reiterated into the nineteenth century. The classical language professor John Popkin (1771–1852) linked gentlemanly status to eloquent rhetoric in 1823:

In pleading, says Cicero, though we do not always employ the liberal arts, yet the hearer immediately discovers whether we understand them; and the benefits of classical literature, though not always brought forward by the possessor, are never long concealed. . . . In our literary compositions, in our public speaking, and in our familiar conversation, it will always contribute to the clearness and precision of our ideas, and, to the correctness and elegance of our language.

The classically educated man, in sum, "enjoys that consciousness of superiority" over those deprived of classical education.[48] These assumptions accounted for the clubbiness created by a classical education, a set of common values cloaked by an aura of ineffable accomplishment.

Knowledge of the Greek and Roman classics was especially important in the gentlemanly culture of the South through the antebellum era. There especially, Richard Lounsbury has observed, "antiquity was not something you received or enjoyed only; it was something you did."[49] Because there were few colleges in the South, boys of genteel families were often tutored at home, after which they went off to northern colleges or to England. From the metronomic reading of Greek and Latin that characterized the daily ritual of the planter William Byrd of Westover (1652–1704) to the all-encompassing classicism of Thomas Jefferson (1743–1826), southern gentlemen perceived the immediate utility of ancient example in their politics, their architecture, and their professional and domestic affairs. Philip Greven has described the gentlemanly education of George Washington's stepson, John Parke Custis, in the late eighteenth century. With his tutor and then at King's College (Columbia) young Custis was urged to acquire through a "liberal, manly" classical education what his tutor called "that easy that elegant that useful Knowledge which results from an enlarged observation of Men and Things."[50]

A monument to the expansive classicism that southern culture could produce was the learned and beautifully illustrated book *Grecian Remains in Italy* (1812), by the wealthy South Carolina planter John Izard Middleton (1785–1849). The son of Arthur Middleton, a signer of the Declaration of Independence and a member of the Second Continental Congress, the younger Middleton grew up in Arcadian splendor at Middleton Place, where the gardens had been designed by a French botanist and the library was stocked with rare books, engravings, and watercolors.[51] On his grand tour of Italy, accompanied by the English antiquarian and artist Edward Dodwell, Middleton painted a series of serene views of the Roman landscape, dotted with toppled columns. The accompanying text was critical and learned, citing and comparing with "laborious research" the various testimonies of ancient and modern authorities, and sprinkled with Greek and Latin quotations. Nonetheless, this was no scholar's dry tome; it was produced "to give the public an accurate idea of objects so highly worthy of their notice."[52]

Though politically, socially, and professionally useful to gentlemen, the classical tradition was problematic for women. Classical republican thought, acquired through direct reading of the ancients and through modern filters such as Montesquieu (1689–1755), identified the political sphere with the masculine virtues of independence and self-reliance, qualities that shielded the fragile republic from corruption. In this formulation women threatened the masculine political sphere: their ostensibly more emotional, passionate natures, their devotion to luxury above self-denial, and their economic dependence were linked to political corruption and therefore posed a threat to the republic. Moreover, the skills required in political life—eloquent speech, appropriate historical allusion, and the like—were imagined as fundamentally masculine skills. "Let the parent . . . fortify his [son's] soul with that masculine energy, . . . that manly and dignified eloquence that becomes the advocate of liberty and independence," counseled one schoolteacher in 1815.[53] In the Renaissance, the acquisition of Latin was part of a boy's puberty rite, something he did partly because it was difficult and therefore exclusive.[54] A woman of great classical learning risked becoming dangerously unfeminine, what authors variously called *virilis femina, une homasse* (man-woman), a virago.[55] Such fears echoed in colonial and early national America, where authors warned readers to beware of what the minister and classics teacher John Sylvester John Gardiner (1765–1830) called "women of masculine minds."[56] "I know no way of rendering classical knowledge ridiculous," affirmed an anonymous writer in 1793, "as by cloathing it in petticoats."[57]

Iconographic tradition, which by the late eighteenth century represented the nation as a classical woman, spoke volumes about the politically exclusive effects of classical republic thought. Though Revolutionary America was represented in civic ceremony and iconography by such classical goddesses as Columbia, Liberty, and Minerva, flesh-and-blood women by contrast enjoyed few civic rights. Mary Ryan has argued that these female symbols of public ideals performed two necessary functions in classical republican thought: they deflected private male interests from the civic sphere, on the one hand, while also reaffirming the sexual difference that warranted women's exclusion from actual participation in public life.[58]

Even the most erudite women of the late eighteenth century, such as Abigail Adams (1744–1818), Judith Sargent Murray (1751–1820), and Mercy Otis Warren (1728–1814), were schooled only haphazardly, if at all, in classical learning. Warren, for example, whose brother attended Harvard, was herself taught at home only by his tutor, though with him she read some classical literature in translation.[59] After the establishment of female academies and seminaries, girls' formal schooling offered comparatively little classical instruction because that knowledge was believed to be masculine. Latin and Greek were not routinely offered in female academies and seminaries until the mid-nineteenth century.[60] This practice had been commonplace since the Renaissance, when humane letters were encouraged among women as virtue-building busywork, a kind of verbal embroidery, but their advanced pursuit in public discourse was discouraged lest women appear "threateningly insane and requiring restraint," as one fifteenth-century Italian humanist put it.[61] Though occasionally offered in the spirit of elegant ornament, by the antebellum era the classical languages and history were viewed in women's academies as useful teachers of virtue and of the comparative superiority of biblical history. Educators also hoped that adding classical study would increase their schools' visibility and prestige. It is unclear whether southern or northern academies offered more Latin to young women during the antebellum era. Christie Farnham has argued that it was more prevalent in the South, noting that in the North a classical education "was a threat to sex segregation in the workforce; in the South it was emblematic of high social status."[62] By contrast, Kim Tolley, who used a larger sample size, found that Latin appeared in only 21 percent of North Carolina girls' schools between 1820 and 1830 but in twice that many in Connecticut, Massachusetts, New York, and Maryland between 1820 and 1842. She has speculated that southern social conservatism may have delayed the penetration of Latin into southern girls' schools.[63]

Despite their rarity in politics, civic ceremony, and classical schooling, however, women of the eighteenth and early nineteenth centuries did in fact have frequent commerce with the classical past, just as they did with history *in toto*. A number of American women were prodigious, imaginative readers who constructed a rich mental life despite their exclusion from a college education. This was increasingly the case after the middle of the eighteenth century, when women turned from primarily religious reading—the Bible, psalm books, and other devotional works—to more secular subjects, such as history, biography, travel literature, journals, and fiction.[64] Some, like Catharine Macaulay (1731–91) in England and Mercy Otis Warren in the United States, were actually writers of history, while others, such as Elizabeth Carter (1717–1806) in England, were translators of the classics.[65] In a world where knowledge of Greek and Roman antiquity defined the summa of erudition, drew the perimeter of political discourse, and supplied a vast array of literary, artistic, and architectural motifs, women could acquire at least passing familiarity with some of the major themes and actors of antiquity through secondary renderings of classical themes. Educated women frequently recruited Roman and, less often, Greek imagery to describe their domestic and political situations. In the Revolutionary era Abigail Adams styled herself as Portia, the long-suffering but wise wife of the Roman statesman Brutus, and when her husband was away she encouraged her son John Quincy to read passages from Charles Rollin's *Ancient History* to her.[66] Her friend Mercy Otis Warren, the historian, answered Abigail's letters as Marcia, the wife of the republican orator Hortensius.[67] Warren's plays of the pre- and post-Revolutionary periods in fact drew repeatedly on classical themes to describe politics. In her satirical play *The Adulateur* (1772) Warren cast the Anglo-American quarrel as Roman intrigue, and in *The Sack of Rome* (written in 1785) she gave the central action to a Roman woman, Edoxia.[68] Judith Sargent Murray looked to Helen of Troy and Penelope to argue for greater utility in women's education in her book *The Gleaner* (1798). Murray contrasted the frivolous, seductive Helen, who squandered her talents in dancing and embroidery, with faithful Penelope, who pursued useful activities to make herself an independent and industrious wife attentive to the needs of the young republic.[69]

Oratory was another way that those excluded from a college education could imbibe the culture of classicism. Classical models informed American oratorical standards during an age when persuasive public speaking was believed essential to the body politic, to professional success, and to gentlemanly ideals of eloquent expression. Before 1750 only ministers and magistrates had the authority to speak in public, but with the proliferation of print, increasing literacy rates, and the growth of an independent, well-demarcated public after 1750, oratory flourished as an essential element of civic life in America.[70] The power of oratory to persuade and move was clear not only in overtly political speeches and church sermons but also in the coffeehouses, clubs, private societies, and salons that proliferated after the mid-eighteenth century. These more private venues, thought conducive to a different, more intimate style of sociability than public oratory, nevertheless revealed the prevalence of classical inspiration in American culture, in which speeches, jokes, games, and even club rules drew partly on a fund of neoclassical diction and imagery on the part of both men and women.[71] Plays too used oratory in public venues to link the classical past to a modern political agenda. Joseph Addison's *Cato* (1713), which depicted the Roman statesman's stand for liberty against a tyrannical Caesar, achieved enormous popularity in the two decades preceding the Revolution. Audiences saw in the colonywide performances of Addison's play by professional acting companies a Roman mirror of their struggles against tyranny. It was even performed by General George Washington's soldiers at Valley Forge in the long winter of 1777–78.[72]

Above all other ancient orators, Revolutionary Americans idealized Cicero (106–43 B.C.) as a model of eloquence and style and also as the ideal citizen whose incorruptible morals protected the Roman republic from tyranny. John Adams in 1787 affirmed that "as all the ages of the world have not produced a greater statesman and philosopher united than Cicero, his authority should have great weight."[73] Ciceronian ideals of public speaking, which predominated in eighteenth-century America, revealed through the grace of the speech the moral probity and authority of the speaker.[74] But while the intricacies of Ciceronian diction might be reserved for the college-educated, the Ciceronian motif of the stately, patriotic orator captured the attention of larger segments of society. When Dr. Joseph Warren appeared before the multitude in Boston in 1775 to commemorate the fifth anniversary of the Boston Massacre, not only did he fill his speech with the keywords of republican ideology—*virtue, vice,* and *corruption*—but he addressed his listeners wrapped in a Ciceronian toga, purchased minutes before from an apothecary shop adjacent to the Old South Church.[75] Such physical invocations of antiquity to drive home a rhetorical point suggested the pervasiveness of the culture of classicism in eighteenth-century America.

Colleges contributed to the oratorical culture of the colonial and early national eras both in their formal curriculum and through extracurricular activities such as student clubs and debating societies. In the classroom students studied Cicero, Isocrates, and Demosthenes in conjunction with Hugh Blair's *Lecture on Rhetoric and Belles Lettres,* which after it first appeared in American colleges in 1783 was a staple until well into the nineteenth century.[76] Recitations and declamations formed habits of classically inspired oral interchange in the classroom, though the practice of actually speaking Latin on campus had been abandoned by the early eighteenth century.

It was in the student societies, which dominated American undergraduate life from the 1750s to the mid-nineteenth century, that many American college students imbibed the culture of neoclassical oratory. The often secret societies were so important to student education and socialization that James McLachlan has aptly called them "colleges within colleges."[77] In the 1770s students in Princeton's Cliosophic Society gave one another names invoking the classical tradition—Brutus, Cassius, Socrates, Atticus. Student debates endlessly took up classical idioms that reiterated the dichotomy between vice and virtue, urbane luxury and pastoral simplicity, self-promotion and self-denial. Princetonians in 1815 debated the question, "Ought the Latin and Greek Languages to be made part of a liberal education?" and a senior oration at Yale's commencement in 1848 was entitled "The Scene of Demosthenes' Oration on the Crown."[78] Students stocked their debating society libraries—often much grander and better used, even by faculty, than the official college libraries—with an impressive array of books representing not only the standards of Renaissance,

Augustan, and Enlightenment literature but also the classics of antiquity and modern histories of the ancient world. Students in Princeton's American Whig Society, furthermore, took as their visual symbol a painting of the myth of the choice of Hercules, a parable in which the young Hercules chooses between the seductive path of vice (often represented as a seductively draped beauty, grapes, cards, and other sensual pleasures) and the more rigorous but ultimately more rewarding path of virtue (embodied by Athena, books, and other symbols of learning, duty, and honor). Colleges scheduled commencement exercises loaded with classical imagery on Independence Day and opened them to the public. The University of Pennsylvania in the 1780s thereby schooled its graduating students and the invited public in what one local newspaper called "the habits of thinking and speaking, becoming Republicans."[79]

Also contributing to the culture of classicism in late-eighteenth- and early-nineteenth-century America was the lack of any disciplinary specialization in classical scholarship. The best-stocked classical libraries in eighteenth-century America belonged not to colleges but to private individuals. Possibly the grandest of all classical libraries in the colonial period belonged to the Quaker merchant James Logan (1674–1751). At a time when Harvard's library housed only 3,000 books, Logan's contained more than 400 volumes of classical writing alone out of a total of 2,651 volumes. Likewise, the private library of the great Virginia planter William Byrd of Westover rivaled Logan's in size, and Byrd, like many southern gentlemen, such as Thomas Jefferson and Richard Henry Lee (1732–94), thought of classical learning as an essential component of the South's composite agrarian gentleman hero, Cicero Cincinnatus.[80]

Nor did college campuses house only experts in classical learning. Well into the nineteenth century most of the classical language teachers on campuses were tutors. These tutors often helped a single classical language professor with the daily routine of recitations and examinations. They were usually young college graduates hoping to earn money before moving on to their real professions, and on average they stayed only a few years. Before the early nineteenth century there was little separating a classics professor from a classics tutor besides the former's greater age and longer-term employment.[81] Indeed, college teachers of classical languages knew that they lived in a Sahara of learning, discouragingly remote from the libraries and scholars of Europe. "In America," complained an anonymous contributor to the *Port Folio* in 1801, "our seminaries are more slenderly endowed, and few of their professorships hold out any great temptations to avarice or ambition. Where learning is neither honourable nor lucrative, it cannot flourish."[82]

Professors of ancient languages had little institutional or disciplinary loyalty; classical language teaching was an occupation through which men moved fluidly on their way from or to other occupations, most often the ministry. Few men at the time actually set out to become a professor of classical languages. Professorships in classical languages, as opposed to just tutorships, began to be created late in the eighteenth century, but these were only at a few older and wealthier schools, such as Yale. At most colleges the function and career trajectory of classics professors remained unaltered into the mid-nineteenth century. The positions continued to be filled by ministers and classical school teachers, the two professions that attracted men most skilled in the classical languages. The career paths of the first five classical language professors at Dartmouth College, who served collectively from 1778 to 1833, are illustrative. John Smith (1752–1809), professor of Latin, Greek, Hebrew, and Oriental languages from 1778 until his death in 1809, was first a tutor at Dartmouth. Ebenezer Adams (1765–1841) was a classical language teacher for only one year (1809–10) before becoming professor of mathematics and natural philosophy for the next twenty-three years. Zephenia Swift Moore (1770–1823) served for four years (1811–1815), then taught theology first as president of Williams College, then as president of Amherst College. Fourth was William Chamberlain (1797–1830); although he taught classical languages from 1820 to 1830, his principal occupations are listed as lawyer and treasurer of Dartmouth. The fifth professor of classical languages was Calvin Ellis Stowe (1802–86; husband of Harriet Beecher Stowe), who taught only from 1831 to 1833 before teaching theology at the Lane Theological Seminary, Bowdoin College, and Andover Theological Seminary.[83]

Classical themes, moreover, permeated American art and architecture, reinforcing the palpable physicality of neoclassicism in colonial and early national America. In painting, neoclassical aesthetic theory echoed the lessons of Enlightenment historicism, suggesting that a painter could capture on canvas the timeless moral virtues of humanity and thereby instruct the viewer in civic virtue. The classical themes depicted on the canvases of the American painter Benjamin West (1738–1820) were both overt, as in his *Landing of Agrippina at Brundisium with the Ashes of Germanicus*, and more subtle, as in his *Death of General Wolfe*, which shows the dying general displaying the classical virtues of heroism, courage, and dignity.[84] Neoclassical architecture, which flourished after the Revolution, likewise stated the immediate relevance of classical antiquity to the political agenda of the young republic. Thomas Jefferson, who designed the Virginia state capitol to resemble the Roman temple at Nîmes, argued for the power of public buildings to transmit a political philosophy, stating that they "should be more than things of beauty and convenience; above all, they should state a creed."[85] Most influential, because most widely dispersed, was the staggering quantity of classical imagery that saturated American newspapers, prints, broadsides, pamphlets, and civic iconography. These were so commonplace as to become unremarkable. Minerva, Columbia, Ceres, Mercury, and Hercules symbolized the classical virtues of the new republic: liberty, martial valor, agricultural fecundity, commerce, the path of public virtue over private vice. Just as frequently, classical columns of all three orders framed people, icons, and words in paintings and prints.

THE WORLD OF WORDS

Although a culture of classicism infused late colonial and early national America with a compelling, politically energizing set of symbols and motifs, the classicism practiced within America's college classrooms was quite different. There, it was not icons and allusions that occupied students, but *language*. Students in the years between the founding of Harvard and the early nineteenth century focused to the exclusion of almost all else upon the grammar of ancient Greek and Latin. Their college days—in class, at least—were spent in a complex liturgy of classical language acquisition that included parsing, scanning, recitation, and translation. By comparison, history, literature, and antiquities played a minuscule heuristic role. Although these might be listed in the published curriculum, faculty and student records of actual classroom practice suggest that language ruled the day in American colleges for more than two centuries. What are we to make of this disjuncture between the broadly diffused, palpable presence of the classical world in America and the grammatical focus of the colleges? The question can be phrased more bluntly, in the way an eighteenth-century student might have recognized: given the excitement about the classical world in American culture more broadly, why was its teaching so narrow in the colleges?

We can begin by examining how Americans understood the study of language in the eighteenth century. Although today it is shackled to a narrow scholarly discipline, the study of language in the eighteenth and early nineteenth centuries was broader and much more exuberant. Americans imagined the world of words, philology, as an expansive, fertile field of study. Indeed, the study of language was one of the central projects of the time, offering a number of avenues to be explored: the ways in which language changed over time, the origins of language in the Garden of Eden, proper usage, whether there existed a "universal grammar" that underlay all others. The manner in which professors taught classical texts in colleges reflected this broad view of language. Professors believed that students should begin with a thorough understanding of the classical languages—their grammar, composition, and the like—but that this was merely a prelude to the ultimate goal of classical language study, which was an understanding of antiquity sufficient for taking up the duties of gentlemen, statesmen, and ministers as adults. They also believed that classical texts offered a more authoritative guide to antiquity than did art or artifacts. Although ancient and medieval historians had eagerly sought out confirmation of historical events with visual remains such as pottery, coins, and sculpture, the Renaissance recovery of many ancient texts had pushed these physical remains into the secondary realm of antiquarians. By the eighteenth and early nineteenth centuries, despite new archaeological discoveries such as Pompeii and Herculaneum and increasing acceptance of the value of antiquities, it was classical texts that remained most compelling to American scholars.[86] The Harvard Greek professor John Snelling Popkin aptly described this optimistic view of the powers of language to illuminate the past: "We live in a world of words; which are indeed the signs of thoughts and of things."[87]

A typical rendering of the expansive possibilities of language was articulated by the classically educated Scottish Presbyterian minister Charles Nisbet (1736–1804), who emigrated to America in 1785 to become president of Dickinson College in Carlisle, Pennsylvania. Nisbet possessed a formidable knowledge of the classics, even by the standards of his time, and was widely known as a walking library.[88] The utter vacuity of Dickinson literally sickened him, and he once called America a nation of "Quacks."[89] Though tempted to leave Dickinson, he was convinced by the trustees to stay, and until his death Nisbet made Carlisle a little oasis of classical erudition in America. His writings often refer to obscure participants in the French and English battles between the ancients and moderns, revealing his optimistic expectation that such figures were commonly known in that remote outpost of the republic of letters. Nisbet himself was thoroughly an ancient, suspicious of modern improvements upon antique wisdom. Any true knowledge of the Greeks and Romans, he argued, could be gleaned only from a thorough study of their writings. This knowledge should be expansive:

> To acquire a sufficient knowledge of the celebrated people, we ought to study their Language, their History, their Religion, their Laws, and those customs, that prevailed in private life, which so often throw much light on national characters, and give us a more exact knowledge of remote ages. These are to be discovered chiefly in their poetry, and such performances as describe Life and Manners, as the gravity of History seldom descends to describe the transactions of private life, however interesting they may be to posterity.[90]

Here was a generous view of language's bounty: through language an entire society could be known. Nisbet's faith that digging into the texts of antiquity could uncover gems of private and public experience was widely shared among classicists in early national America. According to the Reverend James Wilson, president of the Bedford Academy in Pennsylvania, Greek and Latin afforded a view "of the manners and customs and modes of thought in ancient times." Wilson opposed translations because they clothed "the republics of Greece and the Roman empire, in an English dress." "We can never acquire an accurate knowledge of ancient times," he wrote, "without a knowledge of ancient language."[91] Another agreed that through the language and literature of ancient Greece and Rome, a study of "the authors and their works," much could be discovered about "the genius and manners," "the civil or political history," and the "Archaeological, the origin, the antiquities, and the mythology of the nation."[92] Partly as a result of these views, language was enthroned in the curriculum as the chief object of study, the avenue to a broad understanding of antiquity.

A look at the method of teaching languages at some colleges around the country, however, shows that viewing antiquity broadly through the telescope of language was in fact only an ideal and that the classical facility acquired by someone like Charles Nisbet in a Scottish university was realized only rarely in America. The reality was that teachers and students became mired in minutiae, or what Nisbet called the study of "mere words, and the rules of construction necessary to be attended to in putting them in order."[93]

We can take one classroom textbook as an example of this grammatical focus. The most widely used textbook for teaching Greek in American colleges for the first half of the nineteenth century was the plump, two-volume *Collectanea Graeca Majora*, popularly known as the *Graeca Majora*.[94] It was a great sea of Greek text: excerpts from Homer's *Odyssey*, Hesiod, the *Oedipus Tyrannus* of Sophocles, Euripides' *Medea*, Theocritus, Bion, Moschus, and the odes of Sappho filled every page. No islands of gloss or grammatical aid broke through these stretches of words. Help came only at the end, where there loomed a mountain of notes in Latin, keyed to author, page, and line. First published in Scotland in 1789 by the Edinburgh professor Andrew Dalzel (1742–1806), the book entered American classrooms on the wave of Scottish learning that spread over the late-eighteenth-century colleges. At Harvard, John Popkin produced the first American edition in 1808 to accolades from the learned community. The minister Joseph Buckminster (1784–1812) in 1809 praised the introduction of the *Graeca Majora* as "a great step towards the improvement of Greek learning."[95] In 1826 the *North American Review* likewise commended it, adding that "America has never produced a scholar more profound in the department of Grecian learning" than Popkin.[96] Soon after Popkin introduced it to his Harvard classes in 1804, other college teachers of Greek in both the North and the South adopted it: Yale in 1805, South Carolina College in 1810, Columbia by 1810, Hamilton College by 1813, the University of Tennessee by 1829; Davidson College, in North Carolina, was still using it in 1854.[97] The *Graeca Majora* went through thirty-three American editions before it finally drifted out of print in 1860.[98]

The *Graeca Majora* embodied the prevailing conviction that the expansive field of philology—the world of words—could be reached only through extensive preparation in grammar. Although they hoped that students ultimately would be conversant in classical history, antiquities, and mythology, professors imagined that these achievements rested firmly on a foundation of linguistic skill acquired through many years of repetition, memorization, and recitation. Popkin described his hopes for the *Graeca Majora* and the pedagogy it represented as follows:

> To speak plainly, I would read the authors, one at a time, and read them throughout, rather than search out a thousand inscriptions, or the title-pages of three thousand books, and take and give a slight and hasty notice. And, to speak truly, these things are the garniture, rather than the furniture, of a college. For after all that is declaimed, "of the spirit of the age, and the wants of society, and the progress of improvement," and so forth, the root of the matter is to be found in the humble and simple, old-school, tedious business of recitation.[99]

One problem with studying the teaching of classical languages during the late eighteenth and early nineteenth centuries is that this teaching was often so laborious and unpleasant for students that it became synonymous with much that was wrong with the colleges of the time. Later reformers singled out this grammatical method in particular in their attacks on the classics and on the so-called classical colleges as a whole. They were joined by complaining students who despised the punitive and often ineffective methods of classroom instruction. This fact has made it difficult to recover the excitement with which many American classical scholars approached the ancient languages, their hopes for how Greek and Latin could ultimately be used. This disjuncture between the hopes of the professors and the reality experienced by students is clear in the response of Harvard students to Popkin's teaching of the *Graeca Majora*. Whereas Popkin imagined the text as a vestibule to the fertile field of philology, students recalled the *Graeca Majora* as a giant grammar exercise, with students engaged in what one called "the same verbal drilling that they had experienced in the first elementary book they had studied."[100] James Freeman Clarke, the Unitarian minister and social reformer who attended Harvard between 1825 and 1829, remembered of the *Graeca Majora*:

> No attempt was made to interest us in our studies. We were expected to wade through Homer as though the Iliad were a bog, and it was our duty to get along at such a rate *per diem*. Nothing was said of the glory and grandeur, the tenderness and charm of this immortal epic. As only a few of the class recited well enough for us to learn anything from what they said, those hours were not only wasted, but put us in a condition of mental torpor.[101]

Another student recalled that Popkin "never seemed to forget that he was not teaching the elements [of language]."[102] At the end of four years, not more than a dozen students, according to Clarke, were able to read a Greek or Latin book.[103] "In all points of grammar," recalled one of Popkin's students, "he was rigid and punctilious; and the drift of his teaching was rather to make exact verbal critics than enthusiastic lovers of scholarship."[104] A contributor to the *North American Review* noted that Popkin "understood the osteology of the language well, and with good opportunities and exact training in early life, would have been an excellent philologer. But he did not seem to move freely in any higher region than that of verbal scholarship."[105]

A sampling of colleges suggests that many professors of classical languages struggled with the difficulties of plowing through basic grammatical exercises in the hopes of entering into the world of words. A contemporary of Popkin's at Yale, James Luce Kingsley (1778–1852), likewise hoped to improve the study of classicism in American colleges. Against Yale president Timothy Dwight's strenuous objections, Kingsley pushed for Homer to be taught to Yale's students. In teaching the ancient languages, he carefully selected those writings that would aid students' religious progress as well as their grammatical prowess. To the junior class, for example, he taught those works of Cicero that discussed "the doctrine of the immortality of the soul."[106] Yet he evoked from students the same mixed responses that had plagued Popkin. Julian M. Sturtevant (1805–86), who graduated from Yale in 1826 and became president of Illinois College, remembered Kingsley "closing a series of readings of Tacitus Agricola, by saying, 'Young gentlemen, you have been reading one of the noblest productions of the human mind without knowing it." Sturtevant felt like retorting, "Whose fault is it?" Sturtevant was critical of the whole curriculum at Yale, in fact, for its emphasis on rote memorization and recitation.[107]

A similarly expansive agenda appeared in the job description of the Reverend Elijah D. Rattoone, a professor of Greek and Latin at Columbia College in the mid-1790s. His position required him to lecture regularly on "the opinions of the ancient philosophers; the religion, government, laws, policy, customs, and manners of Greece and Rome: the whole designed to explain and elucidate ancient learning, and to facilitate the acquisition of liberal knowledge." This goal, however, was part of the larger goal of classical study in early republican America, which was "to make critical and useful scholars—to infuse, from those learned languages, a true taste for propriety and correctness—to teach the value of those tongues which never change nor vary, which the Professor considers as the true standards of excellence in language, and as containing generally whatever is just in thought, elegant in expression, and harmonious in numbers."[108] Yet students remembered classical language teaching at Columbia during this time as dull. Peter Wilson, a professor of Greek and Latin at Columbia after 1797, was remembered by students as a bore and a stickler for grammar.[109] Though he also held the title "Professor of Roman and Grecian Antiquities," the curriculum gives no evidence that he construed the "antiquities" component of his title as an invitation to stray far from texts. In 1810 students marched through four years of Cicero, Sallust, Horace, Xenophon, Terence, Quintilian, Longinus, Virgil, Livy, Demosthenes, the *Graeca Majora*, various exercise in Latin and Greek composition, and only occasionally "Greek and Roman Antiquities."[110]

At South Carolina College the professor of languages was the kindly but feckless Yankee Thomas Park, a former schoolteacher hired in 1806 at age thirty-nine. Largely unassisted, Park taught Greek and Latin at South Carolina College until 1835. So eager was he to help his students through recitations that a boy had only to stumble once before Park rushed in to supply the rest of the lesson.[111] But again, colleagues and students commented on the grammatical focus of the teaching. "There was nothing shining, nothing brilliant, nothing very remarkable in the character of his intellect," wrote a later professor there. "His reading was not extensive, and his knowledge therefore not various. . . . Many, with not half his learning, are judged superior. I will not assert that his reading in Latin and Greek was very extensive, for I have been led to believe that, in this particular, not a few surpassed him. But he had read carefully all that is embraced in our highest Collegiate courses. . . . I think that he was not capable of inspiring much enthusiasm; but he was laborious, pains-taking and conscientious and could make scholars of those who were rightly disposed."[112] Education in the classics became, according to many commentators, essentially synonymous with bad teaching and even punishment at South Carolina College and elsewhere during this period. In 1824 two South Carolina College students who were discovered shooting their guns in town were punished by being forced to recite fifty lines of the *Aeneid* to the faculty.[113]

American college teachers taught Greek and Latin with an overriding focus on language, a practice that they hoped would turn boys into eloquent, moral, and dutiful citizens, but this method bored a good number of students. More troubling to college classics teachers, however, was that the recitation and memorization method was quite often ineffective, for many students graduated from college with little grasp of Greek or Latin. The shocking deficiencies in language instruction, in fact, were a major preoccupation among classicists, many of whom struggled to come up with ways to help students learn Greek and Latin more easily and effectively. But this effort proved to be extremely divisive, for battles over how to teach the languages shaded into battles over what kinds of erudition were beneficial to the young republic. If a certain method were ineffective, then not only would students be classically ignorant but they might fail in the exercise of their civic duties. Conversely, if they were excessively learned, they would pollute the republic with the vice of pedantry. Fights over how to teach the classics, especially the battle over translations, thus became linked to larger concerns about the place of classical learning in the new nation.

How best to teach a language was an old problem. The ancient Romans had pondered the most effective ways of teaching Greek to their students, and the issue was as hotly debated during the Renaissance as it would be in the eighteenth century. The most popular Latin primer of the Middle Ages, for example, was the *Disticha Catonis* (Sayings of Cato), a series of short moral pronouncements whose Latin grammar was easy and predictable. "Supplicate God. Be clean. Fear the magistrate. Get enough sleep," were some of the unimpeachable nuggets in the *Disticha*.[114] Opponents of the *Disticha*, however, argued that boys should receive sacred rather than pagan instruction, though Cato's sound advice was generally amenable to Christian interpretation. More importantly for our purposes, the medieval gloss upon the *Disticha* came under attack by Renaissance humanists eager to reform language instruction. Erasmus had learned the *Disticha* in the medieval way, with notes on vocabulary and syntax printed over each word and a Christianized moral commentary following in a separate paragraph. He condemned this dissected, word-by-word approach, which he associated with the medieval pedagogy of dictation and repetition, and he opposed the heavy-handed Christianization of a pagan author. Erasmus's own edition of the *Disticha*, by contrast, acknowledged the Roman, pagan origin of the proverbs and eliminated the medieval gloss.[115]

Erasmus was only one of a number of grammarians over the centuries who tried to make the study of Latin easier and more pleasant. His example helps to show that revisions of grammar texts were always tied to larger issues, for example, whether an old or new method of teaching grammar succeeded in inculcating ideals of morality and eloquence in students. Self-styled reformers abounded in every century, and many grammars included an introduction that threw sarcastic barbs at their predecessors' deficiencies while trumpeting their own aptitude for securing the desired civic and ethical ends.

Similar debates raged in eighteenth- and early-nineteenth-century America. One of the most important discussions centered on the use of translations in school: whether to make Latin easier by including literal English translations alongside Latin prose and poetry or to let the Latin stand alone and discipline students' minds through the sheer effort of learning a foreign tongue. The most vocal participants in these debates were concerned with translations in the grammar schools, although the discussion also resonated in the colleges, where the classical languages were studied with the same grammatical focus as in the lower schools. The debate rode the latest wave of educational theories but also extended into a contest over the requirements for scholarship and citizenship. This rather narrow discussion, then, had larger implications: What kind of classical knowledge did gentlemen in the republic of letters need? How was a gentleman, as opposed to, say, a shopkeeper or a scholar, to be defined? Which kind of knowledge was commendable, and which condemnable?

On one side of the debate stood those who favored translations because they opposed the rote memorization of grammar. They took as their leader John Clarke (1687–1734), who had been a Latin schoolmaster at Hull, England. Like so many teachers of classical language, Clarke was pragmatic about the realities of teaching a difficult tongue to young boys. He made a name for himself in both England and America in the mid-eighteenth century after editing a number of introductory Latin texts that placed literal English translations of his own creation alongside the Latin texts.[116] Clarke greatly admired the sensationalist psychology of John Locke, whose *Thoughts Concerning Education* (1693) had criticized the rote teaching of Latin grammar inherited from the Middle Ages. Locke urged that literal English translations appear above or next to the Latin so that boys would better understand what they read and would learn Latin in the natural way that they learned their mother tongue. This was not a completely new idea. For at least a hundred years such translations had been available for teachers who wanted to teach reading and speaking before grammar so that students did not mechanically repeat the master "like Parrots."[117] Locke's proposed grammar reforms simply reached a wider audience and became known to American classical language teachers primarily through Clarke, who published two extremely influential essays on the place of Latin in education that drew heavily on Lockean psychology and education.[118] For pages on end the plainspoken and caustic Clarke quoted Locke on education and on human understanding; many Americans, in fact, came to know Locke on education through Clarke on Locke on education.[119] Clarke's literal translations of beginning school texts were used in many American grammar schools and were required for admission into colleges. In 1822 Yale still included Clarke's *Introduction to the Making of Latin* among its admissions requirements, as did Princeton in 1819.[120] Schoolmasters and college tutors probably often used Clarke's texts in conjunction with traditional rote memorization, mixing the old and the new.

To others, however, translations were anathema. The translation dispensed with some of the basic reasons for reading the classics at all: to cultivate discipline and eloquence through the acquisition of a language that epitomized refinement. One critic blamed "empirics in education," by which he meant Locke and Clarke, for the dismal state of American letters.[121] Cloaked by seductive promises of easy and pleasurable learning was a rotten core of ill-taught students ignorant of language. Seminaries and colleges that advertised the use of Clarke's methods, charged these critics, were merely angling for more students who wanted to learn Latin the easy way. Harvard's John Popkin, a vocal opponents of translations, called them "the clandestine refuge of the pupil, and too often the unacknowledged assistant of the teacher," and he criticized Locke for condemning repetition in the classroom. Locke's ideas, said Popkin, were based on "theory alone."[122] John Sanderson, who taught Latin at Philadelphia's Carre and Sanderson Seminary, agreed, arguing that the qualities befitting gentlemen were not acquired through "the *deteriorating* medium of a translation."[123]

Concerned to fortify language instruction, Popkin and his allies also defended the ancient but fading practice of "making verse," or composing original verse in accordance with antique poetic traditions.[124] Clarke had condemned the reading of poetry in schools because it was "quite out of the common Road" and difficult to understand. He mocked the practice of teaching students to write in verse because it made their style "very bombastick and ridiculous."[125] But to others such as Popkin, making verse was an important part of language instruction because it was difficult and required long years of self-discipline. Making verse required students actually to know something about Latin. One anonymous writer in the *Monthly Anthology*, probably Popkin, blamed the "superficial" state of American knowledge on the decline in making verse. "The neglect of prosody [the systematic study of poetic meter] has been so shameful among us, that scarcely a collegian can read a passage of Latin poetry, without some gross violation of quantity; and the scholars of Connecticut are still more defective, in this respect, than those of Massachusetts. This is a subject well worthy the attention of instructors, as it is impossible to relish the beauties of poetry, or even to discover the harmony of prose, without an accurate knowledge of prosody."[126] English schools, noted this writer, encouraged erudition because they taught their students to make verse. Thomas Cooper (1759–1839), a classically educated English scientist who went on to become president of South Carolina College, restated the importance of prosody and verse-making in school. "I will venture to say that a dozen Latin verses composed as they must be composed, will give the boy more knowledge of quantity, more recollection of various meanings, more command of words and the phrases, and more insight into elegant construction of a sentence, and propriety of periphrasis and imagery, then a week's labor at merely construing a classic author."[127]

Critics of translations agreed with Richard Graves, whose book *The Spiritual Quixote* (1773) satirized John Locke's proposal "to teach Children to read, whilst they thought they were only Playing."[128] Graves imagined a classroom in which games and dancing were the medium of classical instruction: "I make eight boys represent the eight parts of Speech," says the instructor. "The *noun Substantive* stands by himself; the *Adjective* has another boy to support him; the *Nominative Case* carries a little wand before the *Verb:* The *Accusative Case* walks after and supports his train. I let the four *Conjugations* make a party at whist; and the three *Concords* dance the *Hay* together and so on."[129]

One of the reasons that translations were at the core of these debates on the nature of pedagogy and erudition was that translations were in fact widely read in America, even among Americans who knew the ancient languages. The Presbyterian minister Samuel Miller (1769–1850), in his intellectual history of the eighteenth century (which he called the "age of translations"), marveled at the "number and value of the *Translations* of classical authors" produced during that time, then listed more than fifty classical authors translated into English alone.[130] Alexander Pope (1688–1744), John Dryden (1631–1700), Anne Dacier (1647–1720), and other translators of the classics had proved to many that a translation could be a work of art in its own right. Neither Clarke nor Popkin, in fact, opposed reading translations after school in adult life. Popkin conceded that Alexander Pope's translation of Homer's *Odyssey* was exquisite, "perhaps the most adequate modern representative of the ancient epic."[131] It was during school that translations could become problematic because they failed to initiate students into the moral and intellectual virtues of immersion in the classical languages.

A whole student subculture dedicated to the propagation of translations flourished, testifying to the extent to which languages dominated teaching. Barred from checking out classical texts from college libraries for fear that they might use translations in their schoolwork, students trafficked in "ponies," interlined copies of textbooks that helped them weather the recitations. Professors zealously plundered the classroom for this contraband.[132] Many students turned to the libraries of the student debating societies to obtain the translation. Student lore eulogized good ponies:

> And when leaving, leave behind us
> *Ponies* for a lower class;
> *Ponies*, which perhaps another,
> Toiling up the College hill,
> A forlorn, a "younger brother,"
> "Riding," may rise higher still.[133]

The effort to stamp out translations was born of a curriculum dedicated to the world of words, and it testified to larger, more troubling concerns about the education of gentlemen, ministers, and statesmen in the early republic. Opposition to interlining, translations, and the decline in making verse—to all shortcuts—stemmed from a fear that if the leaders of the nation were classically ignorant, they would become morally rudderless. Statesmen would lose their classical tether to the example of Rome, and ministers would forfeit their ability to read and interpret Scripture. A classical education was the badge of the gentleman, but aristocracy in all its forms was crumbling; many public pronouncements in journals by classicists can be categorized as defenses of the existence of a heavily classical curriculum that would safeguard the pedigree of the gentleman. Classicists damned the "smatterer" (also known as a "sciolist" or a "quack"), who made a sham of the gentleman and statesman by pretending he knew the classical languages but was in fact "vain of apparent precocity of talent and of knowledge, selfsufficient, and therefore idle and useless."[134] They struggled equally against the pedant, who violated the canons of gentlemanly behavior with his smug parade of erudition. The pedant (also known as a "scholar" or "critick") loved what was singular and obscure; he was vain and self-righteous, reveled in faction and intrigue, and gleefully squashed his opponents. The smatterer and the pedant threatened not just the world of learning but the republic, whose welfare depended upon a morally and politically selfless citizenry made so in part by a classical education properly deployed.[135]

Not everyone agreed that the ancient languages in and of themselves safeguarded civic virtue. In the second half of the eighteenth century a number of influential figures—Benjamin Franklin (1706–90), Benjamin Rush (1745–1813), Thomas Paine (1737–1809), Noah Webster (1758–1843)—launched an attack on prevailing modes of classical education, charging that they were incompatible with the needs of the young nation. They argued that the "dead languages" were useless to farmers, mechanics, and merchants; that they wasted the most important, formative years of a student's life in quickly forgotten grammatical niceties; that the Greek and Roman myths made boys into "Pimps" by reciting lascivious tales offensive to Christian morality; that the time spent in classical language education might more profitably be spent learning more useful subjects, such as English; that the classical languages conferred social cachet for no good reason.[136] "Who," asked Benjamin Rush, "are guilty of the greatest absurdity—the Chinese, who press the feet into deformity by small shoes, or the Europeans and Americans, who press the brain into obliquity by Greek and Latin? Do not men use Latin and Greek as the scuttlefish emit their ink, on purpose to conceal themselves from an intercourse with common people?"[137]

Much is made of these anticlassical attacks as harbingers of the decay of classicism in the late eighteenth century, but it is important to recognize, first, that these critics did not attack the relevance of antiquity to modern America and, second, that their critiques had almost no effect in dislodging Greek and Latin from the college curriculum. Indeed, Franklin, Rush, and Webster warmly appreciated the relevance of the ancient authors to American political and social conditions and urged the study of classical history and translations. It was instead the word-dominated focus of classics teaching that they criticized, a practice that they argued made classical learning inaccessible to many and focused students' attention on those aspects of antiquity least useful in the new nation.[138] By contrast, classical history furnished a storehouse of useful exemplars for modern students. "It is absolutely necessary that a boy should first be instructed in *history* and *geography*," wrote Rush in 1791. "Let him read an account of the rise, progress, and fall of the Greek and Roman nations. . . . The classics are now read only for the sake of acquiring a knowledge of the construction of the languages in which they were written; but by the plan I have proposed, they would be read for the sake of the matter they contained, and there would be enough time to read each book from its beginning to its end."[139] Noah Webster also urged that American students turn from the poets and orators to the historians. "In our colleges and universities students read some of the ancient poets and orators, but the historians which are perhaps more valuable, are generally neglected."[140] Thomas Paine argued that instead of busying themselves with grammar, students should read translations. "As there is now nothing new to be learned from the dead languages, all the useful books being already translated, the languages are become useless, and the time expended in teaching and in learning them is wasted."[141]

These criticisms failed to dislodge Greek and Latin language study from the college curriculum, but they did point to a growing sense in the new nation that ancient learning might be incompatible with modern social conditions. Within the colleges themselves instruction proceeded as it had for almost two centuries. American classics teachers' choice in the early national period to focus on grammar rather than other aspects of the classical inheritance resulted from their primary pedagogical goals: to mold gentlemen who navigated between sciolism and pedantry, ministers who could intelligently read the Bible, and citizens who were moral and dutiful. All this from boys who were mostly neither interested in nor good at learning languages. This was a task that required from teachers a balance of idealism and pragmatism and certainly patience. It was not until the third decade of the nineteenth century that the teaching of ancient language came under real and damaging assault by a new generation eager to make the ancients fit a new era.

❧ 2 ❧

THE RISE OF GREECE

CLASSICS IN CRISIS

Between 1800 and 1860, American colleges embarked upon a remarkable period of growth. The total number of colleges increased tenfold, from about 20 in 1800 to 217 by the 1850s, with the majority of new colleges founded after 1830. Moreover, they spread rapidly across the growing nation, so that by 1850 the Midwest and the South had far more colleges than did the eastern seaboard. Compared with New England's fifteen colleges in 1850, the Midwest could boast sixty-seven. Religious diversity flourished as well, loosening the grip of Congregationalists, Presbyterians, and Episcopalians on American higher education. Whereas in 1800 those older denominations controlled 70 percent of American colleges, by the 1850s that number had dwindled to just 30 percent. During the same years there were huge increases in the numbers of colleges controlled by Baptists and Methodists, from just 6 percent in the first decade of the nineteenth century to 30 percent by the eve of the Civil War. Finally, the total number of students attending college rose fourteenfold, from just over one thousand in 1800 to over sixteen thousand by the Civil War. This marked a doubling of the percentage of white males aged 15–20 who attended, from about .6 percent in 1800 to about 1.2 percent in 1860.[1]

Popular demand and evangelical fervor fueled much of this growth. Many of the new colleges were founded on the sparsely populated frontiers, where local townspeople sought schooling for their children and denominations hoped to train a literate ministry to spread the gospel. Many colleges founded in the antebellum West and South in fact began as academies, which numbered more than 6,700 by 1860. These all-purpose preparatory schools served many different age groups and reflected the practical, urgent educational needs of their founders and students. They brought education to rural regions and to small towns that the colleges founded in the eighteenth century failed to serve.[2]

The democratization of American higher education in the antebellum era was also reflected in curricular changes. The growth of science was the most pronounced of these. Although much of the antebellum American scientific establishment resided outside the colleges, in private institutes such as the Smithsonian, the sciences continued to make inroads in the curriculum, spurred by practical and popular interest and by their compatibility with Baconian thought.[3] At Yale, Benjamin Silliman (1779–1864) was appointed professor of chemistry, geology, and mineralogy in 1802, and he went on to found America's first lasting scientific journal, the *American Journal of Science*, in 1818. His approach to science reflected the religious view that predominated at other antebellum colleges. Handpicked by Yale's devout president Timothy Dwight, Silliman linked piety to learning, teaching sciences as an illustration of the benevolence of the deity. The perceived utility of science to modern society was reflected in the curriculum of the military academy at West Point, founded in 1802, where cadets learned engineering, drawing, chemistry, and mathematics.[4] Older, more established schools also revealed the trend toward viewing science as a useful subject. In 1815 Harvard University received a bequest from the estate of Count Rumford to establish a professorship in the application of the sciences to the useful arts. This professor was to teach "the utility of the physical and mathematical sciences for the improvement of the useful arts, and for the extension of the industry, prosperity, happiness, and wellbeing of society."[5] The first man to occupy that chair was the influential botanist and physician Jacob Bigelow (1787–1879), whose book *Elements of Technology* (1829) applauded the present age as one that reaped the abundant rewards of what he called "Technology": science as useful knowledge.[6]

The expansion and transformation of the college curriculum after the turn of the nineteenth century stemmed from the large-scale shifts in American society, economics, and politics during that time. The market revolution brought more than just canals, railroads, factories, and banks: it enabled the gradual liquidation of the social hierarchies that had buttressed colonial society. Westward migration and a powerful boom-bust economy allowed larger numbers of citizens to pursue economic, educational, and political opportunities that they would have been denied in the colonial era. These changes in turn eroded the habits of aristocratic deference that had characterized the political culture of the colonial era. The two-party system injected politics with a tone of rancor and populist pandering that was offensive to traditional sensibilities. It also corroded the colonial ideal of the gentleman statesmen, whose grounding in classical history supposedly had enabled him to steer the nation disinterestedly and virtuously. The political field now opened to a new class of men who were distinguished less by pedigree than by their own accomplishments.[7]

John Quincy Adams (1767–1848) and Andrew Jackson (1767–1845), although born in the same year and serving as president one after the other, embodied the dichotomy between the older, classically steeped gentleman statesman and the new, practical, self-made man. Almost completely unschooled, Jackson represented the vigorous, natural frontiersman, unimpaired by a lengthy formal education. Though he eventually lived at the Hermitage, an imposing mansion on a large plantation in Tennessee, Jackson successfully cultivated an image as friend of the common man, praising popular democracy and the possibilities of upward mobility for white men. The historian George Bancroft (1800–1891) reflected on what this new natural man could offer the new republic.

> Behold, then, the unlettered man of the West, the nursling of the wilds, the farmer of the Hermitage, little versed in books, unconnected by science with the tradition of the past, raised by the will of the people to the highest pinnacle of honour, to the central post in the civilization of republican freedom. . . . What policy will he pursue? What wisdom will he bring with him from the forest? What rules of duty will he evolve from the oracles of his own mind?[8]

Jackson also appointed more men of lowly educational background to his administration than had John Adams or Thomas Jefferson. Eight men in his cabinet had no more than a secondary education, compared with two men in the cabinets of Adams and Jefferson.[9]

By contrast with the rustic Jackson, John Quincy Adams stood last in the line of classically educated gentleman statesmen from the Revolutionary era. Born to the political purple and educated at Harvard and in Paris, Amsterdam, and Holland, Adams served as president of the American Academy of Arts and Sciences and as Boylston Professor of Rhetoric at Harvard, spoke seven languages, wrote poetry, and tasted fine wines. He was a great admirer of the classics and the republican virtues with which they could instruct modern Americans. Before his election to the U.S. Congress, he spent two hours every day for ten months reading in Latin the complete works of Cicero, whom he described as "not only the orator, but the moral philosopher of Rome."[10] Adams's was not just a political interest in classical antiquity but a literary and artistic one as well. He judged Virgil's *Georgics* "the most perfect composition, that ever issued from the mind of man" and adorned his house with six bronze busts of antique men, calling them his "Household Gods."[11] His classicism contributed to his unpopularity; Jacksonians painted him as a stuffed shirt, and even supporters found him difficult, remote, and awkward.

The populist, commercial spirit of the Jacksonian era led to a renewed outpouring of objections to the classical curriculum. Anticlassicists reiterated many of the themes first articulated by Benjamin Rush and others in the late eighteenth century—that the classics were elitist, difficult, and immoral—but especially emphasized the uselessness of classical learning in a bustling market economy. In few cases did they advocate a wholesale elimination of the classical curriculum, asking instead for more parity between classics and newer studies such as science and modern languages. In New York City, for example, Albert Gallatin (1761–1849) backed a college in 1830–31 that would serve the needs of the growing class of mechanics in the city, who were both too poor to afford a classical education at Columbia College and uninterested in the apparently useless learning it purveyed. Gallatin and his associates envisioned a university that would serve everyone's needs, offering not only classical languages but sciences and modern languages. Such a university would "afford to all classes of the public the education best fitted to aid them in their pursuits, whether intended for the learned professions, commerce, or the mechanical and useful arts."[12] Likewise, the Philadelphian Mathew Carey (1760–1839) noted that while classical education was suitable for those destined to the professions and for men of leisure, extensive education in classical languages was pointless for those destined for "active business."[13] The southern editor James DeBow (1820–67), writing from New Orleans, a city he called "an infant Hercules," a reference to its boundless commercial potential, concurred that Americans needed education for the "MERCANTILE CLASSES."[14] The physician and Transylvania University professor Charles Caldwell (1772–1853) objected in 1836 to the uselessness of classical antiquity to "practical science" and attributed successes in art and literature in both the ancient and modern eras to faithful observation of nature rather than slavish devotion to past authority.[15]

Some of the most virulent objections to classicism in the Jacksonian era came from those educated in Greek and Latin at elite colleges. Among these was the South Carolina legislator and 1803 Yale graduate Thomas Smith Grimké (1786–1834), who compiled a series of anticlassical addresses in the pamphlet *Reflections on the Character and Objects of All Science and Literature* (1831). For Grimké, modern literature, Protestant history, and the "Scriptures of Science" supplied the most valuable instruction in "practical duty and usefulness, private and public" for students in the young republic. "Ours ought to be an education, adapted to our peculiar character, circumstances, and destiny, as a free, educated, peaceful, Christian People," he urged. Grimké did not oppose all classical study—scholars and gentlemen should know it, he said—but it was "totally useless to the great majority," such as the "working classes" and the "man of business." It was not the ancient heathens, inferior in philosophy and science, who would lead Americans to the millennium, but Christian revelation. Students should study a Christian *Graeca Majora* (the Gospel, church fathers, and the history of the freedom-bestowing Protestant Reformation) because such study armed "the sacramental host of God's elect" for its glorious destiny. Grimké's historical starting point was the shallow past of the Protestant Reformation. Like other anticlassicists in the age of reform and millennial optimism, he looked to the millennial future rather than to the remote classical past for guidance.[16]

Against such pragmatic objections, statements in support of classical learning during the Jacksonian era have appeared anemic and unconvincing. The reason is that the best-remembered and most often quoted defense of classicism in American history, the so-called Yale Report of 1828, was made at this time. But the Yale Report was by then a dated document, a fossil of eighteenth-century classicism. Its two authors, Yale president

Jeremiah Day (1773–1867) and the classicist James Luce Kingsley (1778–1852), were born at the cusp of the American Revolution. They defended the study of classical learning in terms that suited the late eighteenth century, invoking well-worn assertions of the value of classics in building the foundations of a gentleman's knowledge and the usefulness of the world of words in forming the citizen. They crafted their report in response to Connecticut state senator Noyes Darling's request that Yale College jettison the "dead languages" in favor of subjects such as modern languages, which were presumably more useful in a modern economy.[17] Jeremiah Day, in the first, most often cited part of the report, laid out an elaborate defense of a traditional liberal education in terms of faculty psychology, which called for the equal cultivation of the mental, moral, and physical powers. Day encapsulated this process in his assertion that "the two great points to be gained in intellectual culture are the *discipline* and the *furniture* of the mind; expanding its powers, and storing it with knowledge."[18] Though significant in itself, Day's portion of the report has completely obscured the equally important contribution of Kingsley, professor of Greek and Latin and representative of the language-dominated mode of teaching the classics that we saw in chapter 1. Whereas Day spoke generally about the role of mental discipline in the college, Kingsley focused specifically on the place of the ancient languages in a liberal education. "Familiarity with the Greek and Roman writers," Kingsley argued, "is especially adapted to form the taste, and to discipline the mind, both in thought and diction, to the relish of what is elevated, chaste, and simple." Anyone without preparation in classical language would immediately feel "a deficiency in his education" when he tried to discuss a literary topic or associate with Europeans and Americans of "liberal acquirements." In other words, to study the classics was to be "liberalized by liberal knowledge."[19] But the age of Jackson could do little with defenses of gentlemanly learning. The Yale Report, in fact, has eclipsed a far more penetrating and effective defense of classicism that was emerging at the same time.

HUMANISTS IN DISSENT

Beginning in the 1820s another chorus of opposition to the traditional methods of teaching the ancient tongues emerged. It came from within the colleges themselves, from a new generation of classical language professors born between 1794 and 1810. Because they taught the classical courses, these critics knew firsthand the blemishes that defaced the ancient tongues in the American college. All had received a lengthy classical education in preparatory schools and in college. Yet their criticisms were of an entirely different nature than the criticisms of those who advocated greater utility within the curriculum. Nor did they defend classical learning in the obsolete terms of the Yale Report. Instead, these young classical language professors were reformers from within, hoping not to jettison the classical languages but to change the way they were taught. This fact made a critical difference to the way they framed their dissent from eighteenth-century classicism. For while the utilitarians might question the relevance of ancient languages to modern life, this new generation of classical scholars sought instead to refashion that connection, to forge anew America's link to classical antiquity.

The accomplishment of these humanist revolutionaries was extraordinary. They were the first scholars to import German scholarship to America and to incorporate modern historicism into the curriculum. Furthermore, they fundamentally transformed the function of classical antiquity in nineteenth-century American culture. Yet, with the notable exceptions of Edward Everett (1794–1865) and George Bancroft, they have been banished from their important place in antebellum American intellectual life. In addition to these two men, other major antebellum reformers include Robert Bridges Patton (1794–1839), of Middlebury College and Princeton; Charles Anthon (1797–1867), of Columbia College; Charles Beck (1798–1866), of Harvard; Theodore Dwight Woolsey (1801–89), of Yale; Cornelius Conway Felton (1807–62), of Harvard; Isaac Stuart (1809–61), of South Carolina College; and Alpheus Crosby (1810–74), of Dartmouth. In this chapter we will examine their specific criticisms of American classicism and how these shaded into a critique of antebellum American culture more broadly. In chapter 3 we will see how their new approach to antiquity transformed American higher education.

These young classicists began their transformation of classicism in America by turning to a revolution in classical scholarship that had begun in late-eighteenth-century Germany. There classical and biblical scholars had begun to apply new tools of philological criticism to ancient texts, drawing attention to the historical particularity of their creation. J. D. Michaelis's *Introduction to the New Testament* (1750), for example, in contrast to prevailing views that the Bible was a unified, divinely inspired text, distinguished among the individual books of the New Testament, showing the historical particularities of their language and formation. Classical scholars also began to examine Greek and Roman texts in a new way, bringing a critical eye to the authoritative texts of classical antiquity. This "New Humanism" figured importantly in the restructuring of German academic life, as classical scholars sought improved intellectual and social status as independent investigators within the universities, freed from clerical control. A giant in German New Humanism was Friedrich August Wolf (1759–1824), whose *Prolegomena ad Homerum* (*Prolegomena to Homer*, 1795) and *Darstellung der Altertumswissenschaft* (Classical scholarship: a summary, 1807) marked a watershed in New Humanism by demonstrating the importance of establishing textual authorship, meaning, and authenticity.[20]

Central to Germany's New Humanism was an infatuation with the art, literature, and other achievements of the ancient Greeks. Although the Romans had been essential in transmitting the remnants of Greek culture to the modern era through transcriptions of texts and copies of sculpture, eighteenth-century German philhellenes looked beyond these facts to find in ancient Greece a quasi-religious realm of the beautiful and the true. Admiration for ancient Greece was part of a cultural revolt against a sterile Augustan classicism, religious oppression, fussy baroque decor, and aristocratic control. Perceiving a relationship between ancient Greece and modern Germany in an ideal world of literature, art, and philosophy, German philhellenes sought to revive a Greek "spirit" *(Geist)* in modern Germany. Hellenism pervaded many aspects of German thought in the late eighteenth and early nineteenth centuries, animating the literary efforts of Goethe (1749–1832) and G. E. Lessing (1729–81) and the aesthetic philosophy of J. G. Herder (1744–1803) and Immanuel Kant (1724–1804).[21]

German New Humanism arrived in America on several fronts, but we can begin by looking at its influence on Harvard and Boston, where its rise was most spectacular. Indeed, in the first half of the nineteenth century Boston was commonly known as the Athens of America. Such classical tags were commonplace in a nation that styled itself as a new Rome or Hellas; in fact, in the antebellum era thirteen towns were named Athens, while others vied for the sobriquets Athens of America, Athens of the South, Athens of New England, Athens of the Southwest, and Athens of a particular state.[22] But Boston had special claim to being the Athens of America: it was the site of the first Athenaeum in America (1807)—modeled on Liverpool's own—and it was home to Harvard College, which nourished several generations of America's most influential classical scholars in the nineteenth century.

In 1810 Harvard entered its so-called Augustan Age (1810–45), when an influx of public and private monies allowed the college to launch an aggressive program of campus building, student enrollment increases, and faculty hiring that soon allowed it to bypass Yale as the largest college in the nation.[23] One result was the foundation in 1815 of the Eliot Professorship of Greek Literature, the fruit of a $20,000 endowment by the Boston merchant Samuel Eliot.[24] The Eliot Professor was assigned, in addition to the normal duties of teaching, to give lectures to the public and to students on "the genius, structure, characteristics, and excellences of the Greek language" to "cultivate and promote the knowledge of the Greek language and of Greek literature" so that "the University may send out alumni who possess a discriminating knowledge of the renowned productions of Grecian authors, and the powers of the Grecian language."[25] With great fanfare, the Eliot Professorship was bestowed upon Edward Everett, urbane, ambitious, and barely twenty-two years old, who was quickly dispatched to Germany to finish his education.[26] There Everett admired the critical historical scholarship of G. E. Schulze, J. G. Eichhorn, and Arnold Heeren.[27] He also traveled with his friend Theodore Lyman (1792–1849) to Greece, where he saw firsthand the sites about which he had so frequently read.[28] Also at Göttingen were three other Harvard students, George Bancroft, George Ticknor (1791–1871), and Joseph Green Cogswell (1786–1871), who, like Everett, returned to America to popularize both Hellenism and the new philology.

Returning in April 1820 with his Göttingen Ph.D. (1817), Everett over the next several years gave a series of polished lectures on Greek art and literature to his classes at Harvard and to the larger Boston community.[29]

In them he spelled out the reasons for the superiority of ancient Greece and why all Americans, not just the learned, should remedy their "deficient" taste in Hellenism. He reiterated these views in an article in the *North American Review* in 1821:

> It is sincerely to be regretted that we have not more means among us for forming a taste for the antique, and for the study of the beautiful remains of Grecian art. It may certainly be maintained, without exaggeration, that these beautiful remains are the most authentic legacy, which we have received from the glorious world that went before us. The admirable writings, which have descended to us from them, are indeed invaluable. It elevates the spirit to think that you are perusing the works of the great masters of wisdom, and poetry, and learning, from ages so long elapsed. But it is impossible to know perfectly more than one tongue, and the mind struggles too often in vain against the obstacles of a difficult language. . . . But a beautiful temple, or column of a temple, or ancient statue, or relievo, is an object on which we can gaze with all the freshness both of sense and emotion, that belonged to the age of its production.[30]

So popular were these lectures that Everett became the toast of Boston in the early 1820s, sparking admiration for German scholarship, German universities, and Hellenism.[31] His student Ralph Waldo Emerson (1803–82) compared Everett's effect on Harvard to "that of Pericles in Athens," admiring the effect his "new learning" had on "our unoccupied American Parnassus."[32]

In framing the contours of Hellenism in America Everett was especially influenced by two Germans: Johann Joachim Winckelmann (1717–68), the historian of art, and August Schlegel (1767–1845), the romantic critic of drama. Winckelmann had become one of the most influential of the eighteenth-century German neo-Hellenists with the publication of his *Geschichte der Kunst des Alterthums (The History of Ancient Art)* in 1764. Here he had argued that the Greek climate and ancient Greek political freedom had given that nation's art transcendent superiority over the art of all other societies. Ancient Greek art, especially ideal rather than realistic statuary, would endow modern German viewers with a quasi-religious, transcendent experience in addition to aesthetic enjoyment and scholarly knowledge. Winckelmann helped to inaugurate in Germany a religion of beauty, in which Greek art moved the viewer into contact with what was universal and eternal. He also helped to focus attention on Greek art as a national, historical production. As Suzanne Marchand points out, Winckelmann "described *the* art of *the* Greeks" rather than individual works by individual artists.[33] This reductionism became a habit in America as well. Everett had become fascinated with Winckelmann's work while in Göttingen and gushed when he returned, calling Winckelmann "the first, who reduced the history of the Grecian art to a scientific form." Greek art was "the most authentic legacy" of Greek glory and far more accessible to the majority of Americans than the language itself.[34]

August Schlegel, author of *Lectures on Dramatic Art and Literature*, translated into English in 1815, likewise achieved some renown in early-nineteenth-century America. Shoving aside the ideal of classical learning as a model of taste, Schlegel argued that ancient art and drama should be viewed historically, with an appreciation for the characteristic merits of each time and place. One should judge a dramatist not by the degree to which his plays resembled those of the ancient Greeks but by the extent to which he fulfilled the promise of his particular national spirit. Imitation was always fruitless, dull and frigid; original genius, on the other hand, was the aim. Like other New Humanists, Schlegel elevated the ancient Greeks to the peaks of genius and reduced everything Greek—art, literature, science, society—to one nationally defined, harmonious whole.[35]

While Everett's brilliant oratory helped to popularize artistic phil-hellenism among the general public, other early Hellenist scholars more quietly helped to transform the textual culture of campus classicism. Robert Bridges Patton (1794–1839) was one of the first to attempt to make American campuses less like grammatical factories and more like laboratories of philological scholarship of the German type. Patton graduated from Yale in 1817 and became a professor of ancient languages at Middlebury College in Vermont the following year. He convinced the trustees there to allow him a three-year leave of absence to study philology at the University of Göttingen. Patton returned to Middlebury College in 1821 with his Ph.D.[36] But if Harvard's sons found it measly when compared to Göttingen, Middlebury looked even worse. The libraries alone tell a story: in 1820 Harvard's library had 24,000 volumes; Yale's, fewer than 10,000; and Middlebury's, about 1,400. Göttingen, on the other hand, had 200,000.[37]

Patton's solution was to bring Göttingen to Vermont by founding a "philological society" at Middlebury. The society was little more than Patton's library of 1,000 books made available to others, with some extra money secured to import "the best periodical works . . . of a philological character, in England and on the continent."[38] At a stroke Patton had doubled the size of Middlebury's library; he even began to teach German. But it was not to last. Irritated by his low (and sometimes absent) salary at Middlebury, Patton moved to Princeton in 1825, taking his library with him.[39] Finding New Jersey as parochial as Vermont, Patton resurrected his literary salon as the Nassau Hall Philological Society, again essentially Patton's library made public, plus meetings for discussion, criticism, and lectures that created what one professor called a "tone of literary excitement" at Princeton.[40] James W. Alexander, professor of belles-lettres at Princeton, marveled at his friend Patton's library. "He has the best editions ancient and modern of all the classics . . . a uniform edition of the whole range of Italian literature and all of the German writers of eminence. His collection of atlases and plates is noble indeed."[41] This from a private collection when Yale's library, according to James Kingsley, was not only small but utterly "deficient in classical and general literature."[42] Not just the sheer number of volumes but also breadth and depth in the collection were critical to maintaining a proper library for college students, argued Patton in a lecture at Princeton in 1825:

> Here we should find elementary works in abundance—grammars of standard reputation, and approved accuracy, and comprehensiveness; dictionaries which leave the student no excuse for his ignorance but his laziness; works illustrative of the idioms, peculiarities of dialect, elliptical phrases, and nicer shades of expressiveness, which occur in his classical studies; works which lay open the whole pantheon crowded with deities, and spread before him the rich field of mythological antiquity; together with extensive and accurate maps, geographies and histories, which pour a flood of light on the classic pages.[43]

Patton wanted not just works by older philologists like Richard Porson, Gronovius, and Richard Bentley but also the new, more general works of Schlegel, Arnold Heeren, and Girolamo Tiraboschi, books that could lead students "from the cautious and circumscribed flights of the fledgling, to the sublime soarings of the bird of Jove, from the playful circles of the inhabitant of the rivulet, to the uncontrolled range of Leviathan in the deep."[44] Patton even went so far as to prepare with his Princeton seniors an edition of Aeschylus's tragedy *The Seven against Thebes* (1826), a task that greatly surpassed in complexity the kind of rote work that most students did in their classrooms at the time. Princeton's fleeting moment as America's Göttingen ended, however, in 1829, when, for reasons that are unclear, Patton left Princeton to teach at Edgehill, a local preparatory school, once again taking his library with him. The Nassau Hall Philological Society shut its doors and sold its furniture.[45]

Along with Edward Everett, George Bancroft, and several others, Patton produced the basic texts that American college students needed to study ancient Greek more thoroughly than they had before. The American publishing record of these books alone is testament to the rapid infusion of German scholarship in American colleges in the first half of the nineteenth century. Both Everett and Bancroft, for example, published editions of the *Greek Grammar* of the University of Berlin professor Phillipp Buttmann (1764–1829) in the hopes that they would elevate "the standard of excellence" in classical study. Buttmann's *Greek Grammar*, wrote Everett, was far superior to the grammars it replaced, "not only for philosophical investigation but learned criticism."[46] Buttmann's grammar remained one of the mainstays of the freshman and sophomore years in American colleges until mid-century.[47] Patton edited one of the first American editions of a Greek-English lexicon, a work vital for any native English speaker hoping to acquire some precision in Greek translations. Patton's fourteen-hundred-page tome rested self-consciously on the latest work of great German lexicographers like Franz Passow, and like Buttmann's grammar, it was directed to "those who push their Greek reading beyond the narrow limits of College study, as well as to those who were just forming an acquaintance with this noblest of languages."[48] The grammar and lexicon were buttressed by the German bestseller, Friedrich Jacobs's *Greek Reader*, first edited in English by Everett in 1823. Filled with extracts from ancient Greek texts, it allowed students to practice the words and syntax they had learned in their grammar and lexicon. Like Patton's dictionary, Jacobs's *Greek Reader* rejected the traditional practice of teaching Greek through Latin, one of the main barriers to higher Greek scholarship, according to Everett. It also dispensed with extracts from the New Testament because the Greek therein differed "so much from that of the heathen writers, that it does not form the best introduction to their study."[49] By 1830, study of Jacobs's *Greek Reader* was required for admission at colleges across the country. It went through more than fifty-five editions over the next half-century, finally ceasing publication in 1872.[50] The scholarly labors of Everett, Bancroft, and Patton were widely praised for their accuracy and for raising the standard of American scholarship. But in terms of the sheer number of German-inspired textbooks produced in the antebellum era no American scholar surpassed Charles Anthon, professor of Greek and Latin at Columbia beginning in 1820. Though repeatedly charged with plagiarism and sloppiness, Anthon produced almost fifty school editions of classical texts that drew heavily on the most recent German editions, thereby contributing greatly to the increasingly Germanic basis of classical language instruction in American colleges.[51]

To this new scholarly interest in Greece, American classics teachers added their more specific critique of the method of classics teaching in America. They began with the preparatory schools. By 1830, thanks to glowing reports about German education in the press over the past decade, many Americans knew that German students arrived at universities both older and far better prepared in classical languages than American students, who not uncommonly entered college at age sixteen, some even before they were fourteen years old. These usually immature young Americans arrived at college unprepared even "to advance beyond the *hic haec hoc* recitations of the academy," as the classicist Robert Patton at Princeton put it, and the freshman year at many colleges was often spent in remedial work.[52]

A detailed catalog of the defects in preparatory education came in 1834 from Henry Cleveland, a young Harvard graduate and teacher at the Livingston County High School in New York. Cleveland had been a student at Harvard under John Popkin, the professor of Greek. His experience in college, combined with his duties as a preparatory school teacher, had convinced him that "the greatest obstacle to the improvement of education in our universities is the imperfect and superficial preparation in schools." Cleveland gave a memorable description of a typical boy's forced march through the classical languages:

> By frequent repetition he is at last able to construe and perhaps parse a few Latin books which are mentioned as necessary for admission into the college; by the help of Ainsworth's Dictionary, he can change an English sentence into Latin words, (I will not say sentence, for not one boy out of an hundred who enters the first college in America has any idea of Latin idiom). He knows a few Latin books, but he is far, very far, from knowing Latin. In Greek it is still worse. The young pupil can perhaps read the Testament and the Graeca Minora, or Jacob's [sic] Reader; but beyond this his knowledge of the language is utterly at fault; ask him to write it; ask him only to pen a sentence from your dictation. It is beyond his knowledge; he cannot even write the Greek characters.

To be sure, Cleveland continued, boys were taught ancient languages, but other branches of ancient study were entirely neglected. "The school-boy is taught Latin and Greek; but how little care is bestowed upon the key to the beauties of these languages, Heathen Mythology, Antiquities and Classic History." A boy's knowledge of ancient geography was so stifled by rote memorization that it was "contemptible compared with that of any tolerably educated sea-captain."[53]

At the college level, similar criticisms were leveled beginning in the 1830s. One particularly revealing critique emerged at Harvard in 1831, when two young faculty members delivered a series of frank, scathing letters to the Harvard Corporation enumerating the defects they saw in the existing language curriculum. One was Cornelius Conway Felton, a twenty-four-year-old tutor in Greek and Latin who had graduated from Harvard in 1827 after studying ancient languages under George Bancroft, Edward Everett, and John Popkin. Felton ultimately became one of the most influential classical scholars of the antebellum era, disseminating the results of the new German learning to generations of college students and to the public at large. In 1834 Felton became the second Eliot Professor of Greek Literature at Harvard, a post he held until 1860, when he became Harvard's president. The other was the German émigré Charles Beck, aged thirty-three, who had become a professor of Latin at Harvard only that year. Beck had studied classics at the University of Berlin and theology at Heidelberg, eventually receiving a Ph.D. at Tübingen in 1823. By different paths, both had become aware of the new German scholarship and used it to frame a criticism of American language teaching.

First, they assailed the grammar-dominated mode of teaching Latin, which made the class routine into what Robert Patton called an unending string "of dactyls, spondees, caesural pauses, accents and quantities, of palpable darkness and nonsense."[54] One of the worst offenders, they argued, was the three-hundred-page *Latin Grammar*, by the Edinburgh schoolmaster Alexander Adam (1741–1809). This grammar, first published in Scotland in 1772, had been in use at Harvard since 1799 and was required for admission at many colleges until the 1830s.[55] It had long been welcomed because its explanatory text was in English rather than Latin.[56] This feature failed to impress Beck, who found the *Latin Grammar* "of no use to a thorough understanding of the laws of the Latin language."[57] The text, made murky by rules and exceptions, obfuscated any existing regularity in the Latin language.

Felton and Beck also criticized the ahistorical nature of Alexander Adam's widely used *Roman Antiquities*, a gargantuan compendium of facts about the ancient Latin world that functioned as students' Baedeker. Adam's object was to join "the explanation of words and things together," which he believed would help students to root their grammatical studies in a wider context. Overwhelmed by the sheer volume of facts about the ancient world, Adam freely directed students to other sources on subjects that threatened to overflow the boundaries of the book. He carefully presented competing opinions on controversial subjects, such as the mythical origins of the "religion of the heathen."[58] But the text presented only a stagnant picture of Roman society, the wheels of change mired in the mud of descriptions, quotations, and citations from ancient authors. Some examples from the examination questions at Harvard in the 1830s give some indication of the kind of information students were expected to glean from Adam's *Roman Antiquities*: "At what times did the Senate meet?" "What was the number of senators until the time of Sylla [sic]?" "What was the number in the time of Julius Caesar? under Augustus?"[59] The *Roman Antiquities* did for Roman life what the grammar did for Latin literature, parceling the past into discrete bits of information to be memorized. "Well do we remember being more thoroughly beaten in attempting to cope with the Roman legion in the pages of Adams [sic], then ever was a Carthaginian army on the fields of Italy or Spain," wrote Felton of the *Roman Antiquities*.[60]

Greek was just as bad. Every problem in classical language teaching in America, argued the young classicists, was symbolized by that best-selling giant of Greek pedagogy, the *Graeca Majora*. The worst thing about the *Graeca Majora* was that like Adam's grammar, it ripped the authors from what Felton called their "proper connection," or context.[61] A mere compilation of short extracts, the *Graeca Majora* sent students on a breakneck ramble through the literary monuments of ancient Greece that left them, according to Felton, with "but little knowledge, and *no* discriminate knowledge, of the various authors from whom the extracts in this work are taken."[62] It was "difficult to create an interest in an extract from anything."[63] In fact, between 1820 and 1850 a nationwide chorus of opposition to the *Graeca Majora* rang out, as though that book alone had come to embody all the defects of classical language education in America. It was too simple, fit only for a boy of twelve, complained one person.[64] Another remembered "plodding heavily through a page of the 'Majora,' formally, mechanically, and doubtingly."[65] A third dismissed it as a "motley assemblage of shreds and patches . . . a collection of scraps" that made the study of Greek in American colleges "a trial of philological skill and grammatical accuracy" rather than one of "the stepping stones to wider views—the perception of universal criticism, the cultivation of taste and imagination, the attainment of a knowledge of the Poetry, the Philosophy, the History, the Oratory."[66] Felton's was a lifelong campaign to stamp out the *Majora*, born perhaps of youthful trauma: he had read its smaller companion, the *Graeca Minora*, so many times as a child that he could recite all of it from memory and suffered from permanent eye trouble because of the effort.[67] As late as 1850 he was still recalling the "imperfect aids" that assisted "us up the slow and toilsome *Gradus ad Parnassum*."[68]

Largely turning their backs on the English and Scottish classicism that had dominated American higher education until the early nineteenth century, beginning in the 1820s and 1830s American scholars exalted "the noble spirits of Germany" who could appreciate the "moral sublime" of the Greeks.[69] American scholars admired a number of things about ancient Greece. First, with democracy ascendant in America, fifth-century B.C. Athens became more acceptable as a model for young men to emulate in preparation for citizenship. As early as 1824 George Bancroft, in an article praising a new Greek grammar from Germany, looked to Homer and Herodotus as being favorable to "virtue and liberty." The poems of Homer "present as a mirror the purest qualities of our nature."[70] An anonymous writer in the *Southern Literary Messenger* in 1839 concurred: "And have not Grecian classics a special claim on the attention of American youth? Were not their authors *freemen*, and their thoughts beating high with the fervor of liberty? . . . Surely we should reverence and study so valuable a memorial of the past—embodying the breathing thoughts of heroes—the vehicle of indignant rebukes of tyranny—and connected, in its history, with the first dawnings of liberty, and the proudest epochs of the ancient world."[71] Moreover, there was the Greek language, which stood "without question at the head of all languages, both ancient and modern," in the words of Alpheus Crosby, a Hellenist at Dartmouth College. "Its fullness of forms, its copiousness of vocabulary, its studiousness of euphony, its flexibility in derivation and composition, and, above all, the unique circumstance that we can trace it as a living language through the varieties of twenty-eight centuries, from a period beyond the reach of secular history, even to the present day, combine to give it a title to this place, altogether indisputable."[72] Finally, American classicists echoed Winckelmann's deification of sculpture. Greek sculpture, argued Isaac Stuart to the South Carolina legislature in 1835, "proved conclusively that the Greek artists are happiest of all in their selection of expression, and most graceful in their marble contours." This made Greek taste and style "superior to those of any other nation."[73]

As Greece ascended, Rome declined. "Latin is among the languages which stand in the second class . . . far below the Greek," wrote the Dartmouth classicist Alpheus Crosby in 1833, four years before he confined his instruction to Greek alone. Because of this "the Latin literature holds a rank below it, similar to the rank of the Latin language."[74] Romans were derivative, not original like the Greeks. "Vain would be his labors, who should essay to comprehend the efforts of Roman genius, without first listening to the instructions of Rome's literary masters," agreed Cornelius Felton at Harvard.[75] At South Carolina College, Isaac Stuart declared in 1836 that Greek's superiority was "by universal acknowledgment," while Latin was "inferior" though "great in strength and richness." Whatever virtues the Latin language had were due to the improvements made by the Greeks after their subjection to Rome.[76] Exhausted by eons of Latin, these scholars determined that "the Roman has had its sway long enough, and it is time the Greek should take its turn."[77]

HELLENISM

American scholars' enthusiasm for German scholarship and philhelle-nism was part of a larger vogue for Greece in American culture during the antebellum era. Beginning in the early years of the nineteenth century Americans renounced their tenacious attachment to republican Rome and turned to the art, literature, and landscape of Greece. Hellenism did not so much cloud Americans' enthusiasm for Rome as offer an alternative to it. Greece now emerged as the province of the spiritual and the ideal, the seat of art and learning, representing what was at once unique and universally true. "As Greece, then, gave the ancient world instruction and culture, so Europe instructs and refines the modern world, and all mankind; and as Rome wrought out the social work of antiquity, America seems called to do the same service for modern times," observed the Princeton geogra-pher Arnold Guyot in 1849.[78] Furthermore, Greece implied political, liter-ary, and artistic exoticism. "Athens was certainly a free state; free to licentiousness, free to madness," remarked Edward Everett in 1824.[79] By contrast, Rome retained its association with nationhood (and later in the century, empire), standing for what was pragmatic, earthbound, and stately. Latin was the language of Roman nationhood, not of the self; it was what one author called "the true language of History, instinct with the spirit of nations, and not with the passions of individuals."[80] The dichotomy between Greece and Rome that emerged in the antebellum era was summed up most memorably in these lines from Edgar Allan Poe's 1831 poem *To Helen:*

> On desperate seas long wont to roam,
> Thy hyacinth hair, thy classic face,
> Thy Naiad airs have brought me home
> To the glory that was Greece
> And the grandeur that was Rome.[81]

The rise of Greece as an alternative locus for aesthetic and literary cultivation was a form of romantic nationalism. Greece became a place where Americans could seek new forms of self-identification. Philhellenism in America rose alongside other newly interesting pasts that also were deployed as compelling nationalist antecedents. Racial Anglo-Saxonism, for example, flourished in the antebellum era as a way to distinguish true-blooded Americans from blacks, Indians, Mexicans, Spaniards, and Asians, who stood in the way of white territorial and political conquests.[82] Ancient Egypt offered exotic religious alternatives and a spare, massive architectural style.[83] The Holy Land, always central to the American self-image, likewise emerged with new clarity in travel, literature, and art in the nineteenth century.[84]

Popular admiration for ancient Greece also emerged in the context of the modern Greek revolution against the rule of the Ottoman Turks (1821–29). Americans saw in the struggle a mirror of their own revolution against Britain a half-century earlier, and they repeatedly compared the two conflicts. Inspired by the poetry of Lord Byron, their own navy's incursions into Turkish waters, and the transatlantic discussions occasioned by Lord Elgin's removal of the Parthenon frieze to Britain (1803–12), Americans allied themselves with the modern Greek cause. Numerous articles and pamphlets between 1815 and 1829 followed the same logic as Henry Ware's address, "The Vision of Liberty" (1824), an appeal for volunteers to aid the Greek cause:

> Oh Greece, reviving Greece! Thy name
> Kindles the scholar's and the patriot's flame . . .
> And is there none to *arm* in thy defence?

No ardent, generous, devoted youth,
　　To pledge his fortunes and his truth,
　　And, nobly exil'd, cross the wave,
　To join the oppress'd, and aid the brave?

Go forth, if such there be, go forth;
Stand by that nation in her second birth.[85]

Colleges also encouraged sympathy for the modern Greek cause. Everett's oration at Harvard in 1821 was just one of many speeches that knit the American Revolution to the modern Greek struggle for independence. In 1819 Gerard Hallock delivered a commencement address at Williams College entitled "Greek Oration, On the Character and Prospects of the Modern Greeks," and in 1821 Nicholas Croghan, at Transylvania University, in Lexington, Kentucky, delivered an oration entitled "Dissertation on the Associations of Visiting Greece and Italy."[86] Women also participated in the alliance of American and Greek freedom. Patriotic women in New York City in 1824 set about trying to construct a Grecian cross on the heights of Brooklyn, to be capped by the Greek wreath of victory. They sent out an appeal to classical scholars around the nation to discover what such a wreath had originally been made of, sparking a small controversy between rival scholarly camps in New York City and Boston.[87] Women's academies likewise contributed to the cause of patriotism. The Female Academy, in Lexington, Kentucky, joined several male colleges in raising money for the Greek cause and issued an "Address to the Young Ladies of the West" calling on the women of America to contribute funds.[88] Leaders in women's education saw in the Greek revolution an opportunity for educating modern Greek women. In the early 1830s Emma Willard (1787–1870) and Almira Hart Lincoln Phelps (1793–1884) appealed for American women to help their "Own Sex in Greece," and Willard helped to found the Troy Society for the Advancement of Female Education in Greece.[89]

　　Americans traveled with increasing frequency to Greece in the early nineteenth century, making the depiction of Greek ruins and landscapes in architecture, literature, and art far more common than they had been in the eighteenth century. Among the earliest Americans to travel to Greece was the aristocratic Philadelphian Nicholas Biddle (1786–1844), who had become enamored of the Greeks while studying at Princeton, from which he graduated in 1801. Convinced that "the two great truths in the world are the Bible and Greek architecture," Biddle set off for a grand tour of Greece in 1806. Upon his return to America he became one of the chief advocates of the neo-Hellenist architectural style that characterized the antebellum era. The Second Bank of the United States in Philadelphia (the so-called Biddle Bank), built in 1819, reflected his preference for the simple, massive Doric style.[90] Travelers to Greece routinely published accounts of their travels and also gave lyceum lectures on them, often drawing parallels between the freedoms of Greek antiquity and the state of the modern Greeks.[91] They preferred by far the ancient Greeks but anticipated the day when the modern Greeks, degraded by Turkish rule, would "show themselves worthy of their glorious descent."[92]

Hellenism also infused the outpouring of romantic literature in the antebellum era that is commonly known as the American Renaissance.[93] Classical referents were part of the literary arsenal of writers such as Nathaniel Hawthorne (1804–64), Herman Melville (1819–91), and their peers. Invocations of ancient Greece appeared not only in their writings but also in the growing number of novels produced by what Hawthorne dismissed as "scribbling women," helping to spread the knowledge of classical Greek history and mythology from college-educated men to growing numbers of women. For example, the best-selling novel in the wartime Confederacy was Augusta Jane Evans's *Macaria; Or, Altars of Sacrifice* (1864), a novel that drew parallels between a modern woman sacrificing herself for the Confederate cause and a self-sacrificing woman in classical Greece.[94]

Another strand of antebellum American Hellenism lay in the Platonic idealism of the New England Transcendentalists, whose philosophical and literary project formed an important part of the American Renaissance.[95] Plato had yet to play a significant role in the college curriculum, but classically trained Transcendentalists such as Ralph Waldo Emerson drew their idealist philosophy from the long tradition established by Plato, Plotinus, and England's seventeenth-century Cambridge Platonists. "Plato is philosophy, and philosophy, Plato," Emerson affirmed regarding the philosophical tradition that schooled the Transcendentalists to shirk external authority, whether empirical or Scriptural, and look to the inner self for divine communion.[96] In the person of the Transcendentalist Margaret Fuller (1810–50) were expressed both the Platonic and the newly feminine sides of antebellum Hellenism. Broadly educated in Greek and Latin by her overbearing father, and uninspired by that "stern composure" she associated with the Romans, in the 1840s Fuller initiated a series of discussions for women on Greek mythology to find a realm of Ideas in the Greek myths that transcended Christian revelation.[97] This idealist position, as we will see in chapter 4, reached the American college curriculum in the teaching of Plato only after the Civil War, but it had deep roots in this earlier period.

Like republican Rome in the Revolutionary era, ancient Greece in the antebellum period functioned as a forum for political instruction, showing that antiquity in the first half of the nineteenth century remained immediately relevant to American political culture. Yet while Americans in the eighteenth century had quarried Rome for lessons in republicanism, antebellum Americans also mined ancient Greece (especially Periclean, or fifth-century B.C., Athens) for a model of democracy. One particularly illustrative episode of antiquity's continuing political didacticism in antebellum America was Harvard's acquisition in 1819 of the large painting *The Panorama of Athens*.[98] As it did for so much of its Hellenism, Harvard had Edward Everett to thank for the Panorama: he had urged his wealthy college friend Theodore Lyman to purchase the painting in London and donate it to their alma mater. The painting was the work of the English painters Robert Barker and Robert Burford, among the most prolific panorama painters of the day. The *Panorama of Athens* was by Everett's reckoning "the most admired" and "valuable" of panoramas, for it offered a "faithful representation of the Athenian remains," from the Parthenon and the Erechtheum on the extreme left to the Temple of Theseus on the far right.[99] Like many panoramas of the day, it was accompanied by a key that supplied the spectator with information about each important site. Viewers of this breathtaking exhibition would believe themselves actually to be looking at ancient Athens from a nearby hill. In Everett's words, "The illusion was Complete."[100]

The American career of the *Panorama of Athens* reveals some of the reasons for the persistent classicism of antebellum American political culture. First, the panorama was explicitly aimed at both the learned community and the general public, to cultivate their civic sensibilities by reference to ancient Athens. As Everett put it in 1823, the panorama was to be "exhibited for the gratification and instruction of the students of the University and the liberal public."[101] This was an important statement of the universal appeal the panorama was to have on Americans. Panoramas, with their expansive vistas of majestic sites such as Versailles, the West, and the Holy Land, enjoyed huge popularity in the United States and Europe between 1790 and 1860 because they were able to reach the public more readily than printed descriptions. John Vanderlyn (1775–1852), an influential American panoramist, praised the medium's ability to "captivate all classes of spectators," requiring "no study or cultivated taste" for its appreciation.[102] The Harvard Corporation in 1821 began to show the *Panorama* to the Boston public so as to join it to the Harvard community in a collective admiration of ancient Greece, one that would delight the senses, cultivate the morals, and instruct the intellect. In 1821 the *Panorama* was exhibited in the New Circus in Mason Street, advertised by Everett himself in a series of public lectures on ancient Athens in the Boston marketplace.[103] The Harvard Corporation then loaned the giant painting to John Vanderlyn, who showed it in his classically inspired Rotunda in New York City and then in a number of other cities. Vanderlyn, who was firmly convinced of the political importance of ancient Greece in modern America, wrote of the *Panorama:* "On such a scene no citizen of a free and enlightened Nation ought to look with indifference."[104] Athens was the birthplace of democracy, literature, and art and so should kindle in the modern American spectator "the warmest sensations of gratitude and admiration."[105] The public exhibitions of the *Panorama of Athens* between 1820 and 1845 coincided with other public pronouncements of the American affinity for making Greece politically relevant to the modern era. When they gazed at the panorama, Americans looked at a mirror of themselves.

Poverty ultimately strangled Harvard's ambitious program for the public display of the panorama. In 1842, after years of traveling exhibition that damaged the painting, it was finally put on permanent display in a fire engine house on the Harvard campus, only to burn to ashes in a large campus fire in 1845.[106] During its quarter-century career, however, it had exemplified the persistent American association between ancient life and the modern American nation.

GREECE AND THE CRITIQUE OF ANTEBELLUM AMERICA

Just as republican Rome served as a model for the young American nation in the late eighteenth and early nineteenth centuries, so ancient Greece began to appeal to a new generation more enamored of populism during the antebellum era. Yet classical Greece also acquired a second function besides that of serving as school for democrats, a function that ultimately helped to undermine the position of the classical world as a template for political instruction. During the antebellum era Americans for the first time began to imagine classical antiquity as modernity's antidote rather than its mirror. Hellenists, as we saw above, still drew direct parallels between the ancient world and the modern, but they also began to conceive of ancient Greece as a corrective to the evils of the Jacksonian era, a remedy for political and civic corruption, materialism, anti-intellectualism, factionalism, and populist mediocrity. Rome, of course, was not exempt from this service. In the art and literature of mid-century America the Roman countryside and the city's ruins sometimes stood as silent rebukes to modernity. But Greece served this function far more extravagantly.

With anticlassicism now construed largely in economic terms, classicism emerged as noneconomic, standing aloof from the crassness of mere getting and spending. Classicism, that is, became a form of antimaterialism. Edward Everett argued in 1821 that Americans, who were hopelessly mired in vulgar, modern concerns, should acquaint themselves with the pure beauty of ancient Greek texts and art. By contemplating "ancient solidity," Americans would purge themselves of the "inferiority" of "modern taste," the "superficial theatrical character in the modern world."[107] His student Cornelius Felton concurred in a lecture at the American Institute of Instruction in 1830. Knowledge of Greece and Rome "may not lead to the invention of a single new mechanical agent; it may not be the direct means of increasing our fortunes a single dollar. But it will give us an enlarged view of our nature . . . it will teach us to judge charitably of others' minds and hearts; it will teach us that intellect, and sensibility, and genius, have existed beyond the narrow circle in which we have moved—beyond the limits of our country—centuries before our age. Such lessons are needed in the every day concerns of life."[108] G. B. Cheever likewise juxtaposed the materialism of physical science with the spiritual elevation of classicism:

> The wide prevalence and success of physical science begets a prevalent tendency to materialism, and multiplies those employments which belong to man rather as a creature of the understanding than as a being of pure reason, and in which the general mind of the age may work so busily as to be delighted by its own apparent activity, while in reality all its deep spiritual energies sleep, its power of self-consciousness is lost, self-ignorance reigns heavy and undisturbed, and it becomes empty of thought, superficial, and indolent.[109]

Among the chief architects of this new use for antiquity were the young classical scholars who criticized the prevailing grammatical mode of classical language instruction. Their arguments went far beyond the classroom. Faulty language instruction, they argued, not only blighted language teaching on campuses, it imperiled the nation by failing to endow students with the intellectual and moral capacity to resist politically corrosive agents such as private ambition, demagoguery, and ignorance. The scholars thus began the process of entirely reimagining the function of classical antiquity in America, of refashioning the ancient past so as to better resist present perils.

Beginning in the 1820s classical scholars offered indictments of American politics that hinged on failures within classical education. Among the earliest and most scathing came from Robert Patton, of Princeton, in a lecture he gave there in 1826, in which he linked failures in classical education to the political decline of the young republic.

> The preservation of our political health and vigour demands that we provide, from within ourselves, an antidote to the widespreading corruption which darkens our political prospects. Between moral degradation and ignorance there is a mutual reaction. . . . In a word, our systems of education are defective. . . . But our citizens may be enlightened—may have a smattering of

science, and even be able to construe and parse a passage in Homer or Thucydides, and still be destitute of that kind of intelligence which peculiarly adapts them to the form of government under which we live.[110]

George B. Cheever recommended "the study of the ancient Greek classics" as "one of the best safeguards to the students of this country against modern degeneracy and a depraved taste."[111] An anonymous southerner specifically connected reform of the classical curriculum to the dangers besetting antebellum America. "With the enormous influx of immigrants, the rapid extension of population and organization of new States, with increasing wealth and power, and with the natural consequences of these—the growing influence of political parties; there must also arise conflicting interests, jealousies, struggles for ascendancy, and corruption in compassing the ends and giving triumph to the policy of party combinations." The author urged Americans to look carefully at antiquity "lest in the aggressions of conflicting interests, or policy, or parties, we repeat the history and share the calamities of those republics of antiquity, whose records Providence has preserved to us as splendid and mournful examples of national greatness and of human error."[112]

Antebellum commentators also offered classical study in the colleges as a remedy for the anti-intellectualism that led to demagoguery. Like Alexis de Tocqueville in *Democracy in America* (1835), classicists and other Hellenists feared the mediocrity and uniformity heralded by populism. "An ignorant community may be virtuous in motive, but cannot be so in practice . . . and you will see your peaceful ignoramus" become "the blind instrument of outrage in its blackest forms," argued Felton in a lecture in New York in 1828.[113] Such concerns meshed with the Whig impulse to use public education as a safeguard against social and political disorder. Daniel Webster (1782–1852), one of the great classically trained orators of the antebellum era, argued in 1837 that education protected American citizens from becoming "dupes of designing men."[114] It was not just Greece that warned against excessive democracy, for anti-Jacksonians also turned to Roman history to express their fears of Old Hickory. Whig leaders such as Henry Clay (1777–1852) routinely painted Andrew Jackson as a modern Julius Caesar, citing Jackson's military background, his charismatic pandering to the populace, and his overweening executive power as omens of tyranny.[115]

Fears of anti-intellectualism and mobocracy manifested themselves in concerns for apparently declining oratorical standards and calls for a return to classical models of public speaking. The early nineteenth century witnessed the spread of oratory beyond the confines of the ministry and the political elite to a much larger and more diverse spectrum of the population. The lyceum movement, public lectures, stump politicking, revival preaching, and antebellum reform movements all caused public speaking to spread far afield. The definition of an informed citizenry shifted as well, from the purely political goal of defending against tyranny to the personal goal of individual fulfillment and career advancement.[116]

With this expansion of oratory's sphere and function, standards inevitably shifted. A "middling" rhetorical style spread among evangelical preachers like Henry Ward Beecher (1813–87), who sought a rapport with his audience through sympathy and emotion rather than the authority bestowed by education or office.[117] Abraham Lincoln (1809–1865) was another antebellum orator who successfully used middling rhetoric. Not educated in the classics as a boy (he had read Aesop's *Fables* in translation), Lincoln turned to English-language classics like the King James Bible, John Bunyan's *Pilgrim's Progress*, and Shakespeare.[118] Lincoln mastered the art of speaking to both the elite and the commoner in simple cadences of such majesty that they in fact recall some of the great orators of ancient Greece, even if they do not appear to have been directly based upon them.[119] In the halls of the national and state legislatures, which were open to many more men who had not received a classical education, middling rhetoric and even boorish slang flourished along with anticlassical diatribes. "I had rather speak sense in one plain and expressive language, than speak nonsense in fifty," declared the Irish-born New York state representative Mike Walsh in 1854, to much laughter.[120] In the South, economic power shifted from the Virginia and South Carolina low country to the West, threatening the domination of the plantation gentry, which had rested in part on their classically imbued rhetorical style.[121]

Classicists and their allies deplored the rise of middling rhetoric because it presaged mobocracy. "Our orators and demagogues pamper the pride of that great despot, the sovereign people, with flattery as fulsome as was ever poured into a tyrant's ear," remarked Felton in 1828.[122] An anonymous writer in the *Southern Quarterly Review* who signed himself "H" noted in 1851 that "the discussions in the Senate of the United States during its last session, were characterized by equal coarseness and vulgarity, but by less point, without the excuse of either the example of Comedy or Dionysia." He despaired that this poor rhetoric spelled political decline. "The remark of Tacitus . . . that liberty is the nurse of eloquence, that oratory languishes and dies if separated from her breast, is not the hollow lament of desponding rhetoricians, but a sound political truth."[123] Even the most distinguished politicians in the Congress, argued J. C. Gray in 1826, were a national embarrassment, prone to indulge in "irrelevant and ostentatious digressions, in cold and trite similes, and a gay confusion of metaphors, in finical circumlocutions, and a studied avoidance of direct and definite language."[124]

In place of middling oratory proponents of classical rhetoric held up the oratory of antiquity, and especially of ancient Athens, as most conducive to freedom because it produced an educated democracy. "It is not to modern ages that we must look for the exemplars of the art of eloquence," one urged. "We must not be content with seeking them in Rome, or even in Greece; but we must go to the single city of the Athenians, for the ripest fruits of this, as of nearly all intellectual excellence."[125] Another anonymous writer pointed to the presidential campaign of 1840 as analogous to popular speaking in ancient Greece because it spread out to the population at large. "We are enacting Greece on a grander scale," he noted. Stump speaking, however, was no excuse for off-the-cuff rambling; the most successful orators in the 1840 campaign prepared themselves "with minute care," just as the orators of antiquity had done.[126]

Demosthenes now surpassed Cicero as the idealized speaker because of his commonsensical, straightforward style, which cut through the lexical thickets of less disciplined speakers. Indeed, Demosthenes emerged as the archetype of the manly, muscular speaker, rivaling and sometimes displacing the more flowery model of eighteenth-century masculinity, Cicero. "We perceive in it nothing vague or extravagant, nothing florid or redundant, nothing strained or ostentatious," wrote J.C. Gray of Demosthenes in 1826.[127] Study of Demosthenes, argued another, "indurates the mental constitution, gives it muscle and energy, makes it like iron, girds the intellect with power, and teaches it to concentrate its energies." Next to Demosthenes, Cicero often appeared "spiritless."[128] Antebellum northerners and southerners both christened their most cherished orators Demosthenes: the southern Hellenist Hugh Swinton Legaré (1797–1843), Thomas Pinckney (1750–1828), and Daniel Webster.[129] Legaré himself admired both Cicero and Demosthenes, the latter for the way he deployed rhetoric for immediate political ends, a trait that accounts for the reason why many Hellenists praised the "business-like" character of Demosthenes even as they disparaged the business character of the nation.[130]

The adulation of Demosthenes paralleled the rise of a new, more emotional style of oratory in the nineteenth century, as orators like Daniel Webster invoked both a rational and a "sentimental" response from their hearers in balanced proportion according to the tenets of faculty psychology.[131] This style also had the effect of drawing in the hearers rather than focusing attention on the speaker alone, an oratorical goal that classicists conceded was necessary in the age of party politics and that even Webster reluctantly deployed at the Whig Party's urging in the 1840 campaign.[132] Demosthenes, wrote an anonymous author in 1852, "combined in his efforts, in admirable proportion, appeals to the reason and the feelings; his passion and enthusiasm were based on the granite foundation of rigid argumentation. Cicero paid more attention to the graces of speech, was more artistic, copious and ornate. Demosthenes had more rugged strength, more of that vehemence which bears away all obstacles. When speaking, Cicero thought more of himself, Demosthenes more of his subject."[133] Another writer concluded that "Demosthenes, therefore, produced the greatest effect on the *auditor*, Cicero on the reader."[134]

As part of their critique of vulgar oratory and corrupt politics this new generation of classical scholars used their classrooms as forums for restoring classical oratorical standards. They recognized that ancient oratory was the most "practically useful" portion of Greek literature, as Felton put it, and they encouraged students to place the orators into both a historical and a modern context.[135] One interlined textbook from mid-century shows that students were directed to the Webster-Hayne debates of 1830 when they read Demosthenes' oration *De Corona*.[136] Others classicists, entering into an ancient scholarly debate over proper pronunciation of the ancient languages, encouraged students to pronounce ancient Greek and Latin authentically so as to reproduce as closely as possible the conditions of ancient democracy in modern America.

Cornelius Felton urged college students to read Demosthenes and other Greek orators in the original in order to "acquire the power of entering into their spirit fully."[137] He despaired of students' dreadful pronunciation, of the effect it might have on a reincarnated Demosthenes:

> If Demosthenes could rise up to day, and go to a council of state in Athens, he would comprehend with tolerable ease the drift of the arguments there used. . . . But if the awful Shade were to enter a classroom in one of our universities, and hear a Freshman glibly construing his own magnificent oration on the crown, would he not stare with amazement, when told that the young gentleman was reciting the very eloquence he had himself, at the height of his powers and renown?[138]

The goal of proper study and accurate pronunciation was actually to *be* a new Demosthenes in the new Athens. "I become loftier, and am no longer the man I was," wrote Felton. "I seem to myself to be Demosthenes, standing upon the tribunal, pronouncing that same oration, exhorting the assembled Athenians to imitate the valor and win the glory of their ancestors."[139]

As long as national and regional identities merged in America, both northerners and southerners could share an admiration for the republics of antiquity. But rising sectionalist tensions in the wake of Nat Turner's rebellion in 1831, the South Carolina slave uprising that had left over sixty whites dead, caused southerners to embark on more studied defenses of slavery and to craft a regional classical identity increasingly distinct from the North's.[140] Turning to both biblical and classical precedent, they invoked ancient Greece, and especially ancient Athens, to justify the nobility of a slave society.

A number of factors made ancient Greece a congenial exemplar for the South. Its warm climate, its latitude, and its small, scattered, independent city-states evoked in many minds the rural, sparsely populated South.[141] Moreover, Greek slave labor supported a landed, cultivated leisure class of statesmen, much as Roman slavery had done. In the 1840s southern nationalists especially began to turn to Aristotle and Herodotus as they shifted from environmental to biological explanations of black inferiority. In his *Politics* Aristotle had asserted that slavery rested in a natural, hierarchical order; some men must always be subject, others must necessarily lead, and the two should be of different races.[142] "Nature has clearly designed some men for freedom and others for slavery:—and with respect to the latter, slavery is both just and beneficial," wrote the University of Mississippi president George Frederick Holmes (1820–97) in reference to Aristotle's *Politics* in 1850.[143] These writers also recruited Herodotus to prove the immutability of blackness over time. If Herodotus showed "Negroes with black skins, and wooly heads," Josiah Priest asked in his *Bible Defence of Slavery* (1853), "how is it to be shown that they were not always so?"[144] Because slavery was written in nature, it supported an organically unified society in which both slave and master benefited. Slaves flourished under the benevolent protection of their masters, and masters were freed from the cares of labor to exercise their political freedoms. Organic justifications of slavery also explicitly condemned the industrializing, competitive economy of the North. The proslavery writer George Fitzhugh (1806–81) called northern workers "slaves without masters," chained to a cutthroat capitalism unsoftened by the benefits of paternalism. Southern writers also cast the North as an overweening Sparta to the South's more democratic Athens, or a licentious Athens to the South's more socially conservative Sparta, or to a modern-day Macedonia threatening Athenian liberties.[145]

Northern and southern colleges in the late eighteenth and early nineteenth centuries had developed similar classical curricula, but this common educational mission began to fracture somewhat with rising sectionalist antipathies. By the 1840s and 1850s distinct abolitionist and proslavery camps could be discerned within the formerly more homogeneous American collegiate landscape. While northern colleges such as Oberlin, Illinois College, and the University of Michigan became known as abolitionist hothouses, proslavery apologists such as Thomas R. Dew (1802–46) at William and Mary and James H. Thornwell (1812–62) at South Carolina College developed a distinct southern voice. The University of the South, in Sewanee, Tennessee, was in fact founded to train true southrons girded against the corrupting influences of the North. One recent effort to link southern nationalism with a shift in classical language teaching at southern colleges is inconclusive, but regardless of how antiquity was taught in southern colleges by the late antebellum period, it appeared in an increasingly anti-northern educational context.[146]

Hellenism, though ultimately deployed for differing political ends in North and South by the eve of the Civil War, testified to a gradual shift in the uses of antiquity during the antebellum era. At the heart of this shift was the change in emphasis from Rome to Greece that emerged as the political and social structure that had supported eighteenth-century classicism began to erode. Democratizing education, a booming market economy, intensifying party factionalism, and the rise of a middling oratorical culture led both critics and votaries of classicism to reconsider the place of antiquity in modern life. Classical scholars formed an important constituency of Americans who imagined a new role for antiquity in American political culture: as antidote to economic and scientific materialism, a bulwark against mobocracy, a corrective to uncouth rhetoric, and, in the South, a compelling model for an agrarian slave society beset by attacks from an industrializing, free North.

❧ 3 ❧

FROM WORDS TO WORLDS,
1820–1870

BEING GREEK

It is an axiom of the history of universities that changing the curriculum is like moving a graveyard. All the more so when that curriculum *is* a graveyard, a repository of political and moral truths embalmed in the timeless authority of classical antiquity. The antebellum era is often termed the heyday of the classical college, a designation intended to evoke the sterility of American higher education by painting classics as the very symbol of retrograde pedagogy and scholarship.[1] This view emerged from the effort to emphasize the astonishing transformation of American higher education after the Civil War, but it is fundamentally misleading with regard to the antebellum era. During those years, young American classical scholars set about reimagining the classical curriculum in America colleges, turning an era that is so often cast as the nadir of American higher education into a period of great intellectual ferment. Moving from a focus on grammar alone to the study of the entirety of the ancient past—from words to worlds—they inaugurated the study of "civilization" in the university. Moreover, they emphasized the national, historical particularity of Roman and Greek societies, drawing parallels between antiquity and modernity that emphasized the possibilities of democracies more than the perils of republics. Finally, under the influence of German historical scholarship, they encouraged students to reimagine their own relationship to antiquity, seeking not so much to imitate the ancients as to absorb their spirit through the critical, historical study of authentic ancient texts. Like their romantic Hellenist counterparts in England and Germany, they imagined the shift from words to worlds as a process of becoming Greek, literally of self-transformation through a historicized encounter with the classical past. "We are all Greeks," Percy Bysshe Shelley (1792–1822) had declared in 1821, a manifesto that echoed in American classrooms for the remainder of the nineteenth century.[2]

What did it mean to move from words to worlds? Of necessity, much of students' time in the classics classroom remained devoted to mastering these two difficult languages through the tedious avenues of memorization and repetition. But now this grammatical facility was viewed as preparation, a kind of verbal tool kit, necessary before embarking on the study of the society and the author that had produced that grammar. The Princeton philologist Robert Patton contrasted the grammatical mode of studying language with the study of literature, a project that allowed the student to see the author's "very soul."[3] "Shall the student confine himself to the abstract and laborious study of grammar, until every form, inflection and syntactical construction, in all their endless variety and nicer shades, are forced into his memory, as if by the operation of machinery; or shall he neglect these minutiae of grammar, and plunge into the vast ocean of classical literature, with nothing but the raw materials of his bark, calculating afterwards to form, adjust and compact it?"[4] Cornelius Felton likewise urged students to consider "the situation of the author . . . the connexion of the passage in question with the context [and] the style of ancient thought" in trying to unravel the meaning of a difficult passage.[5]

As attention to historical context increased, so did scholars' emphasis on the uniqueness of Greek and Roman cultures, that is, on what made the Greeks Greek and the Romans Roman. Rather than emphasizing the similarities and parallels between modernity and antiquity, as Americans had done in the eighteenth century, scholars now demanded attention to what was individual and unique. George Frederick Holmes eloquently encapsulated this new pedagogical goal in 1849: "We must learn to think in their own language as the Greeks thought before we can truly inhale the glorious and inspiring atmosphere of Athenian wisdom—and we must learn to feel as the Romans felt before we can become participants in the profound and practical sagacity of ancient Rome."[6] Emphasizing the national particularity of the Greeks and Romans required that the professor

describe in detail the social context of the texts being taught, a new pedagogical goal that justified the introduction of lectures into the classroom.
"A course of lectures," argued Felton in 1830, "should contain an account
of the physical character, the scenery, the climate and the productions of
Greece, with the early and later mythology, and the fabulous traditions of
the heroic age. . . . Private life in all its forms, opinions in all their shades,
the intellectual character and physical conformation of the people, should
be fully illustrated."[7] Alpheus Crosby likewise recommended that students study the "three great departments" of antiquity: language, history,
and finally "thoughts and feelings."[8] At the same time that classicists
looked for what was unique in Greece and Rome, they also sought the
essential national character of each, the distinctive art, literature, politics,
and people that created a "civilization." Felton argued this point in 1840.
"With all their diversities, the Greek people were singularly homogeneous, both physically and mentally."[9]

The study of unique ancient civilizations relied on a new attitude toward history and time that abandoned the Enlightenment's cyclical view
in favor of a narrative of progressive development over time. The cyclical
theory of history had assumed an imagined affinity between Revolutionary Americans and the republic of ancient Rome. In this view the modern
era recapitulated the ups and downs of antiquity, and historians could
rightly adopt a stern, admonitory tone to warn of incipient decay. As we
have seen, many in the antebellum era continued to draw explicit parallels
between Greece and Rome, on the one hand, and modern America, on the
other. But now a new historical view arose alongside the earlier Enlightenment view, in which scholars imagined less that they would recapitulate
ancient history than that they would develop upward from it. The Renaissance faith in the necessary temporal finitude of the republic, an idea that
had endured through the eighteenth century, began to be replaced by the
idea of progressive development through time. This view was characteristic of romantic historicism, which searched the past for confirmation of a
new faith in a benevolent future. Dispensing with the declensions of
Enlightenment history, they forecast progress, and history now took on a
celebratory rather than a cautionary tone.[10] Alpheus Crosby in 1833 re-
futed the Enlightenment's cyclical historicism, which he called "the old
belief that the world is deteriorating," in favor of romantic progressive

historicism, which he termed a "general law of improvement." Crosby reasoned that even given the perfections of ancient literature, America would produce a literature "superior to any the world has ever yet seen."[11]

Paradoxically, romantic historicism marked the first step in Americans' gradual abandonment of classical antiquity as a guide to the present. The historicization of ancient texts pioneered in the antebellum classroom was on the one hand an effort to meet the ancients in an authentic, critical way. Students would surrender their objectionable modernity by immersion in an authentic past. Yet on the other hand romantic historicism required that students desert their imagined affinity with classical antiquity, that they abandon the premise that ancient society was a mirror of the modern era. Instead, they were to dwell on the differences between their era and ages past so that they could properly position a text in a historical context. By the late nineteenth century, as we shall see, romantic historicism had the effect of making classical antiquity appear inconsequential to moderns precisely because it was so alien. In the antebellum era, of course, no one could foresee this unintended consequence, and classical scholars cheerfully guided their students to an authentic encounter with the distant past. Felton's advice to his students in 1830 captured both the hopeful spirit of romantic historicism and its potential for historicizing the ancients into irrelevance. "The student who would enter fully into the merits of a classical author, must take himself out of the influences immediately around him; must transport himself back to a remote age; must lay aside the associations most familiar to him; must forget his country, his prejudices, his superior light, and place himself upon a level with the intellect whose labors he essays to comprehend."[12] He continued, with a searing indictment of the eighteenth-century practice of making the classics merely mirrors of the present:

> We take them up, with little knowledge of ancient history, and none of mythology; we hurry through them, with or without a grammatical knowledge of the languages, as chance or caprice may direct; we bring them to the standard of modern tastes, and refer them to our own tribunals. Instead of transporting ourselves back to the time when they lived, we summon their Shades to appear before us,—differing in every respect from them, differing in religion, differing in morality, differing in prejudices—to answer for opinions

and systems, put forth ages and ages before our own opinions and systems were thought of. Such is not doing the justice we owe them.[13]

Though arguably conducive to a more accurate understanding of antiquity on its own terms, this view also made antiquity remote and different, emphasizing the gap of time and culture that separated the moderns from the ancients rather than the imagined affinity that linked them.

The historical relocation of antiquity, however, also enabled its new role in the antebellum classroom, which was that of antidote to modern perils. By perusing the literature and art of antiquity, students imbibed its "spirit," thereby purging themselves of modern materialism, anti-intellectualism, and selfishness. Americans, argued Felton, lived in a "self-indulging age" that condoned "a constant reference to self" to the exclusion of anything that may "have existed beyond the narrow circle in which we have moved." This national provincialism was only worsened by materialism and machines; the single-minded pursuit of wealth demeaned any labor not solely directed toward profit, while "labor-saving machines" made a mockery of sustained effort.[14] By contrast, the spirit of antiquity revealed truth and beauty and so cleansed the modern soul. It was described as something into which students entered, as though they were embarking on a journey through time. Alpheus Crosby described the broad study of antiquity as a student's "entering with interest into its prevailing spirit . . . to inspire and cultivate a taste for the beautiful and true."[15]

Imbibing the spirit of antiquity, moreover, remade the individual. Classical study during the antebellum era became a path to the reconfiguration of the inner self. Americans had always focused on improving themselves, but in the nineteenth century they concentrated more on the possibilities of self-development than on those of self-repression, abandoning the grim dogmas of Calvinism for the millennial optimism encouraged by the Second Great Awakening. This was the age of the "self-made man," a term coined by Henry Clay to describe the ability to perfect the self through sustained, concentrated efforts to improve body, mind, and morals. The ideal of the self-made man was not necessarily a materialist vade mecum. It did not apply to Americans who had succeeded by making millions, but rather to those who pursued inner self-improvement, forging a balanced character from the raw stuff given by nature.[16] The study of Greek and Roman literature and society now emerged as a new path to self-formation.

A locution that appears in both European and American Hellenism captured this faith in the profoundly self-transforming abilities of classical study: *being Greek*. "Everyone should be Greek in his own way! But he should be Greek!" Goethe had cried in the eighteenth-century heyday of German neo-Hellenism.[17] This refrain echoed in antebellum America. By surrendering the modern self and entering into the spirit of antiquity through the study of texts placed in their broad historical context, American students might also become Greek and so resist the seduction of materialism and machines. Felton, for example, urged his students actually to "be Demosthenes" by properly pronouncing their ancient Greek.[18] When students in the 1850s recalled the problems with the old grammatical mode of classics teaching practiced by John Popkin of Harvard, they said his mind "was not Greek enough in its mould to feel and interpret all the power and beauty of its literature."[19] Being Greek meant surrendering one's barren modernity to imbibe the authentic spirit of ancient civilization, thereby girding the soul against corrupting modern forces.

Being Greek in antebellum America was thus a form of cultivation or self-culture. Cultivating students was a new pedagogical goal that emerged in the context of troubling economic changes that demoted classical learning in favor of utilitarian knowledge. The words *culture* and *cultivation* derived originally from agriculture, and in the antebellum era they retained their associations in the language of faculty psychology with the development of things that grew, from plants to animals to human minds. But culture now also became a corrective to industrialism and democracy. Culture, Raymond Williams has observed, emerged in the nineteenth century as a higher court of intellectual and moral appeal, a "body of arts and learning" and "values superior to the ordinary progress of society."[20] By the 1850s classical scholars were using the word *culture* not as a synonym for development but to mean a thing in itself, a product of civilization. One could speak, as Felton did in 1852, of the "art, culture, and poetry" of the Greeks.[21] Culture by mid-century became both something that one could do and a thing that one could study (although it was not until late in the nineteenth century that *cultured* was defined as something that one could be). Cultivating the self and studying the culture of the Greeks became synonymous with following a path of inward perfection distinct from chasing Mammon.

The best-known American exposition of the medicinal capacities of self-culture was made by the Unitarian minister William Ellery Channing (1780–1842), who in 1838 described the human ability to "enter into and search ourselves" with the aim of the "unfolding and perfecting of his nature." Self-culture was explicitly made distinct from the desire to "get property and to rise in the world."[22] For antebellum classical scholars, classicism was essential to self-culture. The culture bestowed by a classical education buttressed democracy by creating an educated citizenry elevated above the concerns of mere getting and spending. "The truth is," said Felton at an address to the Livingston County High School in New York in 1828, "that intellectual culture . . . is deeply connected with every principle of virtue and every spring of noble action," creating "a moral, a thinking, an educated community."[23] "The Greek classics," argued an anonymous contributor to the *Knickerbocker* in 1836, "should be read mainly to cultivate the sense of beauty." The student should not be forced to plod laboriously over grammar but rather should be encouraged to make "an *easy* and *rapid* perusal" so that "the reading of it can become a pleasure." Such was the distinction between the grammatical expertise of a philologist and the general culture required by a student. "Philology is a science and profession; the perusal of the Iliad is a means of general cultivation," the writer concluded.[24]

Antebellum classical scholars imagined their new pedagogical agenda not only as a way to raise the level of undergraduate study in America but also as a way to make them comparable in their professional standing to scholars in German universities. They represent a transitional generation between the eighteenth-century world of porous, broadly diffused but unspecialized classicism and the more specialized, professionalized scholarship that emerged in the late nineteenth century. A few studied in German universities, but only a few held Ph.D.'s, nor was the doctorate a requirement for college-level classics teaching.[25] They pressed their scholarship, based on German models of critical historicism, into the service of teaching students rather than communicating with like-minded professionals. In the tradition of the man of letters, some made extensive efforts to disseminate their new learning in the avenues of antebellum public discourse—the lyceum lecture, the general-interest journal, the broadly gauged book. In mid-century these archetypal Victorian institutions of self-improvement reached far broader segments of the population than did colleges, and classicists used them as means to knit themselves and the classical world to the larger community.[26]

In fact, efforts at creating advanced educational opportunities along German models met with little success in the antebellum era, as we saw with Robert Patton's philological seminary and his edited Greek tragedy at Princeton. The same end greeted two more efforts at Harvard, in 1831–32 and 1846–47. In 1831 Felton and Beck launched the first postcollegiate training program in classical study in America. Their Philological Seminary aimed to teach the classics to college graduates, either for the pleasure of the student or as training for future classical language teachers. Its curriculum included lectures and the reading of whole works, innovations that Felton used in his undergraduate classrooms shortly after that. But the seminary had failed by the end of the 1832–33 academic year, perhaps the victim of financial difficulties.[27] A quarter-century later they tried to make classical philology a branch of study in the newly founded Lawrence Scientific School, but this effort too failed, squelched by those who doubted that classical philology was a scientific pursuit.[28]

The shift from words to worlds is clearest in two areas of the antebellum college curriculum, the study of Homer and the study of ancient Greek tragedy. Each shows how a new historical spirit of inquiry subtly changed the methods and purposes of classical study in the antebellum classroom. Moreover, these methods, though imported from German universities (and also from British, as Britain itself adopted German critical methods in the second quarter of the nineteenth century), were adapted to a specifically American agenda and reflected classicists' concerns about American religion and politics in an age of rapidly shifting expectations.

HOMER AND HISTORICISM

Although the rise of Greece in antebellum colleges centered chiefly on fifth-century b.c. Athens, a new approach to Homer, who had lived several centuries earlier, revealed the rise of a new historical spirit. Homer had long been admired in America as what one author in 1796 called "this father of genuine poetry."[29] Until the second third of the nineteenth century, however, the formal collegiate study of Homer was confined to the relatively short extracts that appeared in textbooks such as the *Graeca Majora*. Students reading this patchwork were more likely to get a sense of Homer as grammarian than of Homer as prince of epic song, much as James Freeman Clarke had done at Harvard, remembering the *Iliad* as a bog. This grammar-oriented pedagogy reflected the prevalent eighteenth-century view that Homer had both written and recited his poetry.[30]

After 1820 American classics professors launched a wholly new approach to Homer, one that was based on a revolution in Homeric scholarship in late eighteenth-century Germany that became known as the Homeric question. The Homeric question represented the avant-garde of textual scholarship; it was complicated, daring, and potentially explosive in its implications about the authority of all ancients texts, whether classical or biblical. For Americans, it revealed both the prospects and the perils of their historicized encounter with the classical world. On the one hand, it was exciting and self-transforming to "be Greek" by immersing oneself in Homer's world; on the other hand, the truths revealed by accurate textual study had the potential to conflict with Christian truth as revealed in another ancient text, the Bible.

Controversy had surrounded the creation and authorship of the *Iliad* and the *Odyssey* for centuries. The two epics enjoyed majestic importance even in antiquity, and in the early Christian world they animated discussions of the nature of the divine despite their pagan origins.[31] Yet the meaning of the Homeric poems remained shrouded in part because they were so very ancient. Homer probably lived in the ninth or eighth century B.C., during the so-called Dark Age of Greece, a time that late-twentieth-century scholars continue to find vexing because of the dearth of surviving evidence. Remnants of any kind antedating 700 B.C. are fragmentary; some pots, weapons, and graves are among the only remnants of Homer's day, when he and other bards wandered the land singing long poems. Thus, even in antiquity Homer's epics seemed somewhat mysterious. Critics wondered, for example, whether and when the fantastic events described in the epics, such as the abduction of Helen, the siege at Troy, and the adventures of Odysseus, had actually occurred. Throughout antiquity, however, and well into the eighteenth century it was almost universally agreed that Homer had lived in a literate age, that is, that he had written his poems and that modern texts of the *Iliad* and the *Odyssey* were transcriptions of these documents.[32]

During the Middle Ages, when knowledge of the ancient Greek language declined, Homer also faded from the scene. Interest in Homer rose anew during the Renaissance, with its reverence for classical Greek models to emulate for style and ethical example. Where, scholars asked, should Homer be ranked in the pantheon of Greek and Roman authors? Did Virgil's *Aeneid* outstrip the *Odyssey* in artistic merit? During the Battle of the Books in seventeenth- and early-eighteenth-century England and France Homer was central to debates over whether the ancients had been superior or inferior to the moderns. Charles Perrault, tireless defender of the moderns in France, stirred a huge controversy by arguing that the *Iliad* would have been much superior had it been composed in the seventeenth century, with the benefit of modern knowledge. As it was, argued Perrault, the epic was marred by boring digressions and endless enumerations of people and objects that were peripheral to the narrative, such as the excessively long description of the shield of Achilles.[33] Yet others, such as Alexander Pope, Anne Dacier, John Dryden, and George Chapman, so admired Homer that they penned vernacular translations that stood as small monuments of literature in their own right.

Toward the end of the eighteenth century, interest gradually shifted from the character of Homer and the value of the epics as literary models toward the historical production of these ancient poems. Among the first contributions to this new mode of criticism was Robert Wood's *Essay upon the Original Genius and Writings of Homer* (1775), in which Wood argued that the art of writing did not exist in Homer's time.[34] This take on Homer was new, and it set the tone for debates over the Homeric question for the next century. The question was answered most memorably by two classical philologists in Germany, C. G. Heyne and his student F. A. Wolf, although Wolf's fame in the matter eclipsed that of Heyne in the twentieth century. As Anthony Grafton has shown, Wolf was not sparklingly original in applying the tools of historical criticism to texts, but after the publication of his *Prolegomena ad Homerum* in 1795 Wolf's name became synonymous with the criticism of Homeric epic.[35]

The Homeric question as it emerged from scrutiny by Heyne and Wolf really comprised a number of questions about the authorship and history of the poems. In the *Prolegomena* Wolf stated that the two received texts attributed to Homer bore no resemblance to the original poems sung during the Homeric age: neither Homer nor his listeners could write. Instead, Homer and the other itinerant songsters of his day had wandered the land singing short poems that varied each time they were uttered, although many of these songs cohered around a certain number of themes. It was only much later, under the reign of the Athenian tyrant Pisistratus in the sixth century B.C., and then among the Alexandrian critics, that some of the songs began to be written and sewn into the longer epics that moderns knew as the *Iliad* and the *Odyssey*. From this time onward the texts were further revised—and corrupted. Wolf did not deny that most of the songs that eventually made up the two epics were invented by Homer, but he did claim that Homer had not composed the disparate sections as parts of one great poem.[36] What became clear by 1800 was that the eighteenth-century texts of the *Iliad* and the *Odyssey* only faintly echoed Homer's original songs, and philological efforts to reconstruct an original written text could take the critic back only to some of the first, flawed written transcriptions.[37] The original Homer could never be resurrected; the critical tools of philology could not reach beyond the dawn of writing. Many philologists considered Wolf's theories to be extreme and logically untenable, and during the nineteenth century a lively debate raged on the Continent and in England about the authorship of the poems.[38]

American scholars' interest in the Homeric question arose along with their interest in German classical scholarship and especially a newly historicized ancient Greece. Everett and others began to write about the Homeric question in general-interest journals beginning in the 1820s, and study of the epics soon formed an important staple of the college curriculum. For example, at Bowdoin College in Maine Homer was nowhere part of the college curriculum in 1837, but ten years later sophomores spent a great deal of their time in their Greek class studying the *Odyssey*.[39] Older methods of grammatical recitation now shared classroom time with a historical Homer as professors began to supplement the reading of the *Iliad* and the *Odyssey* with secondary texts that explained the Homeric controversy. The diary of James Hadley (1821–72), Yale's professor of Greek language and literature, shows that in 1850 he "read on authorship of Homeric poems, and made remarks at the recitation."[40] At Dartmouth College, the Greek professor Alpheus Crosby taught Homer using an English work, Henry Nelson Coleridge's *Introduction to the Study of the Greek Classic Poets* (1831). Coleridge's book was almost entirely given over to an analysis of Homer's works and the Homeric question. Designed for use in schools and colleges, it was intended to move students beyond the study of words and give them "the sense of the writer."[41] Classicists also used Felton's American edition of William Smith's *History of Greece*, which contained a chapter on the Homeric poems and the modern controversy over their origins.[42] Late editions of Felton's widely used *Iliad*, which went through a number of editions, gave extended treatment to the English classicist George Grote's recent contributions to the question from his monumental, twelve-volume *History of Greece* (1846–69).

The new practice of putting Homer into a historical context—what antebellum classicists variously called "historical criticism," "critical analysis," and "critical inquiry"—became central to classicists' effort to cultivate undergraduates.[43] In this way students could be made aware of the characteristic features of Homeric epic and so reap the benefits of a liberal, cultivating education. "We must study ourselves into the Homeric age," declared Felton in 1848.[44] Classicists now recoiled from the didactic, moralizing texts of the eighteenth century, such as the "omnivorous farrago" of Charles Rollin's thirteen-volume *Ancient History* (1730–38).[45] After 1820 they offered a substantially different route, suggesting that students must imbibe the spirit of antiquity through a critical, historical reading of the ancients. Students needed to surrender their modern prejudices and immerse themselves in the spirit of this remotest antiquity. Henry Nelson Coleridge recommended "a total rejection of all associations with modern fashions and artificial modes of feeling."[46] Felton's edition of F. A. Wolf's *Iliad* laid out clearly the agenda of the historical Homer for the undergraduate project of self-formation:

> My wish has been to lead the young student to read the poem, not in the spirit of a school-boy conning a dull lesson to be "construed" and "parsed" and forgotten when the hour of recitation is at an end, but in delightful conscious-

ness that he is employing his mind upon one of the noblest monuments of the genius of man. Whatever his conclusions may be as to the merit of particular passages, if any remarks of mine should chance to excite his attention to the real character of the poem, and to promote a habit of analytical criticism, whether his opinions agree with my own or not, the object which I have proposed to myself will be accomplished.[47]

Studying Homer historically also helped students to understand Homer as literature. Though less exalted than fifth-century Athens, the Homeric age appeared to American scholars to have been a kind of preamble to the perfections of the Age of Pericles. One anonymous author writing in the *Southern Literary Messenger* called the Homeric age the "dawn of civilization," during which the "national genius first began to develop itself."[48] Homer had lived during the "national youth" of the Greeks, the age in which the Greek language became, according to Felton, "most fitted for poetical composition." Like the English people during the age of Shakespeare, the Greeks during the age of Homer had "risen above the state of barbarism to a condition of some refinement, yet uncorrupted by luxury." Childlike, natural, and imaginative, the Greeks of Homer's day had expressed these characteristics in the language of their epics.[49] To assist students in cultivating their literary sensibilities through the reading of Homer, Felton inserted the illustrations of the English artist John Flaxman (1755–1826) into his edition of the *Iliad*. Flaxman's art, though modern, represented the spirit of the Homeric age, displaying in the artistic realm what Homer's language revealed in the literary. Art and literature together would help students to understand Homer "in a liberal way."[50]

Homer cultivated students, but he could also corrupt them. The historical criticism of the Homeric controversy also raised questions about the historical origins of the Bible. German historical criticism of the Bible was deeply problematic for a number of American scholars in the antebellum era, many of whom feared its heretical implications, namely, that the Bible might not be a divinely inspired unity, just as Homer's epics might be a mere patchwork sewn in a post-Homeric age.

Drawing on a historical sense of the remote antiquity that had produced both the Old Testament and the Homeric epics, antebellum classicists drew parallels between the two. Like scholars in England and on the Continent, they noted that both biblical and Homeric texts were almost universally known among the educated, supplying an inexhaustible source of allusions and narratives. Homer was known as the bible of the Greeks and stood in relation to the record of profane history in the same way that the Old Testament was related to sacred history.[51] Henry Nelson Coleridge considered the historical setting for the *Iliad* to be coeval with the patriarchal age of the Holy Land. He said that Homeric society and Old Testament society were "almost identical," displaying "a correspondence of spirit and manners."[52] William S. Tyler (1810–97), the Williston Professor of Greek at Amherst College, argued the same point in *The Theology of the Greek Poets* (1867). Homer was an eyewitness to events in Greece during the time that the Hebrew patriarchs also flourished. Homer, and especially the theology of Homer, "cannot but be a study of deep interest to the Christian who, with no narrow or one-sided view, sees one and the same hand, the hand of God, in the history of the whole human race," wrote Tyler.[53] Not only was there a historical correspondence between the two ancient societies but Homer, like the Bible, could guide modern students with his luminous narratives. Indeed, wrote Coleridge, students should approach Homer "with something of the kind of reverence which we yield to the Hebrew Genesis, and be perpetually familiar with its contents as with the secular Bible of mankind."[54]

Yet classicists explicitly rejected insinuations that Homer might be equivalent to the Bible. To one anonymous writer in the *North American Review* it was obvious that Homer would always rank second to the Bible in influence because the old bard was "uninspired."[55] American classical scholars also rejected the idea of multiple authorship of the Homeric poems in a language that showed their concerns to be driven partly by religion. Tyler dwelt at length upon the arguments over Homeric unity "because they are in themselves questions of great interest, whose influence, according as they are seen in a true or a false light, must extend over the entire field of ancient literature, and affect the authority of the Hebrew Scriptures not less than the credit of Greek poetry."[56] A devout Congregational minister, known as "the bishop of Hampshire County," Tyler, like other classics professors of the mid-nineteenth century, idolized the Greeks despite his dismay that heroes like Socrates were not

Christians.[57] This ambivalence was reflected in his study of the Homeric question. Rejecting the idea of multiple authorship, Tyler argued that such a theory was irreligious: "The moderns have gone to the extreme of uncertainty and impiety in the utter dismemberment and annihilation of this divine poem."[58] He thought that the German critics who were undermining Homeric and biblical unity were engaged in "unscrupulous and sacrilegious warfare" and was pleased that some of them had "repented."[59] James Hadley, of Yale, confessed in his diary that he wished that Grote's *History of Greece*, which argued for a separate authorship of the *Iliad* and the *Odyssey*, had "the moral and religious view."[60]

There were limits, then, to the degree to which mid-nineteenth-century Americans pursued historical accuracy, constrained as they were by boundaries of Protestant morality. These concerns were not confined only to Homer. Even as they studied a more historically accurate Homer, American and British students also faced a renewed commitment on the part of their professors to expurgating sexually explicit passages in a number of classical texts so as to safeguard the Christian morals of young people. Tender minds should be protected even if this meant severely distorting the historical authenticity of the text. K. J. Dover has shown that nineteenth-century educators in England zealously altered Greek texts for their students, fearful that even the slightest hint of titillating goings-on would inspire their charges to imitate unchristian behavior.[61] In nineteenth-century America the suspect morality of the ancients became more problematic as the physical and textual remains of antiquity became more numerous. In art, for example, total nudity was common in Greco-Roman sculptures of males, and even goddesses were often draped in materials so gauzy as to be provocative rather than concealing. Nude and partially nude classical figures became common in nineteenth-century America, as casts of originals went on display and American painters and sculptors created modern renditions of ancient themes. These evoked considerable response as Americans wrestled with the problem of representing timeless ideals of transcendent beauty in forms unacceptable to standards of modern social propriety, especially in female statuary.[62]

School editions of classical texts especially demanded scrutiny. Obscene and indecent passages in Greek literature detracted not only from the "moral effect of the study," wrote C. C. Felton, but also from their historical study. The Greek writers were "singularly free from the charge of indecency," and whatever was now "degraded" was surely the result of later writers' hoping to excite the passions. Roman poetry was another matter, "the growth of a dissolute and ribald age," arising from "revelry and debauch." The solution was obvious. "To the scholar we would say, then, expurgate your Horaces and your Ovids, till not an obscene thought shall stain their pages; and you may be sure that nothing will be lost in your inquiries respecting the classic religion."[63] A rising tide of historicism in the mid-nineteenth century, then, was partially blocked by the bulwark of traditional Protestant morality.

GREEK TRAGEDY AS SELF-CULTURE

More even than Homer, Greek tragedies exemplified the new impulse to self-culture in the antebellum colleges. Tragedy had been scorned frequently in America before 1820; James Logan in 1721 had insisted that Aeschylus consisted "but of seven crabbed tragedies of no great use."[64] But after 1820 the Greek tragedies of Aeschylus, Sophocles, and Euripides, as well as the comedies of Aristophanes, rose to prominence in the curriculum, a place they continue to hold today. At the same time, American scholars produced a number of German editions of the Greek dramas for use in American classrooms.[65] These college texts drew from recent German editions of the plays, and the authors alluded explicitly to this fact in their introductions, differentiating between this scholarship and the English scholarship now deemed unsatisfactory. In his editions of *Alcestis* and *Antigone*, for example, Woolsey drew largely on the reprint in Wilhelm Dindorf, *Poetiae Scenici Graece* (1830), which followed the revisions made by Gottfried Herrmann in his *Sophoclis Trageodiae* (1823), from "whose judgment in such matters there lies no appeal," according to Felton.[66] Woolsey dismissed the English school edition of John Brasse as containing "little that is both useful and new."[67]

In the view of American classicists, Greek drama marked the summit of Greek achievement. Just as the natural simplicity of the Homeric epics arose from the characteristics of the early Greeks, so the plays of the Periclean Age sprang from the perfections of the Athenians. Greek drama embodied the Greek nation in a kind of reductionism that made all of Greece into Athens and all of Athens into the fifth and fourth centuries B.C. "This most singular and beautiful manifestation of Grecian genius," wrote Felton of Greek drama in 1830, "was favored by every circumstance that could make it purely and intensely national."[68] One anonymous author writing in the *Methodist Quarterly Review* in 1852 listed the features of Athenian society most conducive to perfect literature. It was important "to indicate the profound influence which the immense expansion of trade and navigation, the rapid succession of the dazzling conquests abroad, the triumphs and constitutional consolidation of the power of the democracy at home, the embellishment of public and private life with every adornment of art, luxury, and learning, and the splendor of that patriotic oratory which created and sustain the widely-diffused and magnificent public spirit of the Periklean age, must have exerted upon the mind of every imaginative and cultivated Athenian."[69] A contributor to the *Christian Review* concurred that the development of Greek tragedy paralleled the development of the Athenians. "Among the many species of composition in which Athens excelled, the tragic drama holds a conspicuous place. The astonishing rapidity of its growth, from its rude beginnings in the days of Thespis to its lofty elevation in the age of Pericles, can be compared to nothing but the growth of Athens itself."[70]

Americans now identified Athenian democracy as the condition that had allowed a noble literature to flourish. "It was for this lawless, merciless, but free people, that the most chaste and accomplished literature which the world has known, was produced," declared Edward Everett in 1824. "With the decline of liberty in Greece began the decline of her letters and her arts."[71] Seen in this light, Greek tragedies emerged as pamphlets for American political and individual liberty. Such views became especially popular among American classical votaries in the wake of Grote's *History of Greece*. In this, the first history of Greece published in Britain to be written with the benefit of German critical scholarship, Grote drew explicit parallels between ancient Athenian democracy and the rise of the liberal state in Victorian Britain.[72] Friends of the classics in America followed suit, explicitly citing Grote but adapting his conclusions to American conditions. Recommending Sophocles' *Antigone* and Grote's

History to American audiences in 1851, an anonymous reviewer assured readers of the importance of Athenian literature to their democracy. "To the American citizen, above all others, is it important that he become familiar with the history of Athens. . . . The similarity of their institutions to our own, the intense love of individual and national freedom which pervaded all ranks of society, render the study of Athenian life of more than ordinary interest to the American citizen." What was more, Americans should not simply read "her laws and her political history"; they should also "become conversant with her poets, her historians, her philosophers, and her orators" in order to understand the "character of her leading men."[73] Another counseled American readers to acquire "mental citizenship of Athens" to adequately make the connections between the Greek and the American experience.[74] The age of Pericles, agreed a third, showed how "the power of the democracy . . . created and sustained the widely-diffused and magnificent public spirit . . . of every imaginative and cultivated Athenian."[75] Greek tragedy also suited American democracy because it knit thought to action. In his *Poetics*, to which American classicists frequently recurred, Aristotle had defined tragedy as "not a representation of men but of a piece of action."[76] Just as antebellum Americans admired Demosthenes because he exemplified the orator as politician, so they lauded the tragedians for mixing the political with the dramatic. Sophocles, after all, had been a general, as had Pericles and Thucydides, and Aeschylus had served in the Athenian army in the Persian wars.

In addition to instructing young Americans in the blessings of democracy, Greek tragedy taught religion and morals. In fact, Greek drama *was* religion, what one author called "a religious service—a sort of liturgy."[77] It was true that the ancient Greeks were heathens, but the expression of their sentiments was so sublime and elevated in the tragedies as to be generally compatible with Protestant doctrine. "In point of morality," observed Felton in 1836, "they reach the highest point of heathen purity." Tragedies showed the remarkable ancients to have glimpsed the essence of Christian revelation centuries before the birth of Christ. "In moments of poetical enthusiasm, the kindling soul, even of the heathen bard, seems to render asunder the veil of ignorance, weakness and doubt, and to have a sudden comprehension of those truths, dimly shadowed out by tradition, but set in broad sunlight by the Christian revelation."[78]

The extreme emotional pitch of the Greek tragedies smoothed their acceptance as a quasi religion by making them compatible with the heart religion of the Second Great Awakening, which gave priority to the extravagant expression of sentiment. Aristotle had contended that pity, fear, and similar emotions characterized Greek tragedy, and Americans thought that these emotions brought the reader closer to the deity.[79] Describing the misdeeds of Creon in his edition of Sophocles' *Antigone*, Woolsey showed how "highly excited feelings" shaded into religion. "Thus pity, resentment, and fear, sorrow for his misfortune, satisfaction with his punishment, and dread of divine wrath are all aroused in the spectator or reader."[80] Tragedies generated fevered emotions, which in turn helped to cultivate students' faculties. "The tragical effect is overpowering," wrote an anonymous reviewer in 1851, "and an analysis of the constituent elements by which this effect is produced, cannot but improve the aesthetic faculties."[81]

Greek tragic heroines most clearly displayed the emotionalism and femininity that made the tragedies fonts of Christian morality. Clytemnestra, Antigone, Medea, Alcestis, and others rose as overwrought nineteenth-century heroines to rival the self-sacrificing Roman matrons so idolized by eighteenth-century Americans. Many of the heroines were described as the incarnation of a feminine emotion rooted in their biology: Medea the scorned lover driven to murder her children; Clytemnestra the depraved wife but loyal mother; Alcestis the devoted wife who dies for her husband; Antigone the dutiful daughter and sister who dies for her convictions. These women became heroic when they acted out the conventions of mid-century Protestant feminine morality. In particular, classicists and other nineteenth-century commentators on Greek tragedy lauded the heroines for their selflessness and grand emotional gestures. These two traits were in fact what made them "exquisitely tender and feminine."[82] Euripides' Alcestis and Sophocles' Antigone, for example, achieved heroic status by subordinating their own desires to those of others in both the domestic and political spheres. Alcestis, according to Felton, embodied "the spirit of a noble-minded woman" because she was "a being with whom all thought of self is merged in an absorbing love of those to whom she is bound by conjugal and maternal ties."[83] Antigone surpassed even Alcestis in feminine heroism because she not only acted selflessly toward her family but also gave up her life for her religious convictions, as befitted a Christian heroine.[84] Greek antiheroines by contrast displayed traits undesirable in mid-century American women, such as sexual passion and ambition. Helen of Troy selfishly allowed her legendary beauty to launch the Trojan War, while lovelorn Medea recklessly pursued her "pleasure or passion" for men to her doom.[85]

This combination of morality, nobility of sentiment, and democratic inclination made the Greek tragedies uniquely conducive to self-culture, that new goal of undergraduate classicism. They made Greek tragedies efficient conduits of taste and style, conceived not in the eighteenth century's definition as imitation but in the mid-nineteenth century's definition as moving the reader to inner perfection of the soul. Isaac Stuart, of South Carolina College, in 1836 explained why tragedies encouraged undergraduate self-culture. "In the delineation of these characters there are situations so suited to the strongest exaction of the sensibilities, such correspondence of sentiment to situation and of manner to sentiment— there is so much of ideal elevation and select nature, such awakening and deepening in the soul of the sense of proportion and harmony, that the taste and style of the Classical Student, by a sympathy the most acute and enchanting, are attracted to form and ripen."[86]

Sophocles seemed to be the Greek dramatist whose works were most conducive to self-culture. In an age when playwrights were believed to express a national spirit, Sophocles was called the Milton of the ancient world for the majesty of his expression.[87] His tragedies appeared to Americans to best embody the spirit of Athens during the Age of Pericles. Not only the art but also the artist was shaped by Periclean radiance. "The beautiful season of his youthful bloom coincided with the most glorious epoch of the Athenian people," Schlegel had written of Sophocles.[88] The political and social circumstances of Athens during its golden age had endowed Sophocles with a refinement of artistry lacking in the other poets. His rhythm had a "smoother polish," the story a "richer complication," and his language was "more polished and sustained" than that of either Aeschylus or Euripides.[89]

To achieve self-culture, a student had to imbibe the "spirit" of ancient tragedy, which required studying the entirety of ancient Greek civilization so as to be able to put the tragedies in context. Just as pronouncing

Demosthenes correctly and studying themselves into Homeric Greece allowed students to transport themselves to another time, so understanding of the minutiae of Periclean Athens brought the spirit of antiquity to the service of modern self-culture. Felton explained the level of detail needed to imbibe the spirit of antiquity through Greek drama as follows in 1830:

> To understand the Greek drama fully, we must not only ascertain the spirit of the people and the light in which they regarded it, but a minute acquaintance with the architectural construction of the theatre, and the scenic details, is absolutely necessary. It is impossible to gain from ancient authors all on this subject which may be desired; but a careful perusal of Vitruvius, with the proper explanations, will throw much light on this part of Grecian learning. The beauty of their climate enabled the Greeks to enjoy theatrical amusements with no roof above them but the sky. It seemed singularly appropriate, that representations in which the gods and heroes of their mythology bore so distinguishing a part, should be held beneath the broad canopy of the heavens. The great interest felt in dramatic exhibitions, and the grave importance they attached to them, called the whole people, or as large a portion of the people as attended any public occasion, into the theatres; which therefore must have been of prodigious size. Indeed, it was to a certain extent a religious ceremony—an exhibition in honor of the divinities to whom, in a half poetical, half religious sense, they paid their adoration.[90]

Here were some of the antecedents for the rise of archaeology in the American university in the late nineteenth century: the desire for authenticity through contact with physical remains of the ancient world and the conviction that textual study alone was inadequate for fully understanding a civilization. In the antebellum classroom the effort remained almost purely textual, but the visual remains of antiquity now loomed as an appropriate object for the fulfillment of undergraduate self-culture.

The changed study of Homer, Demosthenes, and Greek tragedy after 1820 showed the important role that classicists played in transforming the American imagination of classical antiquity in the antebellum era. Within the colleges they reformed the study of classical texts, part of their ambitious goal of reinventing antiquity for use in a modernized America.

They argued that classical learning, long the province of aristocrats, could become part of the general knowledge of an increasingly diverse citizenry. The study of classical culture might be the glue that would hold together a modern republic fragmented by populism, materialism, and industrialization. Most importantly, they introduced classicism as an antidote to modern materialism and civic degeneracy, an idea that resonated both in the colleges and American society more broadly. Linking classicism to a broad program of self-formation that they called self-culture, they recruited the classical past as an ennobling education available to all. It was this achievement of connecting classicism with antimaterialism that helped to sustain Greece and Rome in American higher education during the late nineteenth century.

※ 4 ※

CLASSICAL CIVILIZATION
CONSECRATED, 1870–1910

THE TRIUMPH OF UTILITY AND SCIENCE

"The American boy of 1854," wrote Henry Adams in the early twentieth century, "stood nearer the year 1 than to the year 1900."[1] With those words the historian described the cataclysmic intellectual and social changes that marked the four decades after the Civil War. Like many of his contemporaries, Adams imagined the late nineteenth century as the first truly modern age, distinguished from earlier eras by an almost unbreachable chasm of thought and practice. Between 1870 in 1900 the population of the nation doubled, largely through immigration. Industrialization siphoned American workers from farms to cities and transformed the landscape with railroads, steel mills, and large factories. Huge corporations fundamentally transformed social and labor relations in the country, encouraging the rise of a managerial ethos that sought efficiency in both industry and government. The centralization of expertise in government, industry, and other areas also fractured American culture, splitting the nation into ever more distinct subcultures, to which a nascent culture of advertising catered. The rise of big business, rampant economic speculation, and corrupt politics earned these decades of the late nineteenth century the epithet "the Gilded Age," coined in 1873 by Mark Twain to describe what looked like the shameful opulence and cancerous moral degeneracy of the era.

Central to the transformations of the Gilded Age was the rise of the modern university, which also relied on growing centralization, expertise, wealth, and population. The Morrill Land Grant Act of 1862 increased state aid to new colleges and universities committed to teaching science, engineering, and agriculture, and colleges admitted students with more diverse backgrounds. Although a few new subjects, such as modern languages, modern history, and economics, had begun to appear in the antebellum era, now the number of new disciplines and courses swelled. The number of academic degrees available to students had increased to thirty-nine by 1900, testifying to the wide array of subjects now taught in the colleges and universities. Freed from the prescribed curriculum that had characterized the colleges for about 250 years, students pursued a variety of elective courses that formed part of that modern invention, the major. Huge infusions of private money made possible the founding of new universities such as Cornell University (1868), Stanford University (1885), and the University of Chicago (1892), and at older schools this funding allowed the beautification of campuses, the improvement of scientific laboratories, and the recruitment of more faculty. One of the biggest changes from the antebellum era was the large increase in the number of women who attended college. Their numbers increased from 21 percent of all collegians in 1870 to 40 percent in 1910.[2] They attended coeducational, religious, and secular colleges, single-sex vocational institutions, and new colleges founded exclusively for women, such as Vassar (1865), Wellesley (1875), Smith (1875), and Bryn Mawr (1884). Likewise, Southern blacks in this postemancipation era attended normal schools, industrial training institutes, and also liberal arts colleges. In the latter, missionary philanthropists encouraged a traditional liberal curriculum that included classics; such a curriculum, reformers argued, would provide future black leaders an elite education, a prerequisite for racial equality in civil and political life.[3]

Of course, continuities with the antebellum era persisted. Enrollment figures in colleges in the Gilded Age hardly budged relative to the population, and a college degree remained the province of the elite. In the four decades after the Civil War, the proportion of college-age white men enrolled in higher education increased from 1 percent to 2 percent, while among women it increased from .7 percent to 2.8 percent. Moreover, despite the proliferation of alternative degrees to the traditional bachelor of arts and new subjects offered in regular colleges and universities, a majority of students still chose the regular bachelor's degree program, while only a fifth enrolled for the new bachelor of science degree.[4]

As the modern university rose, the classical languages were dethroned. The proliferation of new studies in the curriculum, such as modern languages, modern history, and social sciences, as well as the advent of elective study, helped to push Latin and especially Greek to the side. Not only was there less time and space for classical study in an increasingly crowded curriculum but students who were not interested in Greek and Latin could simply choose not to study them. Before this time, Greek and Latin had been required for admission, all students once in college had pursued the same language-heavy load, and all students had emerged with the same degree, the bachelor of arts. Beginning in mid-century, new, parallel courses allowed students to elect different groups of subjects in college. Students could eliminate one or both of the classical languages and receive a degree other than the bachelor of arts, signaling the absence of the full dose of ancient languages. The University of Michigan, to take one example, which began to offer parallel courses in 1853, by 1880 offered five distinct courses leading to an alphabet soup of degrees.[5] College admission requirements, which for two centuries had been similar for all entering students, began to vary according to the courses students decided to pursue. When Northwestern University was founded in 1855, all students had to know mathematics, English, Greek, and Latin for admission. By 1870 only students admitted to the classical course had to show a knowledge of both Latin and Greek for admission; those in the scientific course had to know Latin only, and those in the civil engineering course had to know neither.[6]

As the appeal of these other degrees increased, and as the system of electives spread, students spent less and less time studying Latin and especially Greek in college. A glance at the trends at several universities confirms this. In 1883, the last year in which the classical languages were compulsory for Harvard freshmen, all studied Latin and Greek. In the following year only 77 percent elected Latin, and 64 percent, Greek. By 1900 just under a third elected Latin, while only 16 percent elected Greek.[7] Expressed as a function of time spent studying in college, the decline in classical languages is equally apparent. At Yale the ancient languages occupied about a third of a student's time in 1886 but only a fifth in 1899. Moreover, Greek almost vanished, while Latin remained relatively constant. Greek took 7.69 man-year-hours of a student's time at Yale in 1901–2 but only 1.09 in 1919–20; for Latin the figures were 6.98 and 5.36 for those years, only a small decline.[8] The relative enrollment figures at Syracuse University also show that students gradually turned away from the bachelor of arts, which required both Greek and Latin, to the bachelor of philosophy, which required only one of the two ancient languages, and to the bachelor of science, which required neither. Many Syracuse students still opted for at least one ancient language. The percentage of students pursuing only one ancient language, usually Latin, increased from 28 percent to 46 percent between 1879 and 1905, while the number of students not pursuing either increased from 1 percent to 11 percent.[9] By 1905 the majority of American colleges no longer required Greek for admission. Though many colleges continued to ask for Latin at entrance, this too was in jeopardy.

This change had a drastic effect on the study of classical languages in high schools, feeders to the colleges. In contrast to the highly elite colleges and universities, the so-called "people's colleges" served a relatively large segment of the population. The number of students receiving diplomas from public and private high schools increased from 2 percent of the population of seventeen-year-olds in 1870 to 9 percent 1910.[10] Within the high schools, the study of Latin actually increased between 1870 and 1930s along with enrollments. In 1890 roughly one-third of high school students enrolled in Latin; by 1910 half did.[11] In fact, more high school students studied Latin between 1890 and 1915 than studied all other foreign languages combined, a testament to the continuing desire among students for an elite education in classics. Even when the percentage of students enrolling in Latin declined from a peak of 50 percent in 1900, absolute numbers continued to rise along with mushrooming enrollments. For a while, the democratization of secondary schooling allowed the spread of that elite tongue, Latin, and it was not until the 1940s that both the absolute and relative numbers of Latin enrollments began to plummet. High school enrollments in Latin peaked in the decade 1900–1910 and declined thereafter, from 27.5 percent of enrollments in 1922 to just

7.8 percent in 1949, when students of non-Latin languages outnumbered Latin students by almost two to one.[12]

Though Latin held its own for a while, the study of ancient Greek in high school approached extinction by 1910. Greek remained considerably more popular in private schools because these sent a larger proportion of their graduates to colleges and to theological seminaries. In 1890, 7 percent of private and 3 percent of public high school students studied Greek. By 1898 the total number of students studying Greek had almost doubled— increasing faster than the nation's population—but then began a decline that continued over the twentieth century. By 1910 almost 7 percent of private high school students studied Greek, compared with fewer than 1 percent of public high school students. The study of Greek thus became increasingly uncoupled from its traditional partner, Latin.

In the colleges and universities the sciences and social sciences not only physically crowded out the classics; they also recruited new sources of intellectual authority that challenged the traditional claims of classics. In the twenty years after the Civil War there was a renewed assault on the classics in the writings of a number of scientists, university presidents, and industrialists. Among the scientists were E. L. Youmans (1821–87), the founder of the *Popular Science Monthly* (1872), the Harvard chemist Josiah Cooke (1827–94), and the University of Chicago botanist John Coulter (1851–1928). This group also included Jacob Bigelow, who had opposed the classics in the antebellum era and contributed some final anticlassical polemics in his collection *Modern Inquiries: Classical, Professional, and Miscellaneous* (1867). Finally, industrialists such as Andrew Carnegie (1835–1919) and Charles Francis Adams (1835–1915), president of the Union Pacific Railroad, questioned the role of antiquarian studies in a modern age.

American anticlassicism in the late nineteenth century was spurred by a vociferous indictment of classical education that had appeared in England in the 1860s. During that decade the English Schools Commission, dispatched by Parliament to investigate the great classical grammar schools, such as Eton, Harrow, and Rugby, had discovered both ludicrous failures in language study and utter neglect of the study of physical science. Its report, published in 1864, had called forth a wide-ranging discussion of the place of the classical languages in England and Scotland.[13] The argument immediately attracted attention in the United States, prompting a parallel cascade of arguments that invoked the British situation.[14]

Like their English counterparts, anticlassicists in the United States decried the study of classical antiquity as useless, an indictment that acquired new strength in an age dedicated to utility and modernity in education. Ascendant in the Jacksonian era, the ideal of utility in education rang from the rooftops of America's colleges and universities during the post–Civil War era. Utility encompassed a number of hopes, such as the desire to open education to broader sectors of society, as well as the wish to tie college studies more explicitly to the work students would do in their adult lives. The college and university, according to the advocates of utility, should explicitly prepare students for what became known as "real life," as distinguished from the sheltered groves of the college. "Reality and practicality" should shape the undergraduate college, argued Stanford University president David Starr Jordan (1851–1931), a great exponent of utility in the curriculum. A professor at New York University concurred, stating in 1890 that "the college has ceased to be a cloister and has become a workshop."[15]

It was not utility alone but utility conceived as a fundamentally scientific enterprise that corroded classicism. Until the antebellum era, as we have seen, the classical languages had been vigorously and undeniably useful. Although they cloaked their possessor with a mystique of ineffable acquisition, Latin and to a lesser extent Greek also played a bluntly vocational role in training statesmen, ministers, orators, lawyers, doctors, scholars, and republican citizens. Indeed, classical study had been at some level a vocational study since the Middle Ages and the Renaissance. When most state and church business was conducted in Latin, schoolboys and university men learned the language as a weaver would learn to use a loom. "Scholasticism was very much a going concern in the fourteenth and fifteenth centuries," explain Anthony Grafton and Lisa Jardine. "At the level of the high school, it offered literacy in Latin of a sort to thousands of boys. At the higher level of the university arts course, it provided a lively and rigorous training in logic and semantics. At the higher level still of the professional faculties of law, medicine and theology, it trained men for employment in powerful and lucrative occupations."[16] Utility endured as a plausible justification for classical education in America until the early nineteenth century. Not only did it furnish statesmen and ministers with linguistic skills useful in writing and debate but its cyclical patterns of rise and fall instructed the political conscience of the nation well into the mid-nineteenth century. But by the late nineteenth century the emerging construct of "utilitarian science" had armed a new generation of anticlassicists with a powerful new rhetorical tool. In contrast to the anticlassicism of the Revolutionary era, which was also animated by political fears of privilege and tyranny, the anticlassicism of the Victorian era marched under the banner of science and utility.

Such reasoning and the association of the "modern" university with "modern" sciences, necessitated a rhetorical break with the past. Classicism thus became doubly damned in the postbellum era: it looked by definition to the remote past as its object of study, while also symbolizing an antediluvian educational epoch. Many late-century Americans shared the conviction that industrial capitalism had wrought such vast changes as to warrant a collective resetting of historical clocks. Proponents of a new university system that rested on science and utility shared a sense of chronological dislocation, of a need for temporal spring-cleaning in their new universities. Having successfully defined modernity as an age of utility and science, university builders especially attacked Greek and Latin since they appeared neither useful nor scientific.

Among the most famous attacks was that of the Harvard-educated Charles Francis Adams, who in 1883 dismissed the study of classical languages as "a college fetich." "In a utilitarian and scientific age," he complained, colleges failed to fit their graduates "for the work they have to do in the life that awaits them."[17] The science popularizer E. L. Youmans concurred that science trumped classicism for utility in a modern world. The educational system, he argued in 1867, must be brought "into better harmony with the needs of the times. . . . In place of much that is irrelevant, antiquated, and unpractical in our systems of study, there is needed a larger infusion of the living and available truth which belongs to the present time."[18] In place of classicism Youmans offered "the discipline of science . . . because it takes effect upon the realities of experience, because it is a discipline in the pursuit of truth, because it is a preparation for practical life-work and because it brings the mind into intimate and intel-

ligent relation with the system of natural things."[19] Jacob Bigelow likewise defended the advances of the modern age in an address before the
American Academy of Arts and Sciences in 1866. He contrasted the "prof-
itless abstractions" that preoccupied the ancient Greeks with the "general
enlightenment of mankind which exists in the present age."[20] So, too, did
Harvard president Charles Eliot in 1884. "Modern education" demanded
that "new sciences" like history and political science join the group of
ancient studies considered essential to a liberal education. "Are our young
men being educated for the work of the twentieth century or of the
seventeenth?" he asked.[21] The botanist John Coulter echoed the rhetoric
of antimodernism in 1893, contrasting an ignorant and superstitious past
with an enlightened present. "The world contains untold attics-full of
heirloom rubbish, and it needs an incendiary fire now and then to get rid
of it," he wrote.[22] The industrialist Andrew Carnegie lampooned the college student who learned about the "barbarous and petty squabbles of the
far-distant past" even as the captain of industry was "hotly engaged in the
school of experience, obtaining the very knowledge required for his future
triumphs."[23]

As proponents of science and utility in the curriculum allied themselves with modernity they also urged a disciplinary egalitarianism. They
argued that all subjects, if rigorously studied, were equally capable of
forming an educated person. This reasoning justified the introduction of
elective courses, which many colleges and universities adopted to some
extent in the post–Civil War era. On the one hand electives defused the
unavoidable conflicts in the curriculum as new disciplines jockeyed for a
place, but on the other hand they demolished the antebellum unity of
knowledge and destroyed the intellectual legitimacy of the classical core.[24]
Disputes over heuristic equity appeared in debates over the traditional
bachelor of arts, the sacrosanct college degree that had always implied
training in the classical languages. At a 1904 conference of the Association of American Universities leading scholars and administrators debated
whether to allow all the new degrees to be collapsed into the bachelor of
arts or to reserve the degree for those students who had studied Latin and
Greek. The University of Chicago Greek scholar Paul Shorey (1857–
1904) and the Princeton University Latin professor Andrew Fleming
West (1853–1943) both argued that the bachelor of arts should be re-

tained only for those graduates who had studied Greek. Greek, they argued, was the guardian of "a noble and indispensable tradition." Harvard's president, Charles Eliot, in contrast, thought that the bachelor of arts should be given for both scientific and classical courses since "the same sort of power is developed in both courses, the same intellectual grasp is given, the same power of work." There was nothing magical about Greek; what mattered was the quality of mental training, however achieved.[25] Shorey and West were waging a losing battle. In 1912 a survey of 155 public and private colleges and universities showed that 66 required neither Greek nor Latin for the bachelor of arts and only 27 demanded both.[26]

New conceptions of history also eroded the relevance of antiquity to "modern" civilization. In the late nineteenth century the first generation of professional social scientists in the universities adopted a new conception of history and America's place within it. This new historical paradigm offered the present rather than the distant past as social guide, a view that not only undermined antiquity's claim to authority but advertised the findings of social science as eminently more useful for current concerns. This new view of the allegiance of historicism and science had its roots in the eighteenth century, when Enlightenment theorists in France and Scotland yoked the study of society to the utilitarian goal of human moral, intellectual, and economic improvement. Adam Smith (1723–90), J. G. Herder, and Marie-Jean-Antoine-Nicolas de Caritat, marquis de Condorcet (1743–94) saw general laws and particular investigations of human societies as guides for the betterment of human society. Although they might search the past for universal principles of human action or national development, their focus was on reforming the present and building a better future. In eighteenth- and early-nineteenth-century America millennial hopes for future improvement conflicted with the cycles of republican time, which tempered notions of progress with reminders that time inevitably decayed republics rather than propelling them ever upward. By the late nineteenth century, however, American social scientists, influenced by the historicism of British and Continental figures such as Herbert Spencer (1820–1903) and Auguste Comte (1798–1857), jettisoned republican time and replaced it with the idea of progressive, historical time. They sought the ideal society not by escaping time—which is what classical republicanism had demanded—but firmly within history, through a study of the natural "progress of civilizations," which would lead inexorably to a better future.[27] Such reasoning invoked the present rather than the past as a source of authority. The Columbia University economist John Bates Clark (1847–1938) in 1886 explained the purposes to which social scientists should put the past. "History will aid us by furnishing a point of departure, and by indicating the direction of social development, but not by giving facts from which any possible induction can give the principles which we seek. . . . The materials for study lie in the present and the immediate future."[28]

Gilded Age scientists further asserted their legitimacy by clothing their work in quasi-religious rhetoric. They elaborated on the moral efficacy of scientific practice, arguing that studying nature and searching for truths ennobled the investigator. Such reasoning justified the advance of science in the universities both to scientists and nonscientists while also allying science with the beneficial results of progress.[29] These quasi-religious claims emerged even as science itself shed its traditional link to theology. Until 1870 most scientists in colleges were either clergy or recipients of clerical training; they knew their scientific investigations revealed the plan of the Divine Creator.[30] As they abandoned their traditional theological project for naturalistic explanations of phenomena, they deployed a spiritualized rhetoric to imbue their science with transcendent meaning. Social scientists also linked their disciplines to modern progress, claiming that the scientific study of society could resolve the problems that attended industrialization, urbanization, democratization, and immigration. Social science, that is, could improve the moral sphere. John Dewey (1859–1952) in 1899 explained the power of the social and natural sciences to intercede in the sphere formerly dominated by religion. When science "is progressively applied to history and all the social sciences," he wrote, "we can anticipate no other outcome than increasing control in the ethical sphere—the nature and extent of which can be best judged by considering the revolution that has taken place in the control of physical nature through a knowledge of her order."[31]

New philosophies of education that emphasized experience rather than bodies of knowledge further undermined the claims of the traditional Greek and Latin core. Rejecting idealism as alien to the actual experiences of "plain man," Dewey attempted to ground logic in everyday experience rather than linking it to a larger truth. "There is," he argued, "always as antecedent to thought an experience of subject-matter of the physical or social world, or the previously organized intellectual world." The process of reorganizing this information he called "thinking."[32] This so-called instrumentalism called for a new pedagogy that emphasized the experience of the environment rather than the internalization of a body of learning. John Dewey's two groundbreaking works on pedagogy, *The School and Society* (1899) and *The Child and the Curriculum* (1902), emphasized the active involvement of children in their own learning. The role of the teacher was not to furnish the mind with knowledge or to cultivate the faculties through mental exercise but to guide the native curiosity and capability of the child in constructive directions. Dewey described this process in decidedly modern, industrial terms: the child brought to the classroom in-born impulses that were the "natural resources, the uninvested capital, upon the exercise of which depends the active growth of the child."[33]

Dewey was no anticlassicist; he had studied Greek and Latin at the University of Vermont and had recourse to antiquity in his philosophy. Yet the classical curriculum he set up at his University Elementary School in Chicago diverged from traditional Latin language instruction in the primary grades. Dewey gave an important place to Latin but emphasized the need to understand the entirety of its civilization. "It is not the mere syntactical structure of etymological content of the Latin language which has made it for centuries such an unrivaled educational instrument. . . . It is the context of the Latin language, the wealth of association and suggestion belonging to it from its position in the history of human civilization that freight it with such meaning." Students at the school began learning Latin at age nine, but while memorization of vocabulary and some verbal drill formed part of the routine, the emphasis was on joining Latin to the society that had produced it, something Dewey called the "living" method of teaching. Students read stories in Latin, then illustrated them in their art classes, and then printed them and bound them into books. Older students continued this broad-gauged pedagogy: they impersonated someone from Roman society, compared Caesar and Cicero, held spelling bees, and played games. Dewey's methods steered away from the idea of classical civilization as uniquely cultivating. Latin stood in the curriculum not as a representative of the awesome authority of tradition but as a site of experiences.[34]

HIGHER TRUTHS THAN SCIENCE

How could late-nineteenth-century classicists compete with claims that utilitarian science was the intellectual and moral compass of higher education? Although a number of classicists continued to insist on the utility of classics—they disciplined the mind and promoted the acquisition of foreign languages, English grammar, and medical and legal terminology—such claims appeared increasingly desperate and even ridiculous next to the more obvious and remunerative social utility of engines and bridges. A far more successful strategy was to abdicate utility altogether and embrace its opposite: uselessness, construed in its modern sense as having no claim at all to explicit vocationalism, science, or economics. Many classicists now mined the virtue of uselessness, for uselessness opposed many undesirable aspects of the industrial age, what was "marketable" and "railway," all that led to "$uccess," every feature of "vulgar utility," all the trappings of "Franklinism."[35] Classical study bestowed something higher than vocational or exclusively scientific preparation: it offered *culture*.

The idea of culture, as we have seen, emerged in the mid-nineteenth century, when friends of classicism recruited it to combat materialism, industrialism, and civic degeneracy, and it now flourished in the post–Civil War era. One especially fertile field for culture was the undergraduate college, which became known as the *college of liberal culture*. The term *liberal culture* combined the old idea of the liberal arts with the linguistic novelty *culture*. It sprang up at the same historical moment that science and utility also gained a foothold in the curriculum, for culture and utility formed rhetorical bookends, straddling two poles of Victorian educational thought. At one end utility advertised the modern university's alliance with progress and science, while at the other end culture signaled higher education's age-old ties to broadly gauged learning and civic preparation. The word *cultured* appeared in American writing at this time to describe something that one could *be*, marking the apotheosis of the self-transformative possibilities of classicism and liberal learning. The end product of self-culture was to *be cultured*.[36]

Noah Porter (1811–92), the president of Yale from 1871 to 1886, provided one of the most coherent encapsulations of the ideal of liberal culture as expressed within the colleges of the Gilded Age. First, Porter's liberal culture cast human perfectibility in terms of an equal development of the moral, intellectual, and physical aspects of human nature. Liberal culture was "that kind of culture which tends to perfect the man in the variety and symmetry and effectiveness of his powers, by reflection and self-knowledge, by self-control and self-expression." Porter, himself an ordained minister, thus defined human perfectibility in decidedly secular terms for an age that increasingly humanized the divine. Second, this pursuit of human perfection through liberal culture was precisely opposed to vocational pursuits such as "that which brings wealth or skill or fame or power." In this way liberal culture joined the Victorian opposition to the crass materialism of industrial capitalism. Third, liberal culture was heir to the Enlightenment, placing humanity rather than objects at the center of every worthwhile intellectual endeavor. It included knowledge "of man as an interpreter of nature, and therefore as capable of science; of man, also, as a creature of imagination and ideal culture, and therefore as capable of literature, art, and ethics in individual and social life." Liberal culture could include a wide variety of fields, from science to art to literature: Porter assured readers that even "scientific and professional studies may be pursued in a liberal spirit." Finally, liberal culture was the web that joined human society into a united whole. It was "whatever knowledge connects man with his race by a common sympathy . . . as distinguished from that knowledge which exalts or isolates him as an individual." This belief was intimately connected to the transformation of America higher education, for Porter deplored the separation of knowledge into general and special spheres. Any study could become "illiberal when single branches or spheres of knowledge are pursued apart . . . or are esteemed for their utilitarian or selfish value."[37] Liberal culture held fast to a vanishing world in which all knowledge theoretically lay within the grasp of the educated person. Thus, at the very moment when science and utility were claiming more and more adherents, the ideal of liberal culture was offering an alternative path, mixing ideals of spiritual perfection with aspirations to a broadly educated citizenry.

The ideal of classicism as the road to liberal culture shaped two successive generations of classical scholars. Several of these scholars were the first American classical scholars to rise to lasting international prominence; a few produced books of such depth and accuracy that they are still in use today.[38] The first generation, born between 1817 and 1835, had been educated in the undergraduate classrooms of the antebellum era, when Hellenism and Germanic learning were beginning to infuse classical study with new ideas of broad self-culture and rigorous historicism. Building on this tradition by further study in Germany, where a number received Ph.D.'s, this generation invoked classicism in the post–Civil War era as the chief path to an ennobling self-culture. Major figures included Henry Simmons Frieze (1817–89), a Latin scholar at the University of Michigan from 1854 to 1888; George Martin Lane (1823–97), professor of Latin at Harvard from 1851 to 1894; Basil Lanneau Gildersleeve (1831–1924), professor of Greek at the Johns Hopkins University from 1876 to 1915 and founder and editor of the *American Journal of Philology* (1880); and William Watson Goodwin (1831–1912), Eliot Professor of Greek Literature at Harvard from 1860 to 1901. They allied themselves with a somewhat larger group that, while not part of the classics professoriate, also opposed what they saw as the mediocrity of late-century American intellectual life and asserted their commitment to what they thought were the true principles of American democracy by urging leadership by the "best men." These elites, centered in New York and Boston, included the Harvard art historian Charles Eliot Norton (1827–1908), the designer of Central Park, Frederick Law Olmsted (1822–1903), and E. L. Godkin (1831–1902), editor of the *Nation*.[39]

This generation, in turn, helped to train a younger generation of classical scholars born in mid-century, who carried the liberal-culture ideal of classicism into the first decades of the twentieth century. They included Thomas Day Seymour (1848–1907), professor of Greek at Yale from 1880 to 1907; William Gardner Hale (1849–1928), professor of Latin at Cornell from 1880 to 1892 and at the University of Chicago from 1892 to 1919; John Henry Wright (1852–1908), professor of Greek at Harvard from 1887 to 1908; Andrew Fleming West (1853–1943), professor of Latin at Princeton from 1883 to 1928; Benjamin Ide Wheeler (1854–1927), professor at Cornell from 1886 to 1899 and president of the University of California from 1899 to 1919; Paul Shorey, professor of Greek at the

University of Chicago from 1892 to 1927; Herbert Weir Smyth (1857–1937), Eliot Professor of Greek Literature at Harvard from 1902 to 1925; Francis Willey Kelsey (1858–1927), professor of Latin language and literature at the University of Michigan from 1889 to 1927; and John Adams Scott (1867–1947), who taught Greek at Northwestern from 1897 to 1938. Not all vocally supported classicism against materialism, but the most outspoken—Shorey, West, Kelsey—invoked classicism as a remedy for the cancers of modernity.[40] Their criticisms paralleled those of the New Humanists, such as Irving Babbitt (1865–1933), Paul Elmer More (1864–1937), and Norman Foerster (1887–1972), who also rejected the creeping influence of the social sciences in American life, with their emphasis on specialization and on future progress rather than the wisdom of the past, but the classicists, as we shall see in chapter 5, became engaged more critically with the issue of emerging professionalization and specialization in American scholarship.[41]

Classicists' criticisms of the industrial age paralleled those expressed by the English social critic Matthew Arnold (1822–88) in his influential work *Culture and Anarchy* (1869). A school inspector, Arnold set the terms of the discussion of the Victorian appreciation of ancient Greece for the next half-century, and his argument found ready listeners across the Atlantic.[42] Arnold embarked on a speaking tour of America, and some American classicists corresponded with him.[43] Arnold cast Hellenism as a frontal assault on contemporary British culture: Nonconformist religion, social pluralism, materialism, and liberal politics. The modern British, he argued, were "Philistines" (a word whose modern usage he coined): excessively "mechanical and external," wedded to the idea of "individualism" and "every man for himself." To criticize this state of affairs, Arnold identified two impulses that contributed to high Victorian civilization, Hebraism and Hellenism. The aim of both was the same: "man's perfection and salvation." But they pursued this goal by very different means, Hebraism by "conduct and obedience" and "strictness of conscience," Hellenism by seeing "things as they really are" and by "spontaneity of consciousness." Hebraism encouraged intellectual and moral rigidity, a suffocating fear of sin, an enslavement to duty and self-control. These features dominated the Victorian middle classes, encouraging their devotion to materialism and machines. But Hellenism offered a nobler route, one that emphasized not the material world but the "inward condition." Hellenism enlarged the mind and awakened the spirit. "To get rid of one's ignorance, to see things as they are, and by seeing them as they are to see them in their beauty, is the simple and attractive ideal which Hellenism holds out before human nature; and from the simplicity and charm of this ideal, Hellenism, and human life in the hands of Hellenism, is invested with a kind of aërial ease, clearness, and radiancy; they are full of what we call sweetness and light." In other words, Hellenism offered "culture," a kind of wholeness rooted in a knowledge of classical civilization that was "more interesting and more far-reaching" than the "smattering of Greek and Latin" that characterized early-nineteenth-century classicism.[44]

Like Arnold, late-century American classicists recruited classicism as an antidote to materialism, an idea pioneered in the antebellum era that had now fully matured. In contrast to materialist science and utility, the classics offered a higher truth. Basil Lanneau Gildersleeve, commenting on the American "preference of the immediate and practical," urged "an element of culture" as one of "the best methods of checking materialism."[45] "But what is 'the work of life'?" he asked.

> Is it not just here that we need the high ideal of antiquity in order to coun-
> teract the depressing tendencies of modern civilization, and especially those of
> American civilization? . . . Material well-being in more or less refined forms,
> is more or less consciously the main object. But the ideal life of antiquity is
> constructed after a different pattern; and though it is as unattainable by the
> means of mere humanity as the antique ideal of the state, we must confess the
> superiority of the one as of the other to the negative virtues and positive
> selfishness of our modern standards.[46]

The Dartmouth classicist John Henry Wright in 1886 contrasted the glories of antiquity with a decayed modernity. "Ancient civilization and culture was not only more simple than modern: it had a unity, and organic wholeness, wherein it is quite unlike our modern world."[47] The Harvard art historian Charles Eliot Norton echoed these sentiments in 1900. Classical studies, he wrote, were "the most eloquent preachers as to the vanity of material power and possessions."[48]

Classicists also scoffed at anticlassicists' attempts to portray them as hopelessly retrograde, arguing that it was not all modernism that they opposed, just some of its ugliest manifestations. The Baptist clergyman and classics supporter Edward T. Tomlinson expressed a typical view. Americans lived in age of progression, he argued, and needed to look "forward, not backward." But, he quickly added, "I do believe in a sure progress, but careful."[49] Noah Porter discouraged "whining or whimpering about the times in which we live" and applauded the "spirit of progress and of growth" around him.[50] E. R. Humphreys, another supporter of classical education, noted that "America seems now to be entering on a new and momentous era of progress in almost every department of science, art, trade, commerce, and world-influence."[51] Charles Eliot Norton, though widely known as a severe critic of modern vulgarity, also quietly applauded the "very slow & irregular" rise "in the general morality of the race."[52] Moreover, anticlassicists tended to portray the discipline of classics as still mired in exclusively grammatical concerns. Gildersleeve took aim at Jacob Bigelow's 1867 indictment of the classics, saying that "when Dr. Bigelow left off the study of Latin and Greek, the new light of classical philology had not begun to shine on this country, and the department had not been lifted from its former low level and settled firm and high on a foundation too solid to be undermined, too lofty to be battered down. The classical philologian of the present day is not a mere grinder of vocables, not a mere monger of paradigms."[53]

As part of their social critique of the Gilded Age classicists likewise asserted that rampant utilitarianism and materialism resulted partly from the misguided pursuits of an uneducated majority. Like Matthew Arnold and their antebellum predecessors, they looked to an educated minority to lead the masses. The Harvard Latinist George Martin Lane imagined America paradoxically as "an aristocracy open to all."[54] Avidly reading Matthew Arnold, the classicist Henry Frieze, at Michigan, looked to the "democratic nobility" in the American universities to rescue Americans from the "vicious taste" in which they wallowed. The institutions managed by this nobility, such as public libraries and art museums, would become a "legitimate instrumentality for educating and elevating the people." Every interest of the nation—material, industrial, intellectual— would be served by an improvement in America's "aesthetic culture."[55]

Suspicious of materialism, classicists criticized the tendency of some scientists to make exalted claims about the successes of modern science. For centuries, in the battle between ancients and moderns, the moderns had claimed that new discoveries and methods in science outweighed the wisdom of antiquity and that veneration of ancient wisdom shackled science to outmoded ideas. The physician Benjamin Rush had argued this point in 1774. "I honour the name of Hippocrates: But forgive me ye votaries of antiquity, if I attempt to pluck a few grey hairs from his venerable head. I was once an idolater at his altar, nor did I turn apostate from his worship, till I was taught that not a tenth part of his prognostics corresponded with modern experience or observation."[56] By contrast, late-nineteenth-century classicists disagreed with anticlassicists' claims that the experience of centuries had rendered the knowledge of antiquity superfluous, especially when it came to science. Gildersleeve admitted that the ancients failed in some respects when compared with modern advances but asserted their ultimate originality in asking the questions that really mattered. "Admit, then, the imperfect character of their observation, not only in physics but in language, and show how narrow was their range, how imperfect their induction. And yet they propounded all the ultimate questions concerning language—questions which we are grappling with in vain to-day."[57] Moreover, argued Noah Porter, many scientists placed too much emphasis on the material world, or "objects of experience." For Porter, the great issues, the "problems of life," concerned "human relations, and these are quite as important as those which are commonly called facts or phenomena."[58]

We can glimpse an example of the threat that classicists saw in science in the writings of the Platonic scholar Paul Shorey. Shorey was among the most vociferous opponents of the encroach of scientism and utilitarianism in education and society in the late nineteenth and early twentieth centuries. From his post at the University of Chicago he produced a stream of attacks on the growing influence of scientific experts, calling for Americans to resist "the claim of certain 'scientists' to monopolize all intellectual interests and regulate all existence out of hand."[59] In an address in Germany in 1914 he warned of the threat industrialization posed to national health. "The commonplace is now repeated everywhere that the telegraph, the railroad, and the ocean steamer hold together the whole world; and yet just in this cosmopolitan period a most remarkable renewal of nationalism and divisive national feeling is taking place, accompanied at the same time by a renewal of the lesser languages which threatens our entire higher culture with disastrous fragmentation and narrow-minded chauvinism."[60]

Dubious of all social science, Shorey railed in particular against what he called the pseudoscience of educational psychology, which he thought was a sham. Real science was difficult and produced real results, wrote Shorey, and he conceded victory to science in the curricular conflict between science and the classics. But pedagogical psychology promised results in "monstrous disproportion" to its actual achievements and merely trumpeted findings that philosophers had been stating for centuries. Shorey dismissed Edward B. Titchener's *Experimental Psychology of the Thought Processes* (1901–5) as adding no new knowledge to what Mill, Taine, Schopenhauer, Emerson, Quintilian, Cicero, and Plato had already said. Shorey argued that E. L. Thorndike's popular textbook *Educational Psychology* (1903), which purported to reduce mental traits to measurable units, flew in the face of common sense, which suggested that every person brought to their studies different capacities and interests. Educational scientists were "no more experts than we [the generally educated public] are" in determining what form modern education should take.[61]

FROM CLASSICISM TO THE HUMANITIES

The rise of classicism as medicine for modernity coincided with another important development in the post–Civil War colleges, which was the rise of the humanities. The humanities, an area of study that promised some sort of character formation and preparation for civic virtue, included new disciplines such as art history, modern literature, music, and history, as well as older pursuits such as philosophy and the study of classical literature and history. Just as the social sciences sprang from the disintegration of the antebellum moral philosophy course, so the humanities between 1850 and 1900 arose as an important intellectual province in the landscape of the modern university.[62]

The word *humanities* emerged after 1850 in America as a neologism to describe a kind of elevating, holistic study of literature, music, and art. It derived from the academic meaning of the fifteenth-century word *hu-*

manity, which distinguished the secular study of Greek and Latin texts *(literae humaniores)* from theological studies: *humanity* contrasted with *divinity.* Humanity in the antebellum era still meant primarily the study of Greek and Latin texts. But after 1850 it acquired its plural form and hitched itself to those studies that bestowed liberal culture.[63] In 1858 Michigan's classicist Henry Simmons Frieze deployed *humanities* in its modern usage in a lecture to his students on Roman history. Romans in the second century B.C., he said, had witnessed "a cultivation in higher literature, humanities so to speak."[64] Tracing the origins of the word, the classicist John Henry Wright in 1886 affirmed that the new word "Humanities," formerly denoting "the microscope of linguistic investigation," had now "deepened and enriched in meaning with the progress of knowledge."[65]

How did the humanities differ from the new social sciences, which also studied humanity? After all, psychology, sociology, political science, anthropology, and economics were also at their root studies of humanity, and indeed the division between humanities and social sciences would always remain cloudy and contentious.[66] But in the late nineteenth century what most clearly separated the emerging humanities from the nascent social sciences was that the humanities abdicated most readily any claim to immediate social utility when that was becoming a major preoccupation of social scientists. The justification of humanists was an older one, of knowledge for the sake of knowledge, and erudition as a path to inward perfection and responsible citizenship. Whereas sociologists might fear to pursue scholarship unconnected to social betterment, humanists were ready to introduce themselves, promising ephemeral, empirically unmeasurable, and therefore incalculably valuable rewards. Barriers to materialism and civic decline, the humanities suggested that there were other goals in life then chasing Mammon, worshipping at the altar of science, and surrendering to utility. Science and social science might give students the utility increasingly demanded in an industrial society; they might even aspire in their grander moments to impart liberal culture. But the humanities formed the core of the liberal-culture ideal that flourished in late-nineteenth-century colleges.

As they took shape in the final third of the nineteenth century the humanities represented a huge victory for academic critics of the industrial age. For at the same time that colleges began to liquidate Greek and Latin requirements, the humanities quietly wrapped themselves in the mantle of culture previously worn by the classical languages alone. Fewer students might know the classical languages by 1910—indeed most students were resolutely modern—but the victory of the humanities was to bestow upon these moderns the benediction of classicism—of intellectual, civic, and moral culture, of ennobling acquisition—minus the traditional immersion in the ancient languages.

This shift from classicism to the humanities shaped Gilded Age culture and intellectual life in several important ways. First, it helped to erode the highly masculine world of classicism, opening its ranks both ideologically and numerically to women. Culture as earthly self-perfection was a goal toward which both sexes could strive, and indeed women by the late nineteenth century were often perceived as being more open to cultivation than men because of their ostensibly softer, gentler natures. With high culture now defined as the opposite of business and industry, it also became a province for feminine values removed from the masculine sphere of the market. Culture was antimaterialism, antiaggression, antiexploitation. "In a country where men are incessantly occupied at their business or profession," remarked the English visitor James Bryce in 1893, "the function of keeping up the level of culture devolves upon women." Wealthy women became the female Medici to the museums, libraries, and symphonies of the Gilded Age, bringing beauty and refinement to these temples of high culture. But the feminization of culture was not confined to social elites. "Girls whose mothers had never advanced much beyond reading, writing, and arithmetic," noted one author in 1906, "find themselves studying Greek art and German music."[67] In 1909 another commentator concluded that "the whole higher culture is feminized."[68]

The feminization of high culture and classicism was especially obvious in higher education. By 1910 women made up 40 percent of collegians in America, up from just 21 percent in 1870.[69] Greek and Latin loomed during these years as a symbol of women's achievements in the higher reaches of erudition, and some of the most elite coeducational and women's colleges, such as Bryn Mawr, Cornell, and the University of Michigan, offered parity in classical learning for both men and women. During the first decades after the Civil War, women's inadequate preparation in the classical languages often discouraged them from their higher pursuit, and they more frequently chose the literary course that emphasized modern languages. Even M. Carey Thomas (1857–1935), who eventually earned a Ph.D. in English philology from the University of Zurich in 1882, was stymied in her early years as a student at Cornell by her lack of classical language instruction in primary and secondary school.[70] Yet by the early twentieth century women monopolized enrollments in Latin courses at the high school level, which were an important steppingstone to teaching positions in the schools and to classics competence at the college level.[71]

In addition to storming the bastion of classics, women flocked more readily to the courses newly defined as humanistic and high cultural: English, modern foreign languages, history, art history. Even when given the opportunity to study humanities and science on an equal footing with men, women turned to culture studies. Of the women who graduated from Grinnell College between 1896 and 1914, 81 percent received degrees in what were now called the humanities: modern languages, English, Greek, and history. In contrast to the 41 percent of men who received degrees in science, only 6 percent of women chose that path.[72] These changes were mirrored in the high schools, where the gender balance of science and classics was reversed in just twenty years. In 1890 more boys than girls enrolled in the classical curriculum; by 1910 the reverse was true. Educational rhetoric shifted accordingly, abandoning the eighteenth-century association of linguistic skill with masculinity. In 1915 one commentator noted that there was "something inherently attractive to boy-nature in the engineering pursuits," while girls preferred languages because "the intrinsic quality of the subjects makes more of an appeal to the girl-mind than to the boy-mind."[73] Women's shift toward culture and classicism marked an important change from the antebellum era, when sciences like botany had been viewed as intrinsically feminine pursuits and classics had been considered the male study par excellence.[74] In the late nineteenth century science became not only a more masculine pursuit but also an increasingly working-class pursuit, as men from lower-middle-class and farming families entered science courses to train for jobs in industry and scientific agriculture. Culture and classics, by contrast, sidestepped these associations with industry and masculinity.[75] "Women," concluded a commentator in 1912, "are taking over the field of liberal culture."[76]

In addition to opening classicism to women, the humanities also filled the vacuum left by evaporating religion. As the academy was secularized, the humanities were sacralized.[77] Until 1870 American colleges acted as the scholarly arm of Protestantism, and even after that many students and faculty remained staunch believers. But secularization seeped into the academy just as it did into American culture outside the university. The modern administrator-president supplanted the clergyman-president, and scholars divorced their scholarship from the formal, now privatized practice of religion. Fueling the ideological construction of the new humanities was the spread of what George Marsden has called "liberal Protestantism," a kind of expansive, nonsectarian Protestantism that defined Christianity "as broad ethical ideals or even as just the highest principles of civilization."[78] Many university reformers and professors across the disciplines in the late nineteenth century sought to mold academic disciplines to liberal Protestantism, but it was the new humanities that lay closest to liberal Protestantism's spiritual core. Even as the study of classical languages ebbed in the curriculum, the quasi-religious spirituality in the ideal of Hellenism permeated classical study and the other humanities. The humanistic revolution of the antebellum period had transformed what was a grammatical and politically didactic exercise during the Revolutionary era into a platform for internal self-perfection by 1860. Classicism's revolution now spread to its sister disciplines, making literature, art history, music, and philosophy into chapels of culture for earthly self-perfection. Religious dogmatism seldom ruffled the serene waters of liberal Protestantism, as the Homeric question had done in the antebellum era. Instead, the humanities offered culture as what one observer in 1904 called "the modern secular Gospel."[79]

Humanities professors now described their vocation as quasi-ministerial. Many could remain thoroughly committed Protestants while giving themselves over quite seamlessly to the pious incantations of high culture. At the University of Michigan, Henry Frieze taught Roman literature and history from 1854 until his death in 1889, all the while, according to the *Nation*, making "the classical masterpieces of literature . . .

living and real, a means of inspiration and rare culture."[80] An intensely pious Episcopalian who spent leisure hours playing hymns at the piano, Frieze saw no conflict between his formal religion and classicism as inspiration for raising the level of civic virtue and refined morals among the masses. Michigan's president James B. Angell believed that it was "impossible to overstate the influence" that Frieze "exerted in the West through . . . [his] labors at the University of Michigan in diffusing love for the study of ancient classics."[81] Cornell's president, Andrew Dickson White (1832–1918), declared that Frieze "did more than any other man within my knowledge to make classical scholarship a means of culture throughout our Western States."[82]

Students remembered Frieze's teaching of the classics as much for his inspirational style of presentation as for the content of the lesson. Angell, a former student of Frieze's, showed how Frieze's exalted ethics made his lectures into secular sermons:

> In his presence, in his classroom, even the raw and untrained student felt at once the subtle influence of the spirit of culture, which emanated from the instructor. The fineness of literary perception, the delicacy of taste, which revealed themselves through all his interpretation of the ancient masters of thought, polished and elevated, while they instructed the class. His exalted ethical nature led him also to impress upon his pupils without cant or platitudes, but in the most natural and effective manner, the moral, the heroic qualities of the ancient characters of whom they were reading. . . . How many a graduate have we heard say that two impressions above all they brought from Professor Frieze's class-room, namely, that he was the perfect gentleman, and that he had the finest culture.[83]

Many of the classicists of the late nineteenth century described their vocation in such terms, seamlessly stitching together classicism, high culture, and ethics. Cornelius Felton, a Unitarian, late in life dedicated himself to what he called the "holy cause of popular education," propagated through classicism as "a temporal salvation."[84] Simeon North (1802–84), a professor of Greek at Hamilton College, was remembered by a student who graduated in 1870 for being "alive to the poetic or literary sentiment, the ineffable charm and grace of style and diction of the great authors, on whose works he commented." According to this former student, North embodied sweetness and light.[85] William S. Tyler, at Amherst College, noted in 1873 that students then, much more than before, "read the classics more in relations to History and Philosophy and as a means of higher culture in what are justly called 'the Humanities.' "[86] According to a former student, Tyler taught "Greek civilization" as "a necessary act in God's great drama of salvation" and the Greek authors "with the same moral conviction that made his sermons powerful instruments of conversion."[87]

As classics professors assumed a quasi-ministerial role, their gospel changed accordingly, from the New Testament to the idealism of Plato. The study of Plato became hugely popular after 1870 in both English and American higher education, reflecting a drift toward idealism in American thought that, as we saw in chapter 2, had its origins in the antebellum era.[88] Americans were increasingly less disturbed by the fact that Plato, as well as, for that matter, any of the other ancients, was a heathen. As the specifics of Christian doctrine became less important, scholars emphasized what united ancient and modern philosophies more than what separated them. It was not just in classical study that idealism found a home in the late-century university: philosophers such as Josiah Royce (1855–1916), at Harvard, and George Morris (1840–89), at the University of Michigan, turned their attention to questions traditionally addressed by theologians, though these were now freed from orthodox doctrine.[89] The study of Immanuel Kant and Herbert Spencer suffused the late-century curriculum, accompanied by Plato, who provided an instructive historical antecedent to modern idealism. As a young professor of philosophy at the University of Michigan in 1886, for example, John Dewey offered courses on Plato's *Republic* and ancient philosophy (in translation) while also lecturing on experimental psychology, Kant, Spencer, and logic.[90] The description for Yale's course "Plato's Philosophical System" (1900) assured students that "especial attention will be given to the theories of the *Ideas*."[91]

Students in pursuit of culture no longer needed to read the ancients in the original. One writer in 1927 told readers that actually reading Plato was not a necessary prerequisite to becoming cultured: "Can a man be cultured who has never heard of Plato? Probably not. . . . Can a man be cultured who has never read Plato? Assuredly."[92] Women were believed to be especially receptive to Platonic doctrine because it concorded with their idealized, sentimental natures. "Were Plato alive today," wrote the journalist Jane Croly in 1892, "his auditors would be chiefly women. . . . Women are grappling with the problems of pure thought that underlie all other problems, seeking to remove the limits of the unknown but not the unknowable."[93]

Americans now used in the classrooms the English translation of Plato's *Dialogues* made by the most famous Platonic scholar of the Victorian era, the Oxford professor Benjamin Jowett (1817–93). While professing his faith as a Christian, Jowett likened Plato's teaching to those of Christ, viewing both men as mediators between the worlds of the seen and the unseen. Commenting on the end of Plato's *Gorgias*, Jowett wrote: "The myth which terminates the Dialogue is not the revelation, but rather, like all similar descriptions, whether in the Bible or Plato, the veil of another life."[94] Americans absorbed this line of thinking. "Next to the Holy Scriptures," wrote Taylor Lewis, of Union College, in a review of Jowett's *Plato* in 1872, "a young man should be exhorted to make it [Plato] his most ardent study."[95] Others went even further in smoothing over doctrinal differences to assert the commonality in every religion, whether Greek, Hindu, or Christian. In an article in 1885 entitled "Socrates, Buddha, and Christ," one author exhorted readers: "In all opinions, let us find the common ground, the underlying unity, the scientific definition; and so shall we base ethics on sure foundations and make logic the instrument to universal truth."[96] In both England and America this quasi-Christian Platonic idealism also acted as cultural antidote to utilitarianism and vocationalism, a dose of the spirit in a world overwhelmed by the material. Philosophy was now studied in many colleges as it was at Yale, "as a means of culture," as the 1900–1901 catalog advertised.[97]

Not just philosophy but also literature and art assimilated the ancient Greeks into the nonsectarian atmosphere of the late-nineteenth-century college. One advocate of high culture asked, "In an age when the material aspects of life crowd out the spiritual, when art is either a memory or a hope, who does this man of culture find to guide and refresh him, to prop up his soul?" The answer was the Greeks, specifically Sophocles. Among the "hosts of prophets and preachers" available to the moderns, the "man of trained mind and pure spirit" knew to look to the ancient classics, not the Bible, for spiritual elevation.[98] One former Harvard student who had enrolled in a course on the *Agamemnon* of Aeschylus confessed that his professor had given him the "first intimation that the Greek tragic poets might possess a higher wisdom than Biblical prophets, with greater majesty of form and content."[99] Another student tellingly penciled "Amen" at the end of his textbook of *Antigone*.[100]

It was not only classical texts that partook of the drift toward classics as high culture, for ancient art now arose as an undergraduate study in its own right, an essential part of any student's humanities education. The study of antiquities had formed almost no part of a classical education in America until the late nineteenth century, although antiquities themselves—coins, vases, inscriptions—had been the object of great interest and veneration in Europe for centuries. By late in the century, however, the study of classical texts alone—what Harvard's Eliot Professor William Watson Goodwin in 1884 called "mere grammatical study"—was no longer believed to be entirely adequate in a student's classical education. Instead the study of the classics was "the only sure road . . . leading to the higher level of literature and art beyond."[101] The proliferation of art history courses after 1870 testified to the ease with which a new study could robe itself in the mantle of cultivation earlier reserved for textual study alone, leaving language study as just one of a handful of cultivating studies. After mid-century, museums of classical antiquities sprang up at a number of American colleges, making campuses new sites of high culture.

The University of Michigan's art museum, founded in 1856 by Henry Frieze, was typical. Frieze had just been hired as a professor of Latin when he petitioned the regents to grant him a leave of absence so that he could travel to Europe to procure "specimens of Ancient art illustrative of the classics" with the aim of "laying the foundation for a classical museum in the University."[102] In February 1856, after spending four months studying at the university in Berlin, Frieze and his young friend Andrew Dickson White joined two other Americans for a four-month journey through Italy.[103] Although White in his later life spent years abroad in the diplomatic service, he remembered his journey with Frieze as "among the fortunate things in life."[104] When they reached Italy in March, the four men, led by the tireless Frieze, set off on antiquarian excursions to gather books, engravings, plaster casts, and other objects for the University of

Michigan's projected art museum. Frieze's journey to Italy not only cemented his friendship with White, it completed his own classical education. The group visited Venice, Rome, and Naples, as well as the ruined ancient cities of Paestum, Herculaneum, and Pompeii.[105] In Italy, according to one companion, Frieze "gained as thorough a mastery of the whole subject as it was possible for any one to have who had not lived for years in Rome. . . . You can imagine what a treat was the whole time we spent in Rome to a man so fond of Roman Archaeology as the Professor. . . . every day and all day he was exploring the ruins of Rome and the neighboring Campagna, and in the evening what had been seen was discussed by friends who took the liveliest interest in the subject."[106]

Their experiences and impressions of Italy were in no way unusual for the late nineteenth century, when there was so much more of a focus on *seeing* the ancient world than there had been in the eighteenth century. The Roman Forum, for example, which Frieze and his companions visited, had become well known to nineteenth-century Americans through literature, history, and artistic rendition.[107] American visitors varied in their responses to the ruined site, however, some basking in the afterglow of the site of the birth of liberty, law, and virtue, others sneering at what appeared to be little more than a muddy cow pasture. One American guidebook published in 1853 described the Forum as "a desolation which is not beautiful, a ruin which is not picturesque."[108] Nathaniel Hawthorne's visit in 1858 confirmed the impression of Rome as "a dead and mostly decayed corpse."[109] Frieze's record of his contemporaneous visit accorded with these views of a site heavily encrusted by modern buildings and constantly pillaged by current inhabitants. The Temple of Vesta, which stood in the Forum, was particularly disappointing to Frieze. There, three filthy young girls, whom he called "the modern vestals," chipped off pieces of the marble pillars and sold them for a pittance to tourists. Frieze declined to purchase their wares, although "such forbearance will scarcely prevent the gradual destruction of this fine little temple."[110] Frieze's reflections in his diary were conventional for his day: he was reverent toward Greece and Rome, more diffident toward other ancient art. The ancient Greek city of Paestum, noted Frieze, was "a desolate plain, bounded on one side by the sea, on the other by the southern Apennines, almost destitute of human habitation . . . the fitting site of these grand and silent temples of a departed race." Here Frieze and his companions spent hours "walking about, or in quietly contemplating these beautiful specimens of Grecian architecture."[111]

These rituals of solemn admiration contrasted with the Americans' opinion of the remains of many nonclassical civilizations, impressions confirmed by the displays Frieze saw in the British Museum in July 1856. There, Charles T. Newton, the keeper of antiquities, arranged the collections so as to make clear the artistic stages leading to the perfections of Periclean Athens.[112] The ancient Egyptian relics, according to Frieze, were impressive for "the ingenuity and physical force which created such grandeur, and achieved so much at such an early period in the development both of useful and ornamental arts." But Frieze "felt everywhere in these works the absence of that presiding taste which alone can bring art to its highest perfection." The Assyrian objects recently culled from the ancient city of Nimroud by Sir Austen Henry Layard (1817–94) surpassed the Egyptian in some respects, evincing "more character and liveliness." Yet these too struck Frieze as fettered to "conventional modes" of representation and lacking the Greek "ideas of beauty and expression."[113]

Frieze returned to the University of Michigan in the fall of 1856 with "higher ideals of his own work and much broader conceptions of the function of this University."[114] From Italy he believed he had gained the classical knowledge and artifacts to drive home to his students the tangible reality of the ancient world. Upon his return from Europe, Frieze began to add the study of ancient art and architecture to the study of classical language. This was the main purpose of his art museum. Here Frieze, who remained the curator of the little museum until his death, displayed the engravings, books, maps, photographs, and sculpture that he had purchased on his travels.[115] As the years passed, others, often university alumni, also donated artifacts to the museum. Like many nineteenth-century art galleries in Europe and America, the art museum at Michigan placed great importance on copies of originals, either in terra cotta or in plaster casts or reproduced in photographs and engravings. As Frieze and many others discovered, contact with ancient originals was often profoundly disappointing. Pocked marble, toppled columns, and amputated limbs often so distorted the original piece of sculpture or architecture as to make it visually uninspiring. But casts were relatively inexpensive and restored the art to some approximation of the ancient glory eroded by time. "Casts of statuary of the life size, even more perfect than copies in marble, and for all the purposes of art quite as valuable as the originals, can readily be obtained at an average cost of $25," explained Frieze in his catalog.[116] When many of the plaster and terra cotta copies he had purchased from the "moulding establishments" attached to the Louvre, the Museo Borbonico, and the Vatican were chipped in transit, Frieze, with a small grant from the regents, carefully pieced them back together.[117] He assured his visitors of the value of the museum casts and terra cottas: they were "all of the most reliable character" and belonged "to the best periods of art in Greece and Rome."[118]

Plaster casts and terra cottas also created a didactic historical sequence of art, whose study cultivated students. Frieze viewed the growth or decline of art and literature as a measure of the progress or fall of civilization or culture. Such a view was typical of the day and was expressed also by a new breed of scholars on college campuses, the art historians. After the Civil War art history flourished in liberal arts colleges: it has been estimated that by 1912, of the four hundred liberal arts colleges in America, ninety-five, from Washington State College in Pullman to West Virginia University in Morgantown, taught the history of art.[119]

Leading art historians, such as Charles Eliot Norton at Harvard and Allan Marquand (1853–1924) at Princeton, likewise viewed the study of art as a story of stylistic rise and fall, with material artifacts indicative of "national character."[120] One could extrapolate from artifacts the whole character of a people, or "race." Such thinking paralleled that in the social and biological sciences, with their views of the progress of races from primitive youth to cultured maturity. While prehistoric art, in the opinion of Marquand, could be likened to embryology, Greek and Roman art stood at the pinnacle of achievement.[121] At Frieze's museum, casts fleshed out the museum's scanty collections, presenting "to the eye the whole history of architecture in all periods and of every style."[122] Frieze's catalog led visitors on a meticulously numbered walking tour of the galleries. First came engravings and photographs of ancient, medieval, and modern art, as well as views of ancient Rome and Athens. Frieze's catalog provided numbered guides to the vistas, pointing out the relevant detail in each image. Next came copies of classical and modern statues, followed by a collection of copies of gems and medallions from ancient Egypt onward. The catalog also supplied students with the canonical lore attached to each piece—what Lord Byron thought, what Winckelmann had said.

The presence of this museum transformed the way Frieze taught ancient literature to his students. Now the ancient authors could be placed in the proper context by showing students the society that produced them. Frieze's hope was to lead students beyond the study of Latin to give them a sense of Greek and Roman civilization as a whole—of the people who had produced these things. Frieze's lectures reproduced what the museum showed: a chronological study of art from ancient Greece to about A.D. 1600, after which, Frieze and many others believed, art declined. The museum and the classroom now were combined into a single pedagogy. James Angell described Frieze's agenda as follows:

> But upon no point was he accustomed to dwell in these later years with so much fervor as upon the transcendent importance of teaching Latin literature not merely as a collection of works of gifted men, but as the expression of the life of the great Roman nation, uttering itself in history, philosophy and poetry. . . . According to his conception it was not Latin that we should study so much as Roman, the achievements, the spirit, the vital power of the Roman race.[123]

In his courses Frieze assigned the same works that he had used to supply the descriptive apparatus in his museum catalog, among them Sir William Smith's *Greek and Roman Geography* (1857) and Winckelmann's *History of Ancient Art*.[124]

Integrated art and literature flourished elsewhere as well. At Dartmouth College in 1898 sophomores studied "the art of Pheidias and his successors" through photographs, casts, and lectures and then capped the term with a four-day junket to the Boston Museum of Fine Arts.[125] At Amherst College, the Greek professor William Tyler introduced maps, charts, photographs, casts, and terra cottas to his classroom to "lend to classical studies something of the reality and vividness which specimens and experiments give to the Physical Sciences" and to "help students to reproduce men and things as they were in olden times."[126] It even flourished at Catholic universities, with some appropriate variations: at the College of the Holy Cross in 1900, in the "humanities classroom" there were crowded onto the wall "pictures of the Roman world oriented toward drama and death: a chariot race in the Circus Maximus . . . a picture of Death surrounded by a variety of its victims, and a crucifix."[127]

The study of ancient, medieval, and Renaissance art flourished after mid-century because art had acquired those ennobling traits of high culture previously reserved for texts alone. Both art and literature—rather than grammar—had become the road to acquiring the spirit of Hellenism. Any study of Greece that left art out, declared one Greek scholar at Dartmouth, was "one-sided, fragmentary, and essentially defective."[128] This development generated fierce debate among classical scholars. As other courses within the humanities, such as art history and the history of philosophy, commandeered bits of classical antiquity for their own purposes, they necessarily recruited the ideas rather than the exact wording of the ancients. On the one hand, this practice stretched the life of classicism, justifying the presence of antiquity in the modern university. Indeed, a number of classical scholars, as we shall see, argued that the study of ancient art and architecture should form a necessary part of any student's education in the classics. Dartmouth's classical philologist John Henry Wright argued that students would receive "especial culture and expansion from the systematic study of the remains of ancient art, especially in sculpture and architecture."[129] On the other hand, a number of classicists doubted whether classics in translation furnished students with the same level of discipline, knowledge, and culture as the real thing.

Among the most outspoken opponents of the drift toward the visual was Basil Lanneau Gildersleeve. Gildersleeve maintained that the text had spiritually and intellectually redeeming qualities. Grammar itself had "moral and aesthetic" elements and thus provided students with "the fairest theatre for the culture of aesthetic appreciation."[130] Gildersleeve's undergraduate program emphasized studying ancient texts in the original rather than in translation and the perusal of "the great mass of illustrative literature."[131] Students needed "a real grasp of the language," not just desultory reading of texts in translation.[132] Relative to the text, argued Gildersleeve, art receded in importance: "All the advantages of Hellenism for higher culture cannot be gained by the study of casts of the Pan-athenaic procession, or photographs of the Nike of Paionios."[133] "True art" emanated from grammatical laws, just as beauty rose from the mathematical regularities of music.[134]

Moreover, the marriage of culture and classicism should not blind us to the fact that the study of language was developing in both a literary and a scientific direction. Philology, the study of language, had a pedigree that extended not only to classical language but also, for example, to biblical and Indian languages and universal grammar. By the mid-nineteenth century one of its branches especially, comparative philology, was making explicit claims to using a scientific method. Comparative philology emerged in the late eighteenth century with the researches of Sir William "Oriental" Jones (1746–94), one of a group of scholars who began to trace the genealogical connections between languages and to group them into families, such as the Indo-European. These scholars paid attention to regular historical shifts in languages (as in grammar or word meanings) in order to trace the roots of languages and their affinities. These shifts were believed to be reducible to empirical laws like those that governed other genealogical studies, such as comparative anatomy. This comparative study of language could be distinguished from the older philosophical grammar of the eighteenth century, which was highly speculative and chiefly concerned with the theological project of discovering the original language of mankind—whether Adam and Eve conversed in Flemish, French, or possibly Swedish in the Garden of Eden.[135] In Europe, the great practitioners of comparative philology included Friedrich von Schlegel and Franz Bopp in Germany and Friedrich Max Müller in England.

In America it was the Yale Sanskritist William Dwight Whitney (1827–94) who did the most to subordinate the study of language to the classificatory schemes of comparative philology. Asked in the late nineteenth century to define the word *philology* for the *Encyclopaedia Britannica*, Whitney revealed the growing split between the literary side of philology (as in the study of the classics as culture) and the presumably more scientific, comparative side. The philologist, argued Whitney, could either investigate the literature of a people or focus on the peculiarities of grammar. Whitney conceded that no "absolute distinction" separated the two philologies, but he affirmed that they had been "for some time past tending toward greater independence." Comparative philology was more "scientific," classical philology more "literary."[136]

Far from rejecting this scientific comparative philology, many late-century classicists accepted its results, joining Whitney in distinguishing the scientific study of language from the literary. William Gardner Hale, a Latinist at the University of Chicago, saw "the danger of dilettantism . . . in the study of literature and art pursued exclusively," for these were not as "patient in investigation" as "phonetic and syntactic science."[137] Even someone as humanistically oriented as Henry Simmons Frieze welcomed the results of comparative philology. He spent the winter of 1871 at the University of Tübingen studying Sanskrit because he believed that Indo-European languages could enhance the study of classical scholarship "at home and abroad."[138] The great fear by the early twentieth century, however, was that science would overtake humanism in classical study. The University of Michigan Latin scholar Francis Willey Kelsey in 1908 hoped that American undergraduates could blend what he called "the classics as humanities," which were read for their "refining influence," for "revelation," and for "inspiration," and the "scientific" ideal, which he identified as "a critical attitude" toward ancient authors.[139]

Despite this connection to science, classicism as part of the humanities emerged in the late nineteenth century as a moral and intellectual alternative to natural and social science. Classicism and the humanities were cast as explicitly antivocational, thus counteracting the claim that college studies should offer immediate social utility. They also offered "culture" as a moral alternative to the creeping ethical agenda of the sciences, which presumed to solve a growing number of social problems. Finally, classicists put forth a competing vision of the work of the scholar in the undergraduate college at a time when many scientific experts sought to make themselves into the new moral leaders of society. Many humanities professors elevated themselves to the status of gentlemanly purveyors of culture, ministerial in their authority in matters spiritual. As scientists cast the work of science in terms that elevated morals, so classicists cast the work of classical study as one that had ennobling traits, and the humanities professor as one who guided students into the rarefied air of high culture and prepared them for educated citizenship.

THE ALIENATION OF ANTIQUITY

Late-century classicism and the new humanities rested not only upon the idea of culture as earthly self-perfection but also on a revised conception of history. By the late nineteenth century classical scholars, among other Americans, had replaced their fear of the temporal finitude of the republic with a new faith in the idea of progress, of upward ascent over time. The enemy of classical republicanism, time was for the Victorians the benevolent midwife of progress. Time in this new view allowed civilizations to ascend from primitive barbarity to enlightened civilization. Historicism, however, created a major dilemma for classical scholars because it eroded the imagined affinity between antiquity and modernity that had buttressed classicism in the eighteenth century and even into the antebellum era. Then classicists had argued that America could recapitulate the fate of the classical world, and so antiquity had appeared in the American imagination as a useful, instructive mirror of modernity. By contrast, historicism posited linear, directional change over time, not cyclical recapitulation. The lessons of antiquity now lost their didactic clarity. No longer could the classical past instruct Americans to escape from time; no longer could it offer itself as a mirror of the present. Ensnared by deep, historical time, classical antiquity could not remain the mirror of immediate relevance that it had been since the Renaissance. Greece and Rome were now in danger of slipping into irrelevance, a fate exacerbated by their new association with economic uselessness. For classical scholars, the triumph of historicism in the college curriculum demanded a new temporal justification for a discipline that focused resolutely on a past whose utility seemed unclear in a modern world.

Late-nineteenth-century classicists found this justification in the idea of the "progress of civilizations," the intellectual antecedent to the Western civilization courses that flourished on campuses between World War I and the 1960s.[140] The idea of "Western civilization" rested on the assumption that classical antiquity, medieval Europe, and nineteenth-century Europe and America formed a single civilization united by cultural commonality. The idea of studying "civilizations" had emerged in the eighteenth century among the philosophers of the Scottish Enlightenment, who speculated on the origins of humanity. Scottish philosophers had arrayed human societies into an orderly, historical sequence, arguing by analogy to the cycle of human life that societies climbed as on a staircase from the primitive childhood of the race to its sophisticated maturity, from what the Scots termed "savagery" through "barbarity" and thence to "civilization." The evolutionary staircase built in the eighteenth century also propped up the anthropology and history of the nineteenth century, with its rigidly hierarchical assumptions about language, race, and culture. Its analogy to upward movement helped to solidify the idea that the "progress of civilizations" was a story of nations ascending from a state of savagery to one of settled culture.[141]

Classicists recruited these ideas to buttress the study of antiquity in universities that increasingly worshipped modernity and progress. They argued first that studying the march of history from Athens to America illustrated universal laws of progress. Modern society had its roots ultimately in the civilization of Greece, argued classicists in the late nineteenth century, and the story of progress was one that linked the Greeks and Romans to nineteenth-century Europeans and Americans. "It is as futile for a man to try to study the civilization of the nineteenth century, without understanding its sources among the Greeks, as to attempt to practice medicine, without knowing anything of anatomy and physiology," wrote Edward Clapp in 1896.[142] The Dartmouth Greek scholar John Henry Wright explained the exact relationship between antiquity and modernity:

> Modern culture owes to the civilisation of the ancient Greeks a profound debt, which is at once direct and indirect. The direct debt has arisen principally from the place long-held by Greek studies in our system of education. The indirect debt, which is more subtle and less easily recognised, is that of many forces, inspirations, and models, in art, literature, and science, that have been transmitted to us from a remote past, through various peoples and through diverse civilisations.[143]

Having cast Greece and Rome in the curriculum not simply as illustrations of grammatical laws but as entire civilizations, Gilded Age proponents of classicism believed that students should study the "progress of civilizations" over time. "Through the investigation of Greek and Roman antiquities," argued Charles Eliot Norton in 1900, the modern student would "gain fuller acquaintance with the genius of these commanding races, and a truer appreciation of their works, and thus a better understanding of the origins and nature of our own civilization."[144]

In this Darwinian age American scholars turned to organic, evolutionary metaphors to describe the relationship of antiquity to modernity, just as biologists described the evolution of a species or the unfolding of an organism. As eggs developed into chickens, or Anglo-Saxon developed into modern English, so ancient Greece and Rome developed into modern America by regular, progressive stages over time. "Ancient facts are embryonic stages of modern facts," declared William Torrey Harris in 1885.[145] Nicholas Murray Butler, president of Columbia University, argued that "the embryology of civilization is just as significant and important as the embryology of organic forms."[146] Archaeology, noted Charles Eliot Norton, showed the "evolution" of civilizations.[147] President James Angell of Michigan described classical antiquity not "as a beautiful creation of a dead past, but rather as the flowering of an imperishable life, whose vital currents have been flowing through all the western civilization of these eighteen centuries, and are still beating in the pulse of this nineteenth century."[148]

Through these evolutionary metaphors classical scholars found a way to counteract the charge that the classical languages were dead. The languages were indeed dead, but the civilizations lived as the ancestors to the modern era in the same way that a granddaughter inherited the distinctive physical features of a grandparent even though she might speak a different language. The classical past might be culturally and chronologically remote, but it informed the present age by showing how "they" had become "us."

Classicists also defended the study of the progress of civilizations as uniquely cultivating. The act of escaping from modernity into an authentic past gave students a glimpse of the higher world of truth and sentiment. Historicism, in other words, gave students culture. This was a new assumption. Before the 1840s the college curriculum viewed as a collective entity was chronologically static, and its uniting idea was the existence of God. All curricular roads ultimately led to the senior moral philosophy course, which was in essence an exercise in the contemplation of the perfections of the deity. Students were not encouraged to contemplate the idea that societies or literature or ideas changed over time. It was not until the 1850s, and especially after the Civil War, that courses regularly assumed that this was what students should do, whether in the study of French and German literature, art history, modern European history, U.S. history, or the history of philosophy. By the Gilded Age, historicism had become a chief pillar of liberal culture in the colleges. As R. M. Wenley, of the University of Michigan, explained, "Culture studies link man principally with the *past.*" The past "has become *internal* to us; irreducible circumstances have wrought it into our being as an organic part."[149] President Noah Porter of Yale explained how historicism bestowed high culture by taking the student outside of selfish concerns:

> The student of Corneille and Goethe is . . . mainly conversant with modern ideas and modern civilization. However exquisite the diction or masterly the genius of his writer, the sentiments and passions are all modern. But the student of Virgil and of Homer cannot painfully translate a few books of the Aeneid or the Odyssey, without entering into the thoughts and sympathizing with the feelings, and living somewhat of the life of human beings greatly unlike those whom he has ever known or imagined. Their thoughts and feelings do not repel him by their strangeness so much as they attract him by their dignity and truth, and open to him a new world of sentiment and emotion. The people, into whose life he very imperfectly learns to enter, though in many respects so unlike the men of present times, are yet closely connected with them by the civilization, the arts, the literature, the institutions, the manners, and the laws which the ancients perfected and transmitted.[150]

Paul Shorey's first students at Bryn Mawr and the University of Chicago remembered this historical style of teaching as being conducive to culture. George Norton (1871–1942) recalled that what he got from Shorey "above all was a sense of humanism as a continuing tradition," while Emily James Putnam (1865–1944) spoke of the huge stack of books tucked under Shorey's arm as "a life line to keep us from drowning in the great stream of European culture."[151]

By late in the century the modern literary canon had taken shape out of this sense that literature properly historicized had cultivating powers. Certain "masterpieces" from the period stretching from Homeric Greece to the sixteenth century delivered the noblest sentiments of their ages to the modern student. In the "area of culture" Yale's English professor Albert Cook in 1898 positioned the following works: the Scriptures, Homer, Pindar, Sophocles, Lucretius, Virgil, Tacitus, Juvenal, Dante, Ariosto, the French *chansons de geste*, Ronsard, Molière, Rousseau, the *Nibelungenlied*, Goethe, Cynewulf, Chaucer, Shakespeare, and Milton.[152] This new canon hinged on the assumption not only that classical antiquity and the present were part of a continuous narrative but that it behooved students to know such a narrative in order to be considered liberally educated. Historicism had now thoroughly supplanted grammatical knowledge as the foundation of a liberal education; a new canon had been created.

The idea of the "progress of civilization" created a powerful new rhetorical tool in the dwindling arsenal of the Gilded Age classical votaries, justifying the study of antiquity in universities defined by claims to modernity, progress, science, and utility. In substituting the notion of progressive, historical ascent for an achronological, imagined affinity between antiquity and America, proponents of classicism had fundamentally changed the function of classicism within the postbellum universities. What mattered now was not the imitation of antiquity but its location in historical time. Classics as the story of progress from antiquity to the present now stood on the same footing in the Gilded Age university as modern history, biology, anthropology, geology—all disciplines that showed development over time. All these disciplines could be, at some level, "historical sciences." Students at South Carolina College in 1890, for example, learned "laws of development" not only in their Greek history course but also in zoology and pedagogical psychology.[153] As religion evaporated as the epistemological justification within the American university, progress emerged as one replacement, linking disparate disciplines in the university with the chain of historical time. Combined with the notion that classics ennobled the modern student with a dose of antimaterialist spirituality, the rhetoric of progress propped up the discipline of classical study in a new educational climate that threatened to destroy it.

But while the idea of historical progress rescued classicism by linking it genetically with modernity, it also helped to render the past irrelevant. By stressing the chronological and cultural gaps between the past and the present, historical time fractured the old relationship between modernity and antiquity. The past was no longer timeless; it was not a mirror of the present. There could be little imagined affinity between modernity and antiquity. For the first time, the classical past became strange and remote to Americans. "What is to us the experience of past ages?" asked one commentator in 1872.[154] We can recall Cornelius Felton's advice to his students that he "who would enter fully into the merits of a classical author" should "transport himself back to a remote age." Here was something new: classical antiquity, so long the intellectual backyard of Americans, had now become somehow foreign.

Eighteenth-century classicists, of course, had been aware that the classical world was long gone; they believed in the inherent fragility of republics ancient and modern, their perilous suspension in time. And yet they had also been convinced that the great actors of antiquity were somehow also their contemporaries, a mirror for their own selves, a font of morals, a template for virtuous statecraft and peerless expression. In the eighteenth-century curriculum this belief manifested itself in the grammar-dominated mode of studying the ancients, a tireless imitation of their eloquence and ethics. While eighteenth-century moderns might quibble about the lessons that the ancients taught, their temporal closeness to the modern era was undisputed: Cicero was as relevant to the American Senate as he was to ancient Rome.

This unceasing relevance began to be repudiated in the 1820s and was finally abandoned in the Gilded Age. The historicization of ancient texts in the undergraduate classroom after that time required that students desert their imagined affinity with classical antiquity. Paradoxically, imbibing the spirit of ancient society demanded that students forsake the premise that ancient society was a mirror of the modern era. It asked that they emphasize instead the difference between their era and ages past so that they could properly position a text in a historical context. To return to Felton's advice to his students, antiquity was a remote age that required that the student "take himself out of the influences immediately around him"; he "must forget his country, his prejudices, his superior light."[155]

Expressions of the alienation of antiquity from the modern era abounded by the late nineteenth and early twentieth centuries. The classical world was now described variously as "different," "distant," "vanished," "remote," "alien," and "unlike" the modern era.[156] In 1883, in his famous Phi Beta Kappa address at Harvard, Charles Francis Adams had declared that "The classic tongues were far more remote from our world than they had been from the world our fathers lived in. They are much more remote from the world of to-day than they were from the world of thirty years ago. The human mind, outside of the cloisters, is occupied with a class of thoughts—scientific thoughts—which do not find their nutriment in the remote past."[157] Even votaries of antiquity conceded that the classical word had receded into the distance. "Why is it," asked the Dartmouth classicist John Henry Wright in 1886, "that a culture so remote in the past should touch at so many points, with that touch of nature that makes us kin, the culture of the modern world? Why is it that a culture, which in its material aspects, in its outward features, is so alien to ours, should still exercise upon us so potent an influence?"[158] Classical civilization was linked to the modern era in the late-nineteenth-century idea of progress, but this was a different connection to antiquity than had earlier prevailed. The progress of civilizations acknowledged change over time in a way that the imagined affinity of the early modern era did not. Modern civilization might have developed from the classical past, but it was not the modern reincarnation or parallel of the classical past.

The abyss of time yawning between modernity and antiquity also loomed larger because of a revolution in historical time that occurred in two major stages over the course of the nineteenth century. In the first stage, which began in the late eighteenth century, geological time—the span of earth history that explained its present contours—began to stretch far back into the planet's youth. James Hutton, John Playfair, William Buckland, and Charles Lyell had in various ways suggested that earth-shaping forces, whether uniform or catastrophic, had operated in the past as they did now, a scenario that required a gargantuan time span. Geological time was the first historical chronology to burst from the shackles of biblical time: by the early nineteenth century one could respectably argue in scientific circles that the earth was more than four thousand years old, the age suggested by James Ussher in the seventeenth century based on biblical reading. Theologically, geological time posed no insurmountable problems to the standard account of human history given in the Bible. One could simply posit a long time span between the creation of the earth and the creation of humans, plants, and animals that followed. Human history could thus remain embedded within a short chronology, and the biblical and the classical worlds, even by the mid-nineteenth century, could plausibly appear docked in the modern world.

It took a second time revolution, one that Thomas Trautmann has called the "revolution in ethnological time," to begin to sever those chronological ties and reposition the classical world in the past. The revolution in ethnological time, argues Trautmann, occurred in the 1860s, when the discovery of human fossil remains suggested that the first men and women had walked the earth very long ago indeed. Not only was the earth extremely old, these findings suggested, but now life on earth seemed very ancient as well. It became necessary to imagine that some societies—prebiblical, preclassical—were perhaps so ancient that the traditional tool of the philologist, the analysis of texts, was useless for studying them. The word *prehistory* entered the English lexicon in the 1860s to describe a new scenario in which the traditional span of human history as recorded in the Bible or Homer was now preceded by an incalculably long preliterate epoch whose dark recesses these texts could never light.[159] Because Homer, whose work marks the traditional beginning of the Greek story, could not shed light on this "prehistoric" time, the authority of classical texts correspondingly declined and scholars turned instead to material artifacts. In his 1897 book *The Mycenaean Age* the Brown University professor of Greek literature and history Irving Manatt turned his gaze to what he called pre-Homeric Greece. "Until recently," he explained, "the Homeric poems were our sole source of light upon the civilization of the prehistoric or Heroic Age of Greece." But archaeology had changed that, supplementing the "fanciful" descriptions of Homer with the "actual facts" of excavation.[160] The veneration of texts that had characterized the eighteenth-century study of classical antiquity faded as the study of a textless, preclassical antiquity flourished.

Moreover, in the late nineteenth century the study of classical antiquity began to move in what might be called an anthropological direction, a development that undermined the majestic, idealized classical past of people like Matthew Arnold and his counterparts in Gilded Age America. A number of scholars—Friedrich Nietzsche (1844–1900) in Germany, Numa-Denis Fustel de Coulanges (1830–89) in France, Jane Ellen Harrison (1850–1928) and James Frazer (1854–1941) in England, and Lewis Henry Morgan (1818–81) in America—began around the turn of the century to seek what was common to all contemporaneous ancient societies rather than what was distinctive about the Greeks and, moreover, sought in Greek society what was irrational rather than glorious.[161] The interpretation of Greek religion and mythology, for example, were transformed in this new anthropological reading of Greek culture. Long viewed as a calm, decorous, rational component of Greek society, religion to Jane Harrison became a "savage and irrational passion" filled with "fear and deprecation." Scholars in the earlier part of the nineteenth century had neglected the study of ritual in favor of mythology, and even mythology, argued Harrison, occupied an ancillary position as a handmaiden of literature. But ritual revealed what was dark, alien, and disturbing about the Greeks, and it deserved to be studied in its own right.[162] Fustel de Coulanges, in *The Ancient City* (1864), emphasized the cultural abyss that now yawned between the moderns and the ancients:

> In our system of education, we live from infancy in the midst of the Greeks and Romans, and become accustomed continually to compare them with ourselves, to judge of their history by our own, and to explain our revolutions by theirs. What we have received from them leads us to believe that we resemble them. We have some difficulty in considering them as foreign nations; it is almost always ourselves that we see in them. . . . To understand the truth about the Greeks and Romans, it is wise to study them without thinking of ourselves, as if they were entirely foreign to us; with the same disinterestedness, and with the mind as free, as if we were studying ancient India or Arabia. Thus observed, Greece and Rome appear to us in a character absolutely inimitable; nothing in modern times resembles them; nothing in the future can resemble them.[163]

Such anthropological readings of Greek culture did not immediately penetrate the American college curriculum, however, which remained dedicated to illuminating the glories of classical civilization for the cultural uplift of their students. But in the larger scholarly community it did signal the gradual alienation of antiquity from the modern age. "The past," wrote one humanist in 1930, "is more utterly passed."[164]

FROM PUBLIC LIFE TO PRIVATE CULTURE

Sacralized as the core of high culture and sanctified as the Eden of Western civilization, classical civilization secured a place in the modern universities that emerged after 1870. This victory within the university, however, came at a price. The civically oriented classicism of the Revolutionary and antebellum eras now faded, replaced by classicism as the road to internal self-perfection rather than a forum for public participation. Whereas once it had permeated the life of every student who passed through the college and had blended seamlessly with the nation's civic life, by late century classicism had pooled in the custodial hothouses of high culture that we know as some of the monuments of the Gilded Age—museums, libraries, and college and university campuses. There classical antiquity flourished, but it also stood quite apart from the body of images and associations commonly available to Americans. Classical knowledge became esoteric, its possessor marked as a person of rarefied culture. While it might be a source of *high* culture, of inexpressible, ennobling acquisition, it was no longer an exuberant fountain of *political* culture, of a readily accessible frame of reference for understanding the role of the self in the state or the duties of the citizen in the republic. Classical Greece and Rome moved out of the realm of the immediately relevant into the world of elite culture, where they remain today.

By the early twentieth century classicism in the colleges stood for something new that we can recognize as bearing the imprint of liberal individualism. Americans now embraced the liberal rather than the classical republican ideal of the self, extolling not the virtues of self-denial for the public good but the seemingly limitless possibilities of self-development, with a larger civic goal no longer necessarily attached. Where once classicism had tethered the individual to the state in the ideology of republicanism, by late in the nineteenth century classicism stood as an individualized ideal of self-perfection quite unlinked from the fate of the nation as a whole.

In late-century American life classicism ascended to the pinnacle of elite culture, essential as a class marker but increasingly irrelevant to politics. Gilded Age nabobs imbibed a knowledge of classical culture through travel to Greece and especially Italy, as well as through study of museum antiquities. In addition to the campus art museums, the Boston Museum of Fine Arts (1870), the Metropolitan Museum of Art (1870), the Philadelphia Museum of Art (1876), and the Art Institute of Chicago (1879) paraded an array of both originals and copies of classical antiquities to elevate the general public. The ethereally white classically inspired monuments of the World's Columbian Exposition in Chicago in 1893 presented classical architecture as a shrine to the highest civilization, a contrast to the barbarity of industrial America and the uncivilized peoples beyond.[165] Novelists such as Henry James (1843–1916) and Edith Wharton (1862–1937) used the European world of classical high culture to skewer American provincialism and decadent opulence, casting sites of departed grandeur less as political teachers than as escapist fantasy lands for the overcivilized. The founding of the American Academy in Rome (1894) and the popularity of neoclassical building styles, reflected most famously in the firm of McKim, Mead, and White, testified to an enduring association between the classical world and the highest standards of taste and beauty.[166]

Invocations of imperial Rome increased as America itself became a world empire by the 1890s, evoking military and cultural might rather than arcadian republican simplicity. The grandiose neoclassical architecture of the turn of the century, moreover, rested in an increasingly eclectic cultural context that made the classical tradition one among many alternatives for both national celebration and cultural criticism. An enervated antimodern, for example, could embrace medievalism, Buddhist asceticism, tropical primitivism, or classicism as a way to retreat from civilization's excesses.[167] In 1918 Henry Adams called the Gilded Age the "climax of empire." While comparing America explicitly to imperial Rome, he also showed Rome's fading importance in the national consciousness. "In forty years, America had made so vast a stride to empire that the world of 1860 stood already on a distant horizon somewhere on the same place with the republic of Brutus and Cato, while schoolboys read of Abraham Lincoln as they did of Julius Caesar. . . . The climax of empire could be seen approaching, year after year, as though Sulla were a President or McKinley a Consul."[168]

As classicism floated into the realm of high culture, it also permeated a growing middle class eager to associate itself with that elite. Richard Bushman has shown how antebellum Americans became increasingly refined, adopting the personal and material trappings of the eighteenth-century colonial aristocracy even while embracing egalitarianism. In an expanding, commercial economy the middle classes through the acquisition of classical objects could simultaneously discredit the idea of inherited aristocracy while acquiring by purchase its stamp of authoritative nobility.[169] This trend continued as the century progressed. By the late nineteenth century the Victorian middle classes had thoroughly embraced the classical objects prized by the eighteenth-century gentility, placing objects of classical art and literature in their homes and libraries but casting off classicism's older associations with material self-denial and fears of luxury. Richard Jenkyns has called the popularization of classical objects middlebrow or Biedermeier classicism, evoking on the one hand its pretensions to grandeur while on the other its concessions to cozy domesticity.[170] Biedermeier classicism represented an example of the transition from classicism as republican virtue to classicism as liberal individualism. Objects of classical art displayed in late-nineteenth-century middle-class parlors advertised the individual's achievements in the world rather than exalting the health of the republic.

The popularity of classical artifacts among the middle class, moreover, showed how industrialization and high culture proceeded in tandem during the Gilded Age. Mechanization allowed the mass reproduction of classical objects, making them affordable to many. Yet these classical objects, viewed as the antithesis of machines and industry, showed their possessors to be persons of rarefied taste and culture. The machine, in other words, produced an object that symbolically negated industrialism. The Victorian parlor reflected this reciprocal relationship between industrialization and high culture. The small classical statues or other mementos of the ancient world appearing in the homes of middle-class Americans were intended to demonstrate their knowledge of history and art, as well as their travels to shrines of European high culture. Thanks to mechanization, they could purchase small likenesses of famous classical and neoclassical statues cast in snowy white marble, alabaster, terra cotta, and plaster for reasonable sums.[171] Amid the floral wallpaper and potted palms of the cluttered Victorian parlor a bust of Cicero or a pleasingly chipped Greek urn signaled to visitors that the host's admiration for the heady glories of antiquity was tethered to sturdy values of duty and domesticity. Guides to household management likewise domesticated the ancients, giving Victorian women hints from Roman and Greek matrons on how to juggle domestic duties. One illustration from Julia McNair Wright's *The Complete Home* (1879) shows Socrates dispensing advice in the agora to a young mother holding a babe in arms.[172] The turn toward Greek fashions for women after 1860 purported to liberate women for individualist and even bohemian self-expression. Classical ideals of "natural" female beauty as embodied by Venus had infused medical writings on posture and fashion for a century, but after 1860 those who opposed women's wearing corsets became especially vehement in urging women to adopt the less restrictive garments of ancient Greek women. In contrast to the pinched, restrictive fashions of mid-century, Greek clothing presaged the more voluptuous, athletic, expressive woman of the turn of the century.[173]

Late-century middling cultural venues like the Chautauqua movement and women's clubs likewise delivered classicism to huge numbers of middle-class Americans, but they emphasized classicism as a self-perfecting culture and enriching commodity rather than as a guide to self-abnegating civic virtue. Begun at Late Chautauqua, New York, in 1874, the Chautauqua movement spread across America over the next half-century, bringing a kind of informal education in music, art, drama, oratory, and literature to millions of Americans in rural areas who might never attend college.[174] The Chautauqua movement produced a series of "required literature" that guided Americans' reading in appropriately educational directions. One approved novel of the Chautauqua Reading Circle Literature Series was Alfred J. Church's *Callias: A Tale of the Fall of Athens* (1891), which combined a narrative of fifth-century B.C. Athens with frequent textbooklike interruptions informing the reader about key events and practices in the ancient world. Though painstakingly accurate in historical context, the story's characters displayed Victorian virtues of punctuality, duty, and—among the women—demure charm.[175] Such novelistic renderings of classical figures made antiquity both elite and familiar, ennobling but also accessible to anyone. The dethronement and domestication of classical authority continued in the twentieth century. The best-selling novel in America in 1926 was John Erskine's *Private Life of Helen of Troy*, which featured an impenitent Helen ("He never would have taken me if I hadn't wanted to go").[176] Erskine explained that his goal was to show readers that "Helen, instead of being a wicked villainness, was an almost conventional illustration of American life, even in the suburbs."[177]

Women's study clubs, which proliferated beginning in the late 1860s, brought classical culture and education to many middle-class women who were too old to profit from the colleges just now opening for women. Jane Croly, one early club founder, called for culture as a new adhesive in this age of social fragmentation:

> At the time the Cedar Rapids Ladies' Literary Club was formed, the society of the place was in a state of transition, the old and new breaking up into cliques, social, religious, and political, that threatened to annihilate all possibilities of unity on a higher basis. It is not too much to say that the inspiration of the Ladies' Literary Club arrested this process of disintegration, and concentrated the work of the most cultivated and thoughtful women in an effort that became the nucleus of the social growth and intellectual development of a town.

The clubs' persistent recourse to classical motifs showed the centrality of the knowledge of Greek and Latin to the definition of the educated, cultured person in the late nineteenth century. These women wanted culture, and to obtain their knowledge of the classics they defied men who, in the words of M. Carey Thomas, a philologist and president of Bryn Mawr College, "didn't see any good of a womans learning Latin or Greek [because] it didn't make them anymore entertaining to their husbands." Founders of the Minerva Society in 1859 chose the Roman goddess "because we wished to become wise." Many clubs adopted Latin mottoes, evoking the persistent association between classical learning and rarefied self-culture. The Peoria Woman's Club mined Virgil's *Aeneid* for *Dux femina facti,* while the Chicago Culture Club selected *Vis unita fortior.* Moreover, they largely eschewed modern history for Egyptian, Greek, and Roman history in their club readings. They culled their knowledge of antiquity from a bewildering pastiche of sources such as lectures by classics professors, encyclopedias, translated selections from Plato, and Hawthorne's novel *The Marble Faun* (1860) for pointers on Rome.[178]

The spread of classicism as a middle-class marker also papered over class and ethnic tensions that emerged during this age of immigration and proletarianization. The classically cultured middle-class home became a model to which the working classes could strive, an island of taste, calm, and respectability in a world of cheap amusements and deadening routine work. Elite and middling classical culture defined the new image of America; working-class subcultures did not. "The laborer ought to be ashamed of himself," wrote Henry Ward Beecher in 1876, "who in 20 years does not own the ground on which his house stands . . . who has not in that house provided carpets for the rooms, who has not his China plates, who has not his chromos, who has not some books nestling on the shelf."[179] Jane Addams (1860–1935), a pioneer of the settlement-house movement, employed classical culture as a means of uplifting the poor to middle-class respectability. Modern Greek immigrants at Chicago's Hull House in the late 1890s staged the ancient Greek tragedies *Electra* and *Ajax,* part of Addams's efforts to display "the glory of Greece" to "ignorant Americans."[180]

The fate of antiquity on Gilded Age college and university campuses mirrored this transition from antiquity as training for public life to classicism as a path to enriching high culture. This shift was not unique to classicism; it permeated American academic culture as it emerged in the age of the university. As Americans abandoned the inclusive cosmopolitan civic culture of the eighteenth century, a new breed of academic professionals retreated from commitments to general culture into the universities, where closed professional ranks and disciplinary specialization isolated them from public concerns.[181] College rituals withdrew from public venues and became private campus celebrations. Amherst College in the 1850s, for example, moved its commencement activities from the town commons (which had come to be reserved for scenes of falsely nostalgic genteel leisure) to the campus itself.[182]

Students participated in the university's withdrawal from commitments to public life. They abandoned the literary societies of the ante-bellum era, which had schooled them in classically inspired calls to public service, for the more insular attractions of new intercollegiate activities, such as sports, fraternities, and sororities (ironically called Greek socie-ties). These activities focused students' attention on college life rather than on the world around the college even as the curriculum channeled students into an ever-growing number of professions. One Yale under-graduate in the late nineteenth century reflected on this shift: "Now-a-days, there is very little excitement over political matters, and they seldom form a topic of conversation. . . . A loud-mouthed defender of this or that political party, or of any kind of 'ism,' is looked upon by the rest as a sort of curiosity whom it is 'good fun to draw out' by the utterance of sentiments directly opposed to his own."[183]

A vivid illustration of classicism's transformation from preparation for civic duty to platform for private self-culture was in the vogue for produc-tions of Greek plays on college campuses after 1881. Between 1881 and 1936 at least 349 Greek plays were performed on campuses across the country, from large universities like Stanford and the University of Wis-consin to small colleges such as Olivet and Vassar. Popular among stu-dents, faculty, and the general public, they combined aspirations to schol-arly rigor, historical authenticity, and ennobling high culture. But the collegiate Greek plays were not political pamphlets or entertainment so much as cultural didacticism through immersion in the authenticity of the ancient past. They exemplify the waning of the broad culture of classicism that had buttressed American political culture into the mid-nineteenth century and its replacement by the ideal of culture as internal self-perfection.

The first of these performances, Harvard University's 1881 production of Sophocles' *Oedipus Tyrannus,* is representative of what became typical across the nation. Inspired by the Oxford University student production of Aeschylus's *Agamemnon* in 1880, Harvard determined to rival England with its "masterpiece of classic tragedy" presented with "exact scholarship and literary taste."[184] Like Aristotle, many Americans believed the *Oedipus Tyrannus* to be "a perfect play" because of the "universality of its portrayal of men and morals."[185] The Harvard production would recre-ate through rigorous scholarly attention the actual conditions of Greek performance during ancient times. The play was performed in the new Sanders Theatre, which resembled an ancient theater in shape, although it was smaller. (No Greek theaters existed on campuses until 1904, when the first one was built at the University of California, Berkeley, with financing from William Randolph Hearst.)[186] Among the performers were both students and faculty; the grizzled shepherd of Laius, for example, was played by the Latin professor George Martin Lane, clad in fake beard and sheepskin. Since the play was performed in ancient Greek, the performers worked long hours to hone their pronunciation, and they carefully studied their gestures and stage positions with the help of George Riddle, the elocution instructor at Harvard.[187] Costumes, down to the sandals, were chosen "with regard to historical accuracy."[188] The fifteen-student chorus was instructed by a music student, and everyone memorized their lines. Only the music was deliberately modernized. Greek music was considered too dull and monotonous, and it was believed that a modern orchestral rendition would add to the "sympathetic presentation of the great sentiments of the tragedy."[189] The play was a huge success in Boston, playing over the course of five nights to more than six thousand people, including the giants of Boston high culture, Ralph Waldo Emerson, Henry Wadsworth Longfellow (1807–82), and William Dean Howells (1837–1920).

Yet this production, like the hundreds that followed it, revealed the erosion of the imagined affinity between antiquity and modernity that had animated classicism until the mid-nineteenth century. A monument to high culture, the play perfected the self; it did not instruct the political conscience. First, it was produced on campus, in the new Sanders Theatre, rather than in one of the existing public buildings in Boston itself, which were considered "tawdry" and "ugly."[190] This decision testified to the ascent of the university campus as a discrete site of high culture; while embracing classicism, the university also wrenched it from the broader civic life of Boston. This was first of all Harvard's Greek play, and Boston's only second. Adding to this sense of removal from the broader civic life was that the audience had to breach a moat of expertise to understand the play. In the eighteenth and early nineteenth centuries, classical plays, or plays with classical themes, such as Addison's Cato, were performed in English or were sung in operatic versions in a modern European language.

The most frequently performed Greek tragedy in nineteenth-century New York City, for example, was Euripides' *Medea*, staged at least fourteen times between 1845 and 1881, both in Pacini's operatic form and in English translation.[191] Though "inauthentic," these performances were comprehensible to the general public. Beginning in 1881 the quest for authenticity spawned a new breed of classical play alongside this older one, the Greek (or, less often, Roman) play performed in the ancient language itself. But who in 1881 could understand spoken ancient Greek, no matter how accurately pronounced? Even the program was indecipherable. "Some lines translated for the sake of those who do not know Greek," it read in Greek.[192]

Here was the new irony of Americans' growing knowledge about the classical world: while antiquity was ever more authentically revealed to modern eyes, it also became foreign and incomprehensible in a way that it had not been before. This represented more than culture's late-century bifurcation into highbrow and lowbrow, for classicism had always been simultaneously elitist and broadly diffused. Now the classical world was alienated by its cultural and chronological remoteness from modern sensibilities; they were them, not us. Moreover, the effect of Hellenization on ideas of self-formation had turned the classical collegians in on themselves. In the antebellum period, "being Greek" had meant imbibing the perfections of Periclean Athens by reading the literature and studying the history of the period, and debating clubs had helped students knit individual and national agendas. By the late nineteenth century, "being Greek" began to border on solipsism, with students removing themselves from the broader world through historically accurate escapism. The spectator of the play, wrote a reporter reviewing the production for Boston's *Daily Advertiser*, "must have forgotten his country and century, and have felt himself the Greek of the Greeks."[193]

The forces of modernity in the late nineteenth century helped to push Greek and Latin aside in the universities, undermining their claims to timeless authority and wisdom. In the midst of declining enrollments in Greek and Latin courses, however, classical civilization found a new niche in the undergraduate curriculum. While natural and social scientists recruited the ideology of progress to justify their own disciplines, classical scholars and their allies in the new humanities likewise deployed the notion of progressive ascent over time to reposition antiquity in the new universities. Docking the new idea of "Western civilization" firmly in the port of classical antiquity, they celebrated Greece and Rome as the chief sources of beatifying high culture and historicism. In American culture more broadly, classicism now marked its possessor as a person of rarefied taste, even though machine production of classical objects opened antiquity, by purchase, to all. These cultural and academic victories stood in contrast to the fate of classicism in American political culture, where it faded along with the ready parallelism between antiquity and modernity that had buttressed eighteenth-century political thought. Americans now recruited classicism as internal, privatized self-perfection rather than as a template for making virtuous and self-sacrificing republican citizens.

❧ 5 ❧

SCHOLARSHIP VERSUS CULTURE,
1870–1910

THE IDEAL OF CULTIVATED ERUDITION

"Go to, let us centrifugate," wrote a young graduate student at the new Johns Hopkins University in 1882, capturing one of the major intellectual trends of the late nineteenth century.[1] From the civil service to the factory floor, the specialization of skills and knowledge pervaded America after the Civil War. Its handmaiden, professionalization, attended the coagulation of expertise and knowledge into discrete groups of practitioners with internal expectations and codes of conduct. Specialization played a particularly important role in the rise of the American university between 1870 and 1900. During these years, older colleges like Harvard, Yale, Princeton, Columbia, and the University of Michigan established permanent postgraduate training programs. New universities incorporating both undergraduate and postgraduate programs were also founded during these years: The Johns Hopkins University, the University of Chicago, Cornell, Stanford, and the University of Wisconsin. Until 1861 Americans went to Germany to receive the Ph.D., and the number who could afford to do so was of course limited. Yet by 1900 American universities had awarded four hundred doctoral degrees.[2] Scholarship itself became a viable lifetime profession for increasing numbers of Americans, as the number of professors multiplied by four in just thirty years. In 1870 there were 5,553 professors in America; in 1890, 15,809; and in 1900, 23,868.[3] American universities became centers of research and specialization, not only for faculty but for graduate students, who in laboratories and seminars learned to conduct original research and produce new knowledge according to the scientific method. Within academic disciplines, the launching of learned journals and scholarly societies and the adoption of various professional norms signaled the establishment in America of the modern profession of scholarship. By the end of the century the Ph.D. had become the badge of competence in academic research and the prerequisite for teaching in many universities and colleges.

That the specialization of knowledge figured importantly in the rise of universities between 1870 and 1910 is undisputed. But just what role specialization played in inaugurating that distinctive feature of the modern American university, the graduate program, remains less clear. For these programs illustrated the expectations that an older generation of scholars had for the upcoming one, and they reveal more clearly than the newly founded professional journals or scholarly societies the constellation of qualities that began to be expected of young scholars. In retrospect, the impulse to require students to master ever more specialized fields of knowledge stands out sharply, perhaps because this has become an important feature of twentieth-century graduate programs. But the years between 1870 and 1890 still marked the infancy of the idea of graduate education; many aspirations still floated freely, and many innovations were attempted, not all of them lasting. In crafting programs for advanced training scholars also had to contend with an undergraduate college radically transformed by a half-century of reform that had brought to it the ideal of liberal culture as a guiding principle. This new foundation onto which graduate training might be added had an important role in determining what such programs would look like.

As heirs to a study that had stood at the center of university life since the Renaissance, American classicists entered the debates over the new shape of higher education with great vigor. They looked simultaneously to a past in which their field of study had defined true erudition to a cultivated public and to a present that promised to enliven classical study with discoveries and methods drawn from the new academic discipline of archaeology. Because of the great increase in knowledge of the classical world after mid-century, classical study had fractured so extensively by 1885 that the archaeologist Charles Waldstein (1856–1927) saw fit to represent the science of classical antiquity as a branching tree bristling with subdisciplines.[4] On the other hand, a kind of broad knowledge of classical civilizations stood as an integral part of the humanities in American colleges and remained central to the ideal of the cultured person in late-nineteenth-century America. Gilded Age classicists were eager to determine how the new universities would mediate between their traditional functions to cultivate a broadly educated public and to serve a growing constituency of specialized, professional scholars.

The problem classical scholars faced in the age of specialization and science was neatly expressed by the classical philologist Basil Lanneau Gildersleeve, today the best-known classicist of nineteenth-century America.[5] Gildersleeve's scholarly activities mark him as one of a new breed of modern professionals. He received a Ph.D. from Göttingen in 1853, founded the *American Journal of Philology* in 1880 and served as its editor for the next forty years, and was among the first graduate teachers in America, offering advanced courses in Greek at the new Johns Hopkins University after 1876. As we saw in the last chapter, Gildersleeve admired the classicist of broad learning and literary skill. Recognizing that some young scholars, smitten by German models of scholarship, had retreated into "arid specializations," he pushed for what he called a "higher literary culture" among college teachers of the classics to aid in the spread of Hellenism.[6] In the late 1860s he expressed his twin concerns for general learning and scientific specialization, reflecting a broader anxiety among classicists in the Gilded Age: "As on the one hand the classical philologians must not divorce themselves from general culture, so on the other they must see to it that they do scientific work and have scientific work done, that they live in a scientific atmosphere."[7] Gildersleeve, like many in his generation of classicists, stood at the historical moment when learning began to splinter into two worlds, the world of specialized, "scientific" scholarship and the world of cultivated generalism.

In arguing for a "science" of classical study the scholars hoped first of all to resist the claims of the physical and social sciences to be sole inheritors of the prestige of science. William Watson Goodwin, Eliot Professor of Greek Literature at Harvard from 1860 to 1901, who, like Gildersleeve, received a Göttingen Ph.D. (1855), argued that there was "no good authority, in history or in usage," for restricting the words *science* and *scientific* to physical and natural science.[8] Science was not a discipline but a method. In a science of classical philology, according to Francis Willey Kelsey of the University of Michigan, sources needed to be "critically examined," subjected to "rigid tests" for the "facts of language" and the "truth or falsity of statements."[9] The Dartmouth College classicist John Henry Wright in 1886 called "exactness and discrimination" the qualities that made a study scientific.[10] Classicists held up the eighteenth-century German philologist F. A. Wolf as the father of the science of classical philology because he had unified the disparate approaches to antiquity into the study of "Greek and Roman culture" as a whole, giving it what Kelsey called "a scientific coherence and consistency."[11] As they attempted to stake out what a science of classical scholarship was, they rejected those who taught the humanities in what Goodwin called "a less scientific spirit than Physics and Natural History."[12] They feared classicists' becoming vulgar popularizers, "mere *dilettanti*" whose lectures were but a "superficial exposition" of half-understood distillations.[13]

Devotees of specialized classical study created the institutions that characterized the new age of professional scholarship in America, helping to found the American Philological Association (APA) in 1869. In contrast to earlier learned societies, which had diffused knowledge broadly, such as the American Association for the Advancement of Science (1848) and the American Social Science Association (1865), the APA was the first American learned society to structure itself on a disciplinary base.[14] Other disciplinary associations followed, including the American Historical Association (1884), the Modern Language Association (1883), the American Mathematical Society (1888), the American Physical Society (1889), the American Political Science Association (1903), and the American Sociological Society (1905). Although most scholars of this generation continued to go to Germany for advanced education, new graduate programs offering the Ph.D. were founded in the late nineteenth and early twentieth centuries at places like The Johns Hopkins University, Bryn Mawr College, the University of Chicago, and the University of Michigan.

Although these Gilded Age classical scholars were attracted to specialization, they feared its excesses, which would divorce classicism, so long the common currency of the educated in both Europe and America, from general life. "I have spoken of classical philology as a science," wrote Kelsey, "but do not misunderstand me, I mean no pyramid of bricks."[15]

Gildersleeve mocked what he termed "the supersubtle genius of the present day," who made college work excessively specialized and language a "dry and thirsty land."[16] Already, he wrote, "scientific grammar" was "a horror even to a large class of people of cultivation." There was "increasing danger lest philology shrivel up into mere statistics."[17] "If we dissociate classical philology from our general life," he warned, "it has no hope of a future."[18] These fears persisted into the new century. In 1907 a writer in the *Classical Weekly* despaired of "a certain senility in some seminar youths, who can cite dittography and haplography, Arcadian and Cypriote dialects, talk of Phyles and Demes, of Ecclesia and Boule, and whose specialism reveals itself in ignorance of enormous masses of classical literature." He urged readers to "discriminate between the cultural and the eruditional elements" of the classics.[19] No matter how many bricks scientific scholarship added to the edifice of knowledge, classicists needed to remember what Kelsey called the "the higher mission" of the classical scholar in America, "that he is to his day and generation an interpreter not of an isolated group of phenomena, but of a civilization, which in its better moments rose to ideals that are akin to those of our day because we have them as an inheritance."[20]

Between 1870 and 1900 Gildersleeve and other classicists sought to give both cultured generalism and scientific specialization their proper due. Although they never used the term, I have chosen to call this model of learning the ideal of *cultivated erudition*. This term captures classicists' efforts to retain classicism at the core of general knowledge and also acknowledges their admiration for science and specialization. This ideal of advanced study, which navigated between what a modern era thought were the dilettante excesses of generalism and what some classicists believed was the remote aridity of immoderate specialization, characterized the efforts of classicists to create some of the earliest graduate programs at some of the major American universities in the late nineteenth century. The career of the ideal of cultivated erudition during the late nineteenth and early twentieth centuries can illuminate a moment in the renegotiation of ideals of scholarship as Americans abandoned the classically infused, generally learned citizen for the attractions of specialization and expertise. By 1910, however, cultivated erudition as a model for advanced scholarship had become untenable in American graduate programs. This situation led ultimately to the conundrum of the university we know today, in which the general work of the undergraduate college is often institutionally and intellectually at odds with the specialization of the graduate school.

FOUNDING THE ARCHAEOLOGICAL INSTITUTE OF AMERICA

It was in the archaeological excavation of classical antiquity, and especially of classical Greece, that late-century humanists sought to reconnect antiquity to the modern era, imbuing general knowledge with classicism while pursuing the scientific results of the increasingly specialized discipline of archaeology. These hopes were most clearly articulated in the first American society for professional archaeologists, the Archaeological Institute of America (AIA), founded in Boston in 1879. The AIA's first annual report set forth its purpose:

> The Archaeological Institute of America is formed for the purpose of promoting and directing archaeological investigation and research,—by the sending out of expeditions for special investigation, by aiding the efforts of independent explorers, by publication of reports of the results of the expeditions which the Institute may undertake or promote, and by any other means which may from time to time appear desirable. . . . It is desired by the founders and existing members of the society that its lists should include associates from all parts of the country. The objects of the Institute have no narrow local interest. It hopes, by its work, to increase the knowledge of the early history of mankind, to quicken the interest in classical and Biblical studies, to promote an acquaintance with the prehistoric antiquities of our own country, and to enlarge the resources of our universities and museums by such collections of works of art and remains of antiquity as it may be enabled to make.[21]

The AIA's founding membership testified to the new organization of classicism in the Gilded Age, revealing the interlocking worlds of professional scholarship, cultivated amateurism, opulent private patronage, and modern science. Its first president, who served from 1879 to 1890, was Charles Eliot Norton, professor of fine arts at Harvard University. Its vice-president was Martin Brimmer, a friend of Norton's and president of the Boston Museum of Fine Arts. Other members included Alexander Agassiz, a zoologist and the son of the naturalist Louis Agassiz; William Watson Goodwin, successor to Cornelius Conway Felton as the Eliot Professor of Greek Literature at Harvard; Frederic Ward Putnam, the curator of Harvard's Peabody Museum; Thomas Gold Appleton, an essayist and poet; the Harvard history professor Ephraim Whitman Gurney; the art critic Charles Callahan Perkins, who was also president of the Boston Handel and Haydn Society, founder and benefactor of the Museum of Fine Arts, and author of two books on Italian sculpture; and Charles William Eliot, the president of Harvard.[22] More than a hundred enthusiasts, with callings even more diverse than those of the founders, helped to sponsor the new AIA. They included Ralph Waldo Emerson; Francis Parkman (1823–93); Edward Elbridge Salisbury (1814–1801), the Yale Sanskritist; the Johns Hopkins University president Daniel Coit Gilman (1831–1908); E. L. Godkin, editor of the *Nation*; the Yale professor Theodore Dwight Woolsey; and George B. Chase, a professor at Columbia Law School.[23] Originally confined to Boston, the organization sought fertile ground in other cities, and by 1896 there were eleven branches, including one as far away as Washington state.[24]

During Charles Eliot Norton's eleven years as president the AIA reflected much of his outlook on classical antiquity, modern scholarship, and Victorian American society. Norton was an admirer of English letters rather than Germanic scholarship and had not earned a Ph.D. His scholarly background reflected an earlier educational tradition in America, one that was in its twilight as German-trained Ph.D.'s became more common among American classicists by the turn of the century. Yet the organization he founded helped to open a radically new era in American classical scholarship. Norton and other leaders of the AIA were chiefly concerned to bring the benefits of high culture to Americans at large through the study of antiquity. They believed that acquisitiveness and corruption had distracted Americans' attention from the elevating and ennobling truths epitomized in the art and literature of the ancient Greeks. Labeling ancient Greece and Rome "sites of high culture," they called upon Americans to forge their connection to antiquity anew through direct exposure to classical literature and artifacts. The first annual report of the AIA, published in 1880, revealed these concerns:

> The conditions of American life, separating us in great measure from direct acquaintance with the works of past times, and breaking for us many of the threads of tradition and association by which the successive generations of men are bound one to another, interfere with the influence of many of the most powerful stimulants of the intelligence and the imagination, and tend to beget indifference to one of the chief sources of culture. The same barbaric spirit that asks, "What have we to do with abroad?" asks also, "What have we to do with antiquity?" . . . The existence of this spirit is not surprising, in view of the comparative neglect among us of ancient studies, and especially of those relating to the archaeology of Greece, in which is comprised the study of the origin and development of those arts which gave just expression to the Greek intelligence and sentiment, and afford such an image of national life and character as no other people has ever left of itself in its works.[25]

The acquisition of new knowledge of the past was for the AIA completely connected to its aim of inculcating high cultural ideals in modern America.

Yet while the classical Greeks were uniquely civilized, in the estimation of the AIA, their glories could be transported across the ages to reform a corrupt America. The Greeks had only perfected "qualities common to civilized man," wrote the AIA's leadership in 1884. The superiority of the Greeks was not therefore a one-time achievement but could be replicated by societies willing to cultivate the "even balance, fair proportion, and healthy development" of their civilization.[26] Through classicism Americans could find an antidote to civic and moral decline.

Such high-minded goals were not unique to the AIA. Though it was the first American institution devoted explicitly to classical archaeological pursuits, the AIA was just one of the many interlocking educational and cultural institutions flourishing after the middle of the nineteenth century that were dedicated to public elevation. The Boston, Chicago, Philadelphia, and New York elites by this time were increasingly tied to the Europe-dominated world in which museums systematically collected antiquities in hopes of spreading high culture and science to the population at large.[27] The Boston Museum of Fine Arts, for example, had been founded in 1870 on the assumption "that nations as well as individuals should aim at that degree of aesthetic culture which, without passing the dividing line between general and special knowledge, will enable them to recognize and appreciate the beautiful in nature and art." A museum housing "acknowledged masterpieces" of classical antiquity could "elevate men by purifying the taste and acting upon the moral nature."[28] New York's Metropolitan Museum of Art, also founded in 1870, had in 1873 acquired a large collection of classical antiquities thanks to the labors of an irascible Italian-born count, Luigi Palma di Cesnola (1832–1904), who directed the Metropolitan from 1879 until his death in 1904. While in Cyprus as American consul, Cesnola had uncovered thousands of remnants of Phoenician, Egyptian, Persian, Ptolemaic, Roman, and Byzantine civilizations that formed, in the estimation of Metropolitan president John Taylor Johnson, "the most complete illustration of the history of ancient art and civilization . . . the key to the origin and development of civilization."[29] American classical philologists such as Basil Lanneau Gildersleeve applauded Cesnola's efforts, noting that only in the study of Cypriot antiquities could America rival Europe.[30] Finally, in 1888 the University of Pennsylvania, together with the Babylonian Exploration Fund, sent a small group of archaeologists to the ancient city of Nippur, near Baghdad. Funded by wealthy patrons, the Nippur expedition combined what it called "Christian enlightenment" with "scientific inquiry" to investigate the physical reality of the Old Testament and to disseminate the results to a public in need of culture.[31]

The AIA was established in a climate of growing resentment toward European domination in the field of archaeology. The late nineteenth century was the age of spectacular, grand-scale archaeological excavations at the major cities and shrines of ancient Greece, Asia Minor, and the Middle East. Germany led the world in what the Roman historian Theodor Mommsen (1817–1903) called *Großwissenschaft* (big scholarship): huge, highly technical, specialized archaeological projects backed by the powerful support of a bureaucratized, centralized state and a willing corps of diplomats abroad.[32] In 1875 the Germans began the excavation of Olympia, followed soon by digs at Pergamon, Priene, Miletus, and Thera. Capping them all in the public's mind were the excavations of Heinrich

Schliemann (1822–90) at Hissarlik, which he believed to be the site of ancient Troy, begun in 1870. Schliemann, a wealthy industrialist and autodidact, actually had little involvement with Germany's nationalist archaeology: he paid for his own excavations and zealously fashioned a legend around his own name. Dismissed by trained archaeologists as a truffle hound scrounging chaotically for gold, Schliemann nevertheless captured the popular imagination by exhuming the treasures of the Bronze Age, making Troy historically real again for a generation schooled by the Homeric question to regard the ancient city as a myth rather than an actual place.[33] Other nations, such as Austria, France, and England, also began excavations in ancient Greece and Rome, though of more modest scale and results.[34] As others have noted, such excavations were intimately connected to the rise of nationalism and imperialism in the late nineteenth century. To excavate the classical past was to assert the modern nation on the stage of world imperial powers. Europeans jostled fiercely with one another and with the ruling Ottoman Turks for access to cherished sites that would bring glory to their major cities. The famed Pergamon altar found its way to the Royal Museums in Germany as a way for the Germans to display, according to their education minister, "art of dimensions that are equal (or nearly) to the great rows of Attic and Asia Minor sculptures in the British Museum."[35]

Americans, with imperial designs of their own in the West and the East, soon entered the fray. Though accustomed to German superiority in classical philology, many American scholars now chafed at the prospect of being what Gildersleeve described as "forever slavishly dependent on Germany for results."[36] The impressive findings at recent European excavations in classical lands only added to this sense of nationalist urgency. In 1880 the AIA's vice president, Martin Brimmer encouraged Americans to claim their share of classical antiquities without delay. "America," he wrote, "should not lose its share . . . for lack of enterprise."[37] But enterprise was not always enough. In March 1881 the AIA learned that the Turkish government had refused its proposal to dig at Knossos and Kortyna, two ancient sites on the island of Crete. The loss was a bitter disappointment to AIA members, representing the first of several fruitless negotiations with the inscrutable and seemingly arbitrary administrators of the Ottoman Empire.[38]

The AIA, finally, demonstrated to American cultural elites the importance of excavating the classical past rather than the indigenous American past, which members referred to as "prehistoric." At its founding, the AIA had been devoted not only to the excavation of classical sites but also to the study of biblical and American antiquities. But ultimately, the classical Mediterranean agenda overwhelmed all others, and many AIA members heaped scorn on indigenous American archaeology. Tempers flared even at the first AIA meeting in 1879 as these two agendas conflicted. The ethnologist and historian Francis Parkman, famous for his book *The California and Oregon Trail* (1849), urged study of indigenous American remains, saying that "the acquisition of Knowledge and not the acquisition of objects or works of art" was the true object of the AIA. Others disagreed: one member retorted that knowledge of Indians was "simply curious" rather than useful. He went on, "The Indians are low in the scale of civilization—Mr. Parkman's own books showed us that—and if we possessed all the pottery ware, kitchen utensils, and tomahawks which they had made, it would be no better for us."[39] As a result of these sentiments, the AIA financed only two American expeditions in the early 1880s, to the Southwest and to Mexico, and thereafter largely ignored the field until the AIA opened a school in Santa Fe, New Mexico, in 1908, years after it had established schools in Athens (1882), Rome (1895), Palestine (1900), and elsewhere. Its major American excavator, Adolph Bandelier (1840–1914), lamented American archaeology's underdog status, calling it "that Cinderella among scientific researches."[40]

Many early AIA members sneered at the archaeology of indigenous Americans because they espoused the rigidly hierarchical, evolutionist assumptions at the heart of Victorian classical study and anthropology. In this scheme, Native Americans remained what Charles Eliot Norton called "semi-barbarians."[41] Conversely, classical archaeology investigated what was "most closely associated with our own culture," according to Thomas Day Seymour, a Greek scholar at Yale.[42] The editors of the AIA's journal, the *American Journal of Archaeology*, summed these views up succinctly for their members in 1888:

The archaeology of America even when it has to do with the remains of the former life of still existing native tribes, is essentially prehistoric archaeology,—that is, it is busied with the life and work of a race or races of men in an inchoate, rudimentary and unformed condition, who never raised themselves, even at their highest point, as in Mexico and Peru, above a low stage of civilization, and never showed the capacity of steadily progressive development. . . . The evidence afforded by their works of every kind . . . seems all against the supposition that they had latent energy sufficient for progress to civilization.[43]

Although the Americanist agenda continued to be promoted within the AIA by Francis Parkman and others, the core leadership remained enamored of the classical Mediterranean, choosing to excavate the pinnacle of civilization rather than the depths of savagery. The New York art critic Russell Sturgis (1836–1909) spoke for many in the AIA when he privately declared his preference for urns over tomahawks: "My interest is perhaps too exclusively given to those antiquities which are lovely and full of thought: . . . Grecian ones!"[44]

The AIA thus combined the multiple strands that made up high culture in Gilded Age America. Its members saw in classical antiquity, especially Periclean Greece, the site of the noblest genius of humanity, a genius they sought to resurrect in late-century America to purge it of corrupting plutocracy and ugly industrialism. These moralistic concerns shaded into scientific and imperial ones. Calling classical archaeology "an exact science," they hoped to stabilize America's still-wobbly scientific reputation abroad while also shoring up their own reputations as empirical investigators in a university increasingly wedded to the pursuit of specialized science.[45]

EXCAVATING HIGH CULTURE AT ASSOS

These aspirations to moral and civic regeneration through high culture and to scientific imperialism to rival European achievements revealed themselves in the AIA's first major archaeological project, the excavation of the ancient Greek city of Assos in Asia Minor between 1881 and 1883. The institute undertook the excavation "with a hope of making a valuable contribution to knowledge, and of quickening and deepening an interest in the subject."[46] AIA members hoped that the fruits of these classical investigations would rescue Americans from archaeological provincialism while enriching the collections of the Boston Museum of Fine Arts, the Metropolitan, and American colleges rather than those of the Louvre or other European museums. "To surrender what has been found to another country," wrote Brimmer to Norton about the Assos finds, "would act as a wet blanket on our slowly kindling fires—which will need careful tending for some time to come."[47] In addition to securing a place for America in the world of classical archaeology, the Assos excavation was also an attempt to counteract modern materialism and civic degeneracy through the observation and study of ancient Greek literature, art, and architecture. The artifacts retrieved from Assos would elevate the general public by exposing them to the remains of a past glory.

The abandoned ancient city of Assos lay at the western edge of Asia Minor between two of the century's most celebrated archaeological excavations—Troy, about thirty miles to the north, and Pergamon, fifty miles to the southeast. It was a sterile, inhospitable site. Perched atop a steep volcanic hill that jutted abruptly from the sea below, Assos was blasted by searing winds in the summer and icy rains in the winter. But in antiquity its hilltop location had made it an easily defensible port city, and by the sixth century B.C. Assos thrived as one of the chief emporiums of the ancient Greek world. Because of its happy situation, it had been inhabited at least since the Bronze Age, and it saw occupation by a great variety of powers over the centuries—Phoenician, Assyrian, Persian, Gaul, Roman, Byzantine, and finally Ottoman after the thirteenth century A.D. The great elevation that gave Assos its strategic importance also made it breathtaking to behold. At the summit of Assos stood the acropolis, so high above the sea that one could gaze from it directly down into the holds of ships docked far below. Arrayed along the hillside beneath the temple were a theater, a gymnasium, and other ancient structures, the whole encircled by mighty fortifications. Also dotting the site were the remains of the other peoples who had occupied Assos over the ages, such as a Byzantine church and medieval graves.[48] The tranquil routine of trade had been the role of Assos in antiquity, and the city did not often feature in ancient writings.

Assos beckoned to Victorians preoccupied with the glories of Hellenic civilization because it stood at the threshold of the Orient. Assos seemed an ideal site for investigating the progress of Greek art from its primitive Orientalism to its Hellenic grandeur. In an age intrigued by progress and evolution, the problem facing classical archaeology was to determine Greek origins among what an early excavator called "older and foreign races," such as the Mesopotamians.[49] The acropolis, a shrine to Athena, was the key to this effort. Its epistyle and metopes were sculpted with reliefs of sphinxes, lions, boars, and centaurs that represented the earliest stages of the Doric order. Parts of these animals displayed "fine mastery," while others were marred by "Oriental stiffness."[50] As such, the sculptures could be considered "the most important link in the chain connecting the carving of the early civilizations of the East and the unequalled sculptures of Greece," showing "the path followed by the early Greek artists in the progress toward supreme excellence."[51]

There were also, however, difficulties with Assos as an archaeological site. First was its anonymity; everyone had heard of Pergamon and Troy, but who had heard of (or cared about) Assos? Just as important for Americans mindful of archaeological glory was that many of the acropolis reliefs—by every estimate the most magnificent of the ruins—had been stripped in 1838, when the French archaeologist M. Raoul-Rochette received them as a gift from Sultan Mahmoud II. The French navy had conveyed the lot to the Louvre, where they attracted international attention: to study Assos, one went to Paris. But the French were not the only plunderers of Assos. Many peoples over the centuries had commandeered bits of the ruins for their own purposes, and as recently as 1864 the Ottoman government itself had quarried them to build a dock in Constantinople. The ancient theater, disemboweled during this latest project, was now a rubbish heap. The only positive outcome of this most recent activity, from the American standpoint, was that the Turks had built a road from the hilltop ruins down to the sea so that sledges could convey stones efficiently to awaiting vessels. Earthquakes and torrential rains had also sent blocks and columns tumbling down the grassy hillsides. In the whole of the ancient city fewer than six columns still stood, and on the acropolis itself not one stone above the steps remained in its original position.[52] This generation, of course, was schooled to wax elegiac at the sight of departed grandeur, but Assos was quite ruined even for their tastes.

In advertising the excavation to its sponsoring readership, the AIA leaders made clear their awareness that Assos, though appealing, paled next to the breathtaking sites being exhumed by the Europeans. The Assos acropolis presented "interesting architectural problems," while the ancient city walls afforded unparalleled opportunities for "the study of fortification and defence adopted by the Greeks." But there was also "no reason to anticipate any such brilliant discoveries, or any such finds of treasure, as rewarded the labors of Dr. Schliemann, General di Cesnola, or Herr Humann."[53]

Furthermore, the AIA faced financial obstacles to excavation. Unlike the Deutsches Archäologisches Institut, the centralized, government-supported archaeological arm of the German state, the AIA received almost no assistance, either financial or diplomatic, from the American government. Late-century Americans did not develop the "big archaeology" of the Germans, massive projects staffed by trained archaeologists, engineers, and hundreds of laborers. A representative of the U.S. Department of State in the Ottoman Empire could be called upon to intervene on the AIA's behalf to secure a digging permit, but on the whole the AIA was left to its own devices. As a result, the AIA, like many Gilded Age institutions, was forced to rely on subscriptions from its membership to support its work. The costs of digging permits, salaries, equipment, and export fees added up, so that AIA president Charles Eliot Norton expended much of his energy in niggling administrative and fund-raising details that rivaled those of any American college president at the time.[54]

In christening their new organization the Archaeological Institute of America the founders had declared broad, national ambitions. In fact, however, for its first years it was centered largely in Boston, with ancillary support from the tightly knit, wealthy cultured elite in other cities, such as New York. These "rich friends," as one member bluntly described these patrons, helped to finance projects and broadcast results.[55] To those with high cultural pretensions, the tightened purse strings of the U.S. government were simply further evidence of American national philistinism. Nathaniel Hawthorne had reflected wistfully about this from Florence in 1858. "I wish our great Republic had the spirit to do as much, according to its vast means, as Florence did for sculpture and architecture, when it was a Republic; but we have the meanest government, and the shabbiest—and, if truly represented by it, are the meanest and shabbiest people—known in history."[56]

The team sent to Assos reflected the difference between the big archaeology of Germany and the smaller archaeology of America. Its leader was Joseph Thacher Clarke (1856–1920), a student of Charles Eliot Norton with no other qualification than an interest in writing a history of Doric architecture.[57] His second in command was his friend Francis Henry Bacon (1856–1940), an architecture student at the Massachusetts Institute of Technology and a draftsman of "fine taste."[58] The two had originally planned to travel together down the Mississippi River; Assos presented itself as an equally interesting alternative. We might usefully compare these two young unknowns with Ernst Curtius (1814–96), the German instigator of the excavations at Olympia, who was one of the most famed philologists of his day. Curtius held a coveted faculty chair at the University of Berlin, tutored Crown Prince Friedrich Wilhelm of the Hohenzollern, and maintained personal and professional ties with the Prussian military.[59]

Clarke and Bacon led a ragtag group of about eight college graduates culled from a search advertised in the newspapers. Norton received more than fifty responses, most of them evidence of the prevailing cultured amateurism that characterized the expedition. One recent Yale graduate, for example, who was ultimately rejected, described himself to Norton as "an enthusiastic Hellenist," a "jolly pagan, a pure idealistic pantheist," "Damned to all eternitie." What he lacked was "leisure for keeping up in the profounder parts of the new archaeological and philological work."[60] Eventually the AIA settled on a handful of young volunteers; most of them, like Clarke, were students of Charles Eliot Norton's. Among the volunteers were Maxwell Wrigley and Charles Howard Walker, two New York architects; Edward Robinson, an 1879 Harvard B.A. who later became the first curator of classical antiquities and then the director, in 1902, of the Boston Museum of Fine Arts; Charles Bradley, an 1880 Harvard graduate; and Joseph S. Diller, an 1879 graduate from the Lawrence Scientific School.[61] Later, J. R. S. Sterrett, the only Ph.D. on the expedition; William C. Lawton, who studied the Assos inscriptions; and John H. Haynes, who served as the photographer, were added. Also aboard for a few months in 1881 was Norton's eldest son, eighteen-year-old Eliot, whom Norton hoped to bring into association with the men of "character and acquisition" at Assos.[62]

The digging permit required almost a year of irritable negotiations with the Ottoman authorities in Constantinople, but a two-year permit was finally secured in May 1881.[63] Members of the Assos expedition prepared themselves for the dig by studying the Assos antiquities at the Louvre and other ancient Greek artifacts at the British Museum in January and February of 1881.[64] Eventually, in mid-April, surveying at the Assos site began, although excavation, hindered by a number of inconveniences, was delayed until August. Digging for a total of eleven weeks with the assistance of local laborers, the group closed the excavations in November 1881. They returned to Assos for two more years, closing the site upon the permit's expiration in May 1883.[65]

Considering that these young men were thought to be genteel, it was a rude shock to AIA leaders in America to discover in November 1881, after a half-year of excavation at Assos, that Joseph Clarke was a scoundrel and that low morale plagued the expedition. Norton and others publicly continued to praise Clarke's high character and scientific spirit even as they received ominous letters from the young expedition volunteers about Clarke's numerous improprieties. One described Clarke as "a libertine of the lowest tastes," alluding to a romantic entanglement in nearby Smyrna. There were frequent, lengthy, unexplained absences. When actually at the dig, he whiled away the long, hot days plucking his banjo and once fired his pistol in the direction of a student's head.[66] Adding to the low morale of the expedition was the professional disgrace felt by the young Americans. One likened Clarke's digging to Schliemann's jumbled scratchings at Troy, dreading to think what Carl Humann (1839–96), the "trained archaeologist" who headed the Pergamon dig, might make of the work at Assos. Humann evidently took pity on the struggling youths at Assos and sent over a small band of helpers.[67] They were not so fortunate in their relations with the excavators at Troy. In May they received an unannounced visit from Schliemann, who was attempting to determine whether Assos was one of the cities described in Homeric epic. "He wouldn't talk about anything but prehistoric remains and cared nothing for our work here," reported Bacon.[68]

Such behind-the-scenes difficulties, however, did not mar the public success of the expedition. Clarke successfully balanced the two tasks of the Assos work: on the one hand, to export antiquities to the Boston Museum of Fine Arts as a public, cultivating exercise; on the other hand, to do what he called "scientific" work at Assos, which meant exhuming antiquities from all of the ancient Greek sites that were representative types rather than objects of spectacular beauty or great material value. By the laws of the Ottoman authorities concerning antiquities, only one-third of antiquities discovered on the site were granted to the finder; the remainder were divided between the owner of the land and the Turkish government. At the negotiations with the Turkish commissioner, Clarke repeatedly relinquished specimens of coins, pottery, and terra cotta that were of what he called "greater intrinsic, but of less scientific value." Mindful of French glory, however, the Americans negotiated ferociously for two blocks of the sculptured epistyle, giving up to the Turkish government in exchange all fragments of bronze sculptures. In this way the Boston Museum of Fine Arts acquired centaurs and sphinxes rivaling those in the Louvre.[69]

AIA leaders were thrilled when the Assos investigations, if not as spectacular as Pergamon, did attract some European attention. The English classicist Richard Jebb (1841–1905) reported that the expedition had "completely and scientifically determined" the plan of the temple and called the discovery of more bas-reliefs among "the most important links yet found between Oriental and Greek art."[70] The French were sufficiently impressed to encourage further American archaeological pursuits in Greece.[71] Assos seemed to confirm what one German classicist had claimed of America in 1873: "Even that country, utterly swallowed up as it is in the solution of material and social problems of the most elementary sort, is beginning to realize that some attention to the antique is essential to the prosperity of its industrial arts."[72] The American expedition to Assos achieved one important goal of the AIA, which was to use a classical site to elevate Americans. In addition to securing the antiquities for the Boston Museum of Fine Arts, Clarke embarked on a lecture tour of the East Coast to advertise the AIA's successes. Edward Clarke Cabot (1818–1901), president of the Boston Society of Architects, summed up the success of Assos, saying that the expedition "seems to have brought nearer to our sympathies and comprehension that spirit which the conditions of modern architecture require as a corrective and purifying force."[73]

THE AMERICAN SCHOOL OF CLASSICAL STUDIES AT ATHENS

The Assos artifacts displayed for the general public in Boston attacked only half the problem of Americans' "barbaric" indifference to culture, according to AIA members. An ultimately more potent remedy lay in the treatment that humanists in the antebellum colleges had prescribed half a century earlier: educational reform. In their early reports, AIA members frequently bemoaned "the comparative neglect among us of ancient studies and especially of those relating to the archaeology of Greece, in which is comprised the study of the origin and development of those arts which gave just expression to the Greek intelligence and sentiment, and afford such an image of national life and character as no other people has left of itself in its works." No universities or colleges provided regular instruction in this field, even though "to encourage a cultivation of it . . . might well be considered as among the chief aims of an enlightened scheme of education."[74] While the display of classical artifacts in museums and the prosecution of archaeological investigations could go far in cultivating barbaric Americans and competing with European finds, a school of classical studies could go further.

To address these concerns, in 1881 the AIA founded the American School of Classical Studies at Athens (ASCSA).[75] The school had a number of aspirations. The first was to create what was still a rarity in America, a national intellectual venture that would transcend the merely local. The AIA itself was such an organization, and the Athens school could possibly go even further. The AIA created a committee to manage the school that included classical scholars from around the country: John Williams White, of Harvard, who served as chairman; Princeton's William Sloane; Yale's Lewis R. Packard; Henry Drisler, of Columbia College; and Basil Lanneau Gildersleeve, of Johns Hopkins.[76] The committee enlisted support and subscriptions from twelve American universities, which the AIA saw as "natural feeders" for the Athens school.[77] Lacking the means to secure a permanent director and to create a permanent endowment of $100,000, the school's managing committee settled for an annually rotating directorship and a small startup fund of about $3,000. "The close union of colleges in the promotion of a common object," wrote the founders, "is a spectacle unique in this country, where the relations between colleges are far too slight."[78] That unity was "creditable to American scholarship."[79]

The school was not only a national venture but a nationalist one, displaying Americans' growing appetite for competition with Europeans in the area of classical archaeological training. Several European nations had already founded archaeology research institutes. Germany had established one in Rome in 1829 and one in Athens in 1874, and France had established its own school in Athens in 1846.[80] The French and German schools were staffed by renowned archaeologists, filled with students, and housed large libraries—all at the expense of the home government. "Pour La Science, Pour La Patrie," declared a commemorative medal struck for the École Française d'Athènes, encapsulating the sentiment behind this state-supported classicism.[81] The French school, wrote the American school director William Watson Goodwin, showed every visitor to Athens that "the French Republic never forgets to cherish ancient arts and letters, amid all its distractions at home and abroad." American museums, he admitted, could never rival those of Naples, Paris, and London, except of course in indigenous American antiquities and natural history. But, he pointed out, most of the spectacular classical archaeological treasures, such as the Pergamon altar in Berlin, had been found in the last decade. Had Americans possessed an "advanced post" in Athens along with the Germans, they could have better positioned themselves to reach Pergamon first and made a better case to the "imperial treasury here at home" for the necessary funds. Americans "cannot afford to be behind other nations in improving our methods and enlarging and elevating our instruction," Goodwin concluded. "We Americans need such a school even more than any other nation."[82]

A monument to American scholarly nationalism, the Athens school also testified to the shift within classical study from an emphasis on texts to an emphasis on objects as accurate testimonials of truth. Since the Renaissance, as we saw in chapter 1, texts had been the major avenue to knowledge of the classical world. Not only were these texts numerous but they were believed to be the most authoritative guides to antiquity. This reliance on texts slowly declined during the eighteenth and especially the nineteenth centuries as historians became more convinced of the ability of images to evoke the reality of the past.[83] By 1880 the visual remains of the past had achieved new importance. Seeing antiquity with one's own eyes had become an equally sure guide to antiquity. This transfer from the textual to the visual as the repository of truth was one result of the humanistic revolution begun in 1820, which had stressed the need to know about the complex entirety of the classical past. For these antebellum scholars, as we have seen, "knowing" a tragedy of Sophocles meant not just mastering the Greek text but also learning about the theater in which it had been performed. The school at Athens, originally christened the American School of Classical Literature, Art, and Antiquities, reflected this new faith in the power of images and objects to resurrect the truth about the past. "To be convinced of facts on testimony," argued Thomas Day Seymour, of Yale, a member of the ASCSA managing committee, "is very different from having experience of our own and the witness of our own eyes."[84]

Finally, during its early years the school at Athens embodied a now forgotten ideal of postgraduate education: cultivated erudition. The founders of the Athens school saw no conflict between generalism and specialization, believing that advanced work in classical study must always rest upon a solid foundation of general culture. The school was intended for two groups of students: those with "a definite object in view, such as professional study," and those "general students of classical antiquity, who come rather for general cultivation in Greek studies than for special research in a particular department."[85]

For the future specialists, the Athens school offered firsthand archaeological knowledge that was unavailable in late-nineteenth-century America. In tandem with the AIA, the school was to offer access to archaeological sites so that students could make "original researches" in antiquity.[86] The school did not offer a Ph.D., and most students remained for only one year; rather, it gave students a certificate showing that they had completed a thesis approved by the director. Those students who did go on to careers in academic classical archaeology and philology used the school as an opportunity to perform original research of the kind needed for a doctorate. For example, J. R. S. Sterrett (1851–1914), who went on to head the Department of Greek at Cornell after 1901, received a Ph.D. from Munich in 1880 and then spent the 1882–83 academic year at the school at Athens. He used his time there to edit the inscriptions that he had helped to uncover at Assos. Many in the first generation of professional classicists, archaeologists, and philologists, born in the years around the Civil War, passed through the school between 1882 and 1902: Edward Capps (1866–1950), Mortimer Lamson Earle (1864–1905), Harold North Fowler (1859–1955), Joseph Clark Hoppin (1870–1925), Gonzalez Lodge (1863–1942), Richard Norton (1872–1918), and Paul Shorey. Of the 128 students who attended during those two decades, 79 went on to teach at the collegiate level and 26 entered the school with a Ph.D. already in hand.[87] The ASCSA was thus a major step in the professionalization of classical archaeology in America.

Yet professional, scientific archaeology was only one of the school's missions. Its other constituency, according to Goodwin, comprised those "general students of classic antiquity, who come rather for general cultivation in Greek studies than for special research in a particular department." These students would become high school teachers, for example, or would simply remain cultured generalists. They would profit from vivid illustrations of scenes and the battles described in literature. Even if the students wrote no thesis during their time there, they would have improved themselves through "the delightful associations of Athens."[88] In a speech in 1890 on the achievements of the Athens school, the University of Wisconsin professor Charles Edwin Bennett emphasized the school's contribution to high culture through immersion in classical civilization.

Most of them (former students of the school) now hold positions as instructors in the leading colleges and schools of the country, where they are making themselves felt as the vehicles of a higher and better culture. They are making their students feel as they have been made to feel themselves, that a classical education does not end with the grammatical interpretation of a prescribed round of Greek and Roman authors, but that its province is broader, including the whole domain of Hellenic and Roman civilization. It was to secure such results as that that it was founded; to subserve the practical end of a higher education of our people rather than to enable individuals to win distinguished reputation by purely scientific work.[89]

This commitment to cultured generalism remained prominent throughout the school's early decades. Charles Waldstein, the ASCSA's director from 1888 to 1892, reminded readers of the annual report that the "encouragement of a general interest in classical antiquity" at the school was intended for those who were "not intending to pursue this as their chief vocation in life" and those who were "not specially prepared for higher archaeological investigation."[90] Likewise, Benjamin Ide Wheeler, of Cornell, who taught at the school in 1895–96, cited the "great diversity in the needs" of the Athens students and reiterated that the school should continue to provide for the "certain number of students whose work is not directed toward specialization in any of the archaeological disciplines, but whose year of residence in Greece is intended to broaden and enrich their preparation for philological teaching and study."[91] Of the 128 students who enrolled during the first two decades of the school's existence, 63 entered with only a bachelor's degree. Forty-nine went on to nonuniversity careers as high school and seminary teachers or administrators or chose careers in other fields.[92]

The ASCSA embodied late-century classicists' concerns for both scholarship and culture. Recognizing that general knowledge must remain moored in classicism if it was to survive into the new century, they also hoped to usher their discipline into the age of the university, with its professionalizing ranks, its specialized disciplines, and its scientific methods.

THE FAILURE OF CULTIVATED ERUDITION

By 1890 many American universities had acquired the internal structure that would remain essentially unchanged over the next century: a flourishing bureaucracy, distinct academic departments headed by chairs, and faculty rankings.[93] Graduate programs now capped the curriculum of many colleges, from the older eastern schools to the new universities that had spread across the western states. No longer the exotic newcomers that they had been in the 1870s and 1880s, postcollegiate training programs by 1900 generated more than seventeen hundred master's degrees and close to four hundred Ph.D.'s. Such programs rested atop ever-growing undergraduate colleges, which awarded bachelor's degrees in numbers far greater than the numbers of master's and doctor's degrees.[94]

The relationship between these graduate and undergraduate programs was significant. By 1900 graduate education in America was conceived as being institutionally separate from undergraduate education. The nomenclature that came to distinguish graduate from undergraduate programs makes this statement now seem too obvious to require explanation. But the triumph of the institutionally distinct graduate school by the turn of the century signaled the death of the options that had sprung briefly to life in the 1870s and 1880s. At the University of Michigan, for example, the classicist and interim president Henry Simmons Frieze had envisioned a "university system" by which the Ph.D. would be awarded after five years of post–high school study. By 1890 the institutional embodiment of this idea, the School of Political Science, had shriveled away. In its place stood the graduate school, formally separated from undergraduate education both institutionally and philosophically. Unlike the School of Political Science, the graduate school did not demand broadly integrative knowledge; it required pure "research" and "an independent scholarly grasp of one or two subjects."[95] Nor was the example of the ASCSA imitated. There, professors hoped to open archaeological doors both to future professionals and to cultivated amateurs through a program of study that included wide reading and specialized work. But by 1900 the cultured amateur had become increasingly unwelcome in the training programs of American universities. The undergraduate college would house "preparatory" education, while "advanced" education, now conceived as specialized research training, would characterize the Ph.D.-granting graduate program. The ideal of cultivated erudition, which contended that the most advanced education should incorporate both general and specialized knowledge, had quietly retreated.

Few shed tears over the demise of the ideal of cultivated erudition as a goal of Ph.D. programs. In fact, hardly anybody by 1900 even seemed to recall that it had once been a compelling model for organizing higher education. The German model of the university now stood less for raising the level of the undergraduate college, as it had for antebellum university leaders, than for specialized training in independent research to be pursued either late in college or altogether after college. In becoming professionalized, academic scholarship assumed the shape of the older professions in America, separating the general work of the college from the more technical study of the professional.

Even among classicists who had witnessed the transformation of higher education in the 1870s and 1880s, the substitution of specialized research training for cultivated erudition was quickly normalized. William Watson Goodwin's example is instructive. Following Everett, Popkin, and Felton as the Eliot Professor of Greek Literature at Harvard and a key figure in the early years of the ASCSA, Goodwin in 1900 celebrated the new style of graduate training as though it had emerged uncontested over the decades. He characterized the graduate school at Harvard not as a home for liberal culture and advanced work but as "the professional school of the Arts and Sciences, as the Schools of Divinity, Medicine, and Law are the professional schools of those faculties." More significant still was the way he articulated the mission of this professional school for scholars.

> The highest instruction will always be technical, adapted to those who intend to make teaching, writing for the press, or public life a profession. The demands for scientific professional training for all these are rapidly growing in all parts of our country. . . . The Graduate School must answer these calls, and it must take its stand with our other professional schools as a home of advanced learning, where the best and the highest which each department can offer will be found, and where all students will learn also (what is much more important) the scientific methods of investigation by which all sciences have been advanced, that they may become leaders and not mere followers in the great march of the world's progress of learning.[96]

Goodwin carefully explained that others could also attend the graduate school, such as those "students who simply want more of that general liberal culture of which they have laid the foundation in college, and who have no idea of preparing themselves to be teachers or writers." But providing students with more liberal culture was not the main function of the graduate school as now conceived by Goodwin, who argued that "scientific and methodical investigation must always be its highest object, that for which the School primarily exists."[97]

It was characteristic of this new era that one of the major critiques of scientism and specialization in the first decades of the twentieth century came from the New Humanists, several of whose most outspoken members—Irving Babbitt, Paul Elmer More, and Norman Foerster—did not complete the doctoral course leading to the Ph.D. The New Humanist movement rejected the creeping influence of the social sciences in American life, their emphasis on future progress rather than the wisdom of the past, and its members continued to advocate a classics-based ideal of cultivated erudition long after it had become a hothouse curiosity in graduate schools. Frank Jewett Mather Jr. (1868–1953), one New Humanist who did complete a doctorate in philology at Johns Hopkins in 1892, called the program "the mill" and said that he had emerged from it "with much of the juice squeezed out of me, but with enough left to know that I had been squeezed." In 1930 at Harvard he tried to establish an "AM with Honors" that emphasized "assimilative reading" rather than "original research" so that students would gain "discipline in ideas" and not just "discipline in facts." This proposal was defeated. At the University of Iowa a similar program was established by Norman Foerster, a major voice among the New Humanists. As the new director of the School of Letters and Science in 1930, Foerster proceeded to restructure the doctoral program, which he believed had descended into pedantry and failed to train qualified literature teachers. Under Foerster's aegis, the school announced in 1931 that in lieu of original research leading to the Ph.D. it would accept "imaginative or critical writing"—even of as few as fifty pages.[98]

But such graduate programs were exceptions in the new century. By 1900 the structure of American higher education worked against the simultaneous prosecution of general culture and research. The closest that universities would come to approaching the ideal of cultivated erudition was in the advanced courses available to juniors and seniors, which introduced undergraduates to the kind of research that reached its apotheosis in graduate school. Even in 1883, when he suggested such courses for American colleges, however, the classicist John Henry Wright already regarded them as somehow out of place, as belonging more appropriately to graduate programs. "Is there not something in the very structure and object of American college education that would make such methods out of place with us?" he asked rhetorically. Wright worried that it would be "ill-judged" to "introduce into a college course, where mental discipline and the acquisition of general literary and scientific culture are the ends in view, methods of instruction which consist, essentially, in special studies." These special studies were more appropriate to "our post-graduate courses of study, in the professional departments of our universities."[99]

In this new scheme, specialization in classical studies emerged as an enemy of general knowledge, and classicism retreated further from the civic culture of America to the realm of academic and elite arcana. Implicit in the new structure of American higher education was the idea that erudition must necessarily divide knowledge into popular and expert kinds. The men of letters who had populated American learning earlier in the century had seen their specialized knowledge as a contribution to general learning, not a threat to it. They did not believe that the growth of knowledge led to specialization, but instead that specialization led to the growth of knowledge. The men of letters reasoned that as a new field of learning became more minutely cultivated, more knowledge could be channeled into the public sphere. The assumption that specialized learning could enhance general knowledge was what had propelled some late-century scholars to conceive of the Ph.D., indeed all advanced learning, as a united, integrating venture. But slowly the connection between specialization and general knowledge frayed as scholars increasingly stressed what they saw as the methodological distinction between the acquisition of liberal culture and the prosecution of "scientific" research. The college was properly the home of liberal culture, while the graduate program was where one actively pursued knowledge through independent, specialized scientific work.

EPILOGUE

The reinvention of classical antiquity in nineteenth-century America played an important role in determining the role of the ancients in the twentieth century. It is not my object in this epilogue either to endorse or to bemoan these developments but rather to reflect on how the Victorian inheritance shaped the modern reception of antiquity. From the perspective of the eighteenth century, the resolute modernity of the twentieth is remarkable, and yet some of the major intellectual monuments of this century have been shaped by the classical tradition. Freudian psychology, the literature of James Joyce, T. S. Eliot, and Ezra Pound, modern revisions of classical tragedies (by Jean Anouilh, Bertholt Brecht, and others), stunning archaeological finds and their popularity in museums, and various architectural revivals of classicism testify to the classical world's ongoing presence in the twentieth century.

More central to our purposes, however, is the fate of classicism within higher education and how its position there connects to modern notions of citizenship and selfhood. There, I would argue, the Victorian notion of classical antiquity as uniquely cultivating has been unable to weather the general trend of twentieth-century education, which is toward ever more egalitarianism. This is a radical simplification, of course, and there are many other factors that have contributed to undermining the position of classical antiquity in the modern university. But there is clearly a fundamental incompatibility between the egalitarian ethos of the twentieth-century university and the elitism traditionally associated with classicism. This conflict has its roots in the late eighteenth century and continues today to animate debates over the canon.

By 1915 the major trends in American higher education had been set, and developments later in the twentieth century reinforced and expanded upon these. Most significant was the continuing expansion and democratization of higher education. There were 563 institutions of higher learning in America in 1870; 1,409 in 1930; 2,000 in 1960; and 3,595 in 1990. The number of students also continued to climb. In 1870, 52,000 students were attending college in America; by 1990 there were 15.3 million. The percentage of the college-aged population attending institutions of higher education grew from barely 1 percent in the late nineteenth century to 40 percent by 1990.[1] Clearly, higher education in America no longer serves just the elite, as it did even into the late nineteenth century, but an ever-growing sector of the population. Within the universities, trends that began in the Gilded Age have continued unabated: an elective system at the undergraduate level; graduate schools that produce specialists; the reorganization of knowledge into autonomous disciplines organized along professional lines; the consolidation of research rather than pedagogy as the chief goal of the university; the separation among both faculty and students of scholarly work from the private practice of religion; the expectation that faculty have a doctorate in their field and publish in order to advance professionally; and a flourishing administrative structure.

The classical languages, now confined entirely to educational institutions, have continued the decline that began in the late nineteenth century. For a while, Latin held its own in the high schools. In 1915 Latin still accounted for the largest enrollments of any subject besides English, history, and algebra, and nearly every public high school and private academy offered Latin. (By contrast, Greek ranked twenty-eighth in popularity in the list of thirty subjects offered by high schools in 1915).[2] The strength of Latin in the high schools was in part a consequence of its being required for admission to American colleges and of its popularity as a major among college women destined for high school teaching. The popularity of Latin also testified to a renewed interest in Rome between the world wars. Anti-German sentiment in the context of World War I diverted some attention away from the ancient Greeks, who for so long had been identified with German New Humanism. Two of the major American classical scholars of the early twentieth century—Paul Shorey, of the University of Chicago, and John Adams Scott, at Northwestern University—vociferously opposed Germanic scholarship, which they associated with cultural narrowness and excessively specialized scholarship.[3] By the 1960s, however, Latin was beginning a sharp decline in the high schools, from nearly 7 percent of enrollments in 1960 to just 1 percent in 1978. In colleges, enrollments in Latin shrank over the same period from about .7 percent to .2 percent.[4] The number of college majors in classics likewise declined by 30 percent in the two decades after 1971. One observer has estimated that of the 1 million bachelor's degrees awarded in 1994 only 600 were granted in classics.[5]

As classics enrollments continued to subside, so did the idea that Greek and Latin were uniquely cultivating. One testament to the chastening of classicism's pretensions appeared in that monument to twentieth-century notions of liberal learning, Harvard University's *General Education in a Free Society* (1945). "The somewhat mystical superiority of intellectual discipline which has been claimed for these languages, especially Latin, may be largely false," intoned the authors in 1945, grouping classical languages with other foreign languages. This statement also reflected the collapse of the sanctity of the B.A. as the degree that symbolized immersion in classical antiquity. In the 1940s many universities adopted the B.A. as *the* undergraduate degree, regardless of whether a student had learned a classical language. Whatever programs they offered, colleges asserted that everyone deserved the B.A. for completing their university studies: everyone was cultured, whether they had had contact with the classics or not.[6]

Yet it would be a mistake to assume that classical antiquity vanished from the colleges and universities in the twentieth century. It thrived, in fact, in the compulsory Western civilization courses that flourished at many colleges and universities between World War I and the 1960s. These courses were responses to several factors, most importantly the loss of the common classical core and the proliferation of electives, which had left many students and faculty feeling somewhat at sea. In 1890, 84 percent of a student's courses in college were prescribed; in 1940 only 40 percent was prescribed.[7] The erosion of Greek and Latin as a common core spurred the creation of courses that would ostensibly provide commonality and unity in the curriculum. These courses, which typically occupied the freshman year, presented to students a historical sequence of the "rise" or "progress" of "Western civilization" from classical antiquity (or even before) to the modern era. This idea rested firmly on Victorian ideas of evolutionism and historicism. In the Western civilization courses, civilizations evolved upward, and students were believed to be uniquely cultivated by observing this historical change over time.[8]

These courses also reflected a continuing commitment to linking a liberal education to the duties of citizenship, but such ideals became increasingly strained in the egalitarian society of the second half of the twentieth century. As a result, Western civilization courses and the classical history that they brought with them began to collapse in the 1960s as a number of students and faculty adopted the rhetoric of relevance and self-expression. The Western civilization courses had maintained the late-nineteenth-century conviction that high culture and democracy must be made compatible. In 1919 Columbia University introduced the first such freshman course, entitled "Contemporary Civilization," reflecting a commitment to tying liberal learning to democracy. One faculty dean at Columbia expressed the equation between democracy and a liberal education in 1918 as follows:

> It is not surprising . . . that those who have had to do with this course are beginning to ask themselves if it does not constitute the elements of a liberal education for the youth of today. Born of the consciousness that a democracy needs to know what it is fighting for, it has awakened the consciousness of what we, as a people, need to know if our part in the world of today is to be intelligent, sympathetic, and liberal. In the past, education was liberalized by means of the classical tradition. . . . if education is to be liberalized again, if our youth are to be freed from a confusion of ideas and standards, no other means looks so attractive as a common knowledge of what the present world of human affairs really is.[9]

The authors of Harvard's *General Education in a Free Society* continued to insist in mid-century on the importance of a liberal education in an egalitarian, democratic society, easily glossing over the elitist pretensions that liberal education had always had. "The task of modern democracy," they wrote, "is to preserve the ancient ideal of liberal education and to extend it as far as possible to all the members of the community. . . . to believe in the equality of human beings is to believe that the good life, and the education which trains the citizen for the good life, are equally the privilege of all."[10] The decline of classics and the Western civilization course heralded the overall decline in the humanities since the 1960s. Although the absolute number of bachelor's and doctor's degrees in the humanities increased slightly between 1960 and 1990 (amid ever-growing total enrollments), they declined as a percentage of the total number of degrees awarded across the disciplines. In 1966, 20 percent of bachelor's degrees were in humanities; by 1990 fewer than 10 percent were.[11]

These minuscule numbers belie the passion that discussions of the place of antiquity in American intellectual and cultural life continue to inspire. The problem of reconciling the traditional elitism of the classical tradition (shaping gentlemen, ministers, statesmen, and scholars) with the universalist, utilitarian educational values of a liberal, democratic society continues to infuse modern controversies about the classical past, just as it did, with a somewhat different vocabulary, in the eighteenth and nineteenth centuries. These concerns have taken a number of forms in the last twenty years. Should a common core of learning essential to every educated American citizen be located in part within the literature, history, and art of ancient Greece and Rome?[12] Should we assign modern ethnic and racial identities to the peoples of the classical world, and how broadly should that classical world be defined?[13] To what extent can classics and classical archaeology, traditional disciplines charged with upholding "Western civilization" for a century, meet the challenge of poststructuralism, postmodernism, and other literary theories?[14] To what should we attribute the employment and enrollment crises plaguing the modern profession of classics and classical archaeology?[15] Such questions are beyond the scope of this book to answer, but they have their origins in the story told here.

NOTES

ABBREVIATIONS

AIAP   Archaeological Institute of America Papers
HSFP   Henry Simmons Frieze Papers
HUA   Harvard University Archives
JBAP   James Burrill Angell Papers

INTRODUCTION

1. The literature on the American classical tradition in the eighteenth and early nineteenth centuries is vast. Some of the major contributions include Gummere, *American Colonial Mind*; Middlekauff, *Ancients and Axioms*; Colbourn, *Lamp of Experience*; Wood, *Creation of the American Republic*; Kerber, *Federalists in Dissent*; Pocock, *Machiavellian Moment*; Reinhold, *Classick Pages*; Eadie, *Classical Traditions in Early America*; Banning, *Jeffersonian Persuasion*; McCoy, *Elusive Republic*; Reinhold, *Classica Americana*; Robson, *Educating Republicans*; Rahe, *Republics Ancient and Modern*; Pangle and Pangle, *Learning of Liberty*; Richard, *Founders and the Classics*.

2. Jaeger, *Paideia*, 1:xxiii.

3. This view has its origins in the writings of late-nineteenth-century university builders and scientists such as the Harvard president Charles W. Eliot, who successfully waged a rhetorical battle that pitted modernity, construed as science and utility, against antiquity, construed as classicism and generalism. This rhetorical strategy shaped two of the most influential works on the history of American higher education in the second half of the twentieth century, which identify the "classical college" with retrograde pedagogies and classicism: Hofstadter and Metzger, *Development of Academic Freedom*; and Veysey, *Emergence of the American University*.

4. Some recent books have begun to restore classicists and classicism to nineteenth-century American history: Dyson, *Ancient Marbles to American Shores*; Gildersleeve, *Letters*; Briggs and Benario, *Basil Lanneau Gildersleeve*; Briggs, *Soldier and Scholar*; and Turner, *Liberal Education of Charles Eliot Norton*. The major recent books on classicism in

nineteenth-century Europe are Jenkyns, *Victorians and Ancient Greece;* Turner, *Greek Heritage;* Marchand, *Down from Olympus;* and Stray, *Classics Transformed.*

5. On student life, see Harding, *College Literary Societies;* McLachlan, "Choice of Hercules"; Allmendiger, *Paupers and Scholars;* Horowitz, *Campus Life;* Stevenson, "Preparing for Public Life"; and Geiger and Bubolz, "College as It Was."

6. Grafton, *Defenders of the Text;* Levine, *Battle of the Books;* Haskell and Penny, *Taste and the Antique.*

7. Goldgar, *Impolite Learning.*

CHAPTER 1. ANTIQUITY IN THE NEW NATION

1. Quotation from Rowland, *Life of George Mason,* 384. See also MacCormack, "Limits of Understanding"; and Miller, *New England Mind.*

2. Cotton Mather, "An Elegy on Ezekiel Cheever" (1708), in Cohen, *Education,* 1:550.

3. Cremin, *American Education: The Colonial Experience,* 180.

4. Middlekauff, *Ancients and Axioms,* ch. 5; Murdock, "Teaching of Latin and Greek"; Reinhold, *Classick Pages;* Shipton, "Secondary Education"; "The System of Public Education Adopted by the Town of Boston" (1789), in Cohen, *Education,* 2:732–38.

5. Cremin, *American Education: The Colonial Experience,* 207.

6. Reinhold, *Classick Pages,* 4.

7. Clarke, *Classical Education in Britain,* ch. 2.

8. "College Book III," 187.

9. Broome, "College Admission Requirements," 186.

10. Cremin, *American Education: The Colonial Experience,* 216.

11. McLachlan, "Classical Names," 84–85; Nye, *Cultural Life,* 171, 176.

12. Broome, "College Admission Requirements," 39.

13. Broderick, "Pulpit, Physics, and Politics," 50–51.

14. Durrill, "Power of Ancient Words," 472.

15. Cremin, *American Education: The Colonial Experience,* 207, 221.

16. Kimball, *"True Professional Ideal,"* table A2.5.

17. Morison, *Founding of Harvard College,* 432.

18. Cremin, *American Education: The Colonial Experience,* 213.

19. Jay, *New Testament Greek,* ix, 265–66.

20. Morison, *Harvard College in the Seventeenth Century,* 1:197.

21. Ibid., 199.

22. Fiering, *Moral Philosophy,* 19.

23. Reinhold, *Classica Americana,* 235.

24. Morison, *Harvard College in the Seventeenth Century,* 1:176.

25. Reinhold, *Classica Americana,* 235.

26. Ibid., 236; Thacher, "Address Commemorative," 641.

27. Bender, *Intellect and Public Life,* 7.

28. Warner, *Letters of the Republic*, 32, 125.

29. McLachlan, "Classical Names," 85.

30. McLachlan, "American College," 293; McLachlan, "Classical Names," 85.

31. Aronson, *Status and Kinship*, 124–25. These figures include both graduates and those who attended but may not have graduated.

32. Ferguson, *Law and Letters*; Grasso, *Speaking Aristocracy*, 4.

33. Adams, *Papers of John Adams*, 126.

34. Ferguson, *Law and Letters*, 28, 29, 75.

35. Davis, "Augustan Conception of History"; Persons, "Cyclical Theory"; Colbourn, "Thomas Jefferson's Uses of the Past."

36. Levine, *Battle of the Books*, 7.

37. Bolingbroke, *Letters*, 1:170.

38. "Curious Branches of Knowledge Vindicated," 18.

39. Rowson, *Present for Young Ladies*, 53.

40. Adam, *Roman Antiquities*, vi.

41. Strong, "Speech to the Massachusetts Legislature," 115.

42. William Smith, quoted in Reinhold, *Classick Pages*, 185.

43. Reinhold, *Classick Pages*, passim; Gribbin, "Rollin's Histories."

44. Reinhold, *Classick Pages*, 168; see also Richard, *Founders and the Classics*, 85–122.

45. Rawson, *Spartan Tradition*; Reinhold, *Classick Pages*, ch. 13.

46. Morison, *Harvard College in the Seventeenth Century*, 1:179.

47. "Carre and Sanderson's Seminary," 415.

48. Popkin, "On the Study of the Classics," 312. For more on Ciceronian models of speech in America, see Cmiel, *Democratic Eloquence*, 23–54.

49. Lounsbury, "*Ludibria Rerum Mortalium*," 361.

50. Greven, *Protestant Temperament*, 287–88; Wills, *Cincinnatus*; Wright, *First Gentlemen of Virginia*; Marambaud, *William Byrd of Westover*; Bridenbaugh, *Myths and Realities*; Morgan, *Virginians at Home*.

51. Mack and Robertson, *Roman Remains*, 3.

52. Middleton, *Grecian Remains in Italy*, 2.

53. "Carre and Sanderson's Seminary," 416.

54. On women's exclusion from the male world of classical knowledge, see Ong, "Latin Language Study as a Renaissance Puberty Rite"; Lefkowitz, *Heroines and Hysterics*; Fowler, " 'On Not Knowing Greek' "; Kerber, *Women of the Republic*, 189–231; and Winterer, "Victorian Antigone."

55. For *virilis femina*, see Davis, "Gender and Genre," 158; for *homasse*, Smith, *Gender of History*, 16; and for virago, Shuckburgh, *Antigone of Sophocles*, xxv. For more general discussions of learned women, see Brink, *Female Scholars*; Baym, *Feminism and American Literary History*; Kelley, "Reading Women/Women Reading"; Davidson, *Revolution and the Word*.

56. Kerber, *Women of the Republic*, 198.

57. "On Female Authorship," 69.

58. Ryan, *Women in Public*, 52. See also Fleming, "From Indian Princess to Greek Goddess"; Kennon, *Republic for the Ages*; and Kammen, "From Liberty to Prosperity."

59. Hutcheson, "Mercy Warren," 379; Zagarri, *Woman's Dilemma*, 1–3; Gelles, *Portia*; Skemp, *Judith Sargent Murray*.

60. Woody, *History of Women's Education*, 1:418 and apps. 1–3; see also Farnham, *Education of the Southern Belle*; and Tolley, "Science Education of American Girls."

61. Anthony Grafton and Lisa Jardine, "Women Humanists: Education for What?" in Grafton and Jardine, *From Humanism to the Humanities*, 33.

62. Farnham, *Education of the Southern Belle*, 32.

63. Tolley, "Science Education of American Girls," 336–37.

64. Davidson, *Revolution and the Word*; Brown, *Knowledge Is Power*; Kelley, "Reading Women/Women Reading"; Baym, *American Women Writers*.

65. Davis, "Gender and Genre."

66. Gelles, *Portia*, 135; Richard, *Founders and the Classics*, 55.

67. Zagarri, *Woman's Dilemma*, 87.

68. Ibid., 56, 135.

69. Murray, *Gleaner*, 140–48.

70. Grasso, *Speaking Aristocracy*, 2–3; Brown, *Knowledge Is Power*; Cmiel, *Democratic Eloquence*, 24.

71. Shields, *Civil Tongues*, 99–140, 175–208.

72. Litto, "Addison's *Cato*."

73. Adams, *Works of John Adams*, 4:295.

74. Cmiel, *Democratic Eloquence*, ch. 1

75. McLachlan, "Classical Names," 82–84.

76. Cmiel, *Democratic Eloquence*, 40.

77. McLachlan, "Choice of Hercules," 472.

78. Ibid., 484; Pierson, *Yale Book of Numbers*, 317.

79. McLachlan, "Choice of Hercules"; Waldstreicher, *Perpetual Fetes*, 73.

80. Tolles, "Quaker Humanist," 418–19; Davis, *Colonial Southern Bookshelf*, 9; Ferguson, *Law and Letters*, 295.

81. See Finkelstein, "From Tutor to Specialized Scholar," 103.

82. "Philology," 378.

83. Bisbee, *General Catalogue*, 65, 75, 76.

84. Snyder, "Icon of Antiquity," 30–31.

85. Ibid., 34.

86. Haskell, *History and Its Images*; Momigliano, "Ancient History and the Antiquarian."

87. Popkin, *Three Lectures*, 21.

88. Miller, *Memoir of the Rev. Charles Nisbet*, 28.

89. Charles Nisbet to Joshua M. Wallace, Carlisle, Pennsylvania, 8 June 1793, in Hofstadter and Smith, *American Higher Education*, 1:254–55; Miller, *Memoir of the Rev. Charles Nisbet*, 138–39.

90. Nisbet, "Classical Learning" (1807), 386.

91. Wilson, "Classical Literature," 451–53.

92. Popkin, *Three Lectures*, 23.

93. Nisbet, "Classical Learning" (1808), 8.

94. Dalzel, *ΑΝΑΛΕΚΤΑ ʹΕΛΛΗΝΙΚΑ*.

95. Buckminster, "On the Dangers and Duties," 158.

96. "Classical Learning," 142–43.

97. Felton, *Memorial of the Rev. John Snelling Popkin*, lxxxii; Thacher, "Address Commemorative," 641; LaBorde, *History*, 98; *History of Columbia University*, 90; Ibbotson, *Documentary History*, 142; Knight, *Documentary History*, 3:121; 4:331, 309. The catalogs of Bowdoin College, Dartmouth, Dickinson, Middlebury, Princeton, and Yale show that the *Graeca Majora* was used at these schools into the 1830s.

98. *National Union Catalogue*, s.v. "Dalzel, Andrew."

99. Popkin, *Three Lectures*, 24–25.

100. "Felton's *Memorial of Dr. Popkin*," 476–77.

101. Clarke, *James Freeman Clarke*, 36, 41.

102. "Felton's *Memorial of Dr. Popkin*," 476.

103. Clarke, *James Freeman Clarke*, 42.

104. Felton, *Memorial of the Rev. John Snelling Popkin*, lxxv.

105. "Felton's *Memorial of Dr. Popkin*," 476.

106. Thacher, "Address Commemorative," 657.

107. Kelley, *Yale*, 161.

108. *History of Columbia University*, 79.

109. Drisler, *Charles Anthon, L.L.D.*, 6–7.

110. *History of Columbia University*, 90–91.

111. Legaré, *Writings*, 1:xxii.

112. LaBorde, *History*, 181.

113. Ibid., 133.

114. Thomson and Perraud, *Ten Latin Schooltexts*, 58–59.

115. Ibid., 55–58.

116. Clarke published translations of Eutropius, Florus, Justin, Nepos, Ovid, Sallust, and Suetonius. For a discussion of Clarke as an agent of Latin school reform in America, see Middlekauff, *Ancients and Axioms*, 79–86.

117. Webbe, *Lectures and Exercises out of Cicero*, unpaginated 5.

118. Clarke, *Essay upon the Education of Youth*; Clarke, *Essay upon Study*.

119. Smith, *Theories of Education*, 61.

120. Kelley, *Yale*, 156; Broome, "College Admission Requirements," 43.

121. Popkin, "On the Use of Translations," 456.

122. Popkin, "On the Art of Teaching," 316.

123. "Carre and Sanderson's Seminary," 416.

124. On the decline of composing original Latin verse at eighteenth-century Harvard, see Broome, "College Admission Requirements," 29–30.

125. John Clarke, quoted in Smith, *Theories of Education,* 75.

126. "Otis's Rudiments," 222.

127. T.C., "Classical Education," 581.

128. Locke, *Educational Writings of John Locke,* 256.

129. Richard Graves, quoted in Hopkinson, "A New Plan of Education," 61.

130. Miller, *Brief Retrospect,* 2:51–52.

131. Popkin, *Three Lectures,* 130.

132. Felton, *Memorial of the Rev. John Snelling Popkin,* lxxvii. See the University of Alabama's library policies in Knight, *Documentary History,* 3: 262; on student libraries and translations, see McLachlan, *"Choice of Hercules,"* 478.

133. Hall, *Collection,* 358.

134. T.C., "Classical Education," 572.

135. On the problem of the pedant in Europe, see Goldgar, *Impolite Learning.*

136. "Pimps" was used by John Wilson, quoted in Richard, *Founders and the Classics,* 224.

137. Ibid., 200.

138. This point is made in ibid., 196–231; and Wiesen, "Ancient History," 53–69.

139. Wiesen, "Ancient History," 61.

140. Ibid., 62.

141. Richard, *Founders and the Classics,* 221.

CHAPTER 2. THE RISE OF GREECE

1. Burke, *American Collegiate Populations,* 14, 18–19, 22–23, 54.

2. Ibid., 35, 38.

3. Bozeman, *Protestants in an Age of Science;* Hovencamp, *Science and Religion.*

4. Rudolph, *Curriculum,* 62.

5. Quincy, *History of Harvard University,* 2:321.

6. Bigelow, *Elements of Technology,* iii–v.

7. Wood, *Radicalism.*

8. Hofstadter, *Anti-Intellectualism,* 159.

9. Aronson, *Status and Kinship,* 166.

10. Howe, *Political Culture,* 44; Hofstadter, *Anti-Intellectualism,* 157.

11. Reinhold, *Classica Americana,* 239.

12. Bender, *New York Intellect,* 103.

13. Carey, "Learned Languages," 558.

14. DeBow, "Commercial Age," 230–31.

15. Caldwell, *Thoughts,* 128.

16. Grimké, *Reflections,* 4, 19, 42, 156–57, 181.

17. Kelley, *Yale,* 161.

18. Day and Kingsley, "Original Papers," 300.

19. Ibid., 328–29.

20. Wolf, *Prolegomena to Homer;* Diehl, *Americans and German Scholarship;* Brown, *Rise of Biblical Criticism;* Herbst, *German Historical School;* Pfeiffer, *History of Classical Scholarship;* Sandys, *History of Classical Scholarship;* Wilamowitz-Möllendorff, *History of Classical Scholarship;* Marchand, *Down from Olympus.*

21. Trevelyan, *Goethe and the Greeks;* Marchand, *Down from Olympus,* 3–35; Leppmann, *Winckelmann.*

22. See Kane and Alexander, *Nicknames.*

23. McCaughey, "Transformation of American Academic Life," 246.

24. Morison, *Three Centuries of Harvard,* 224.

25. Popkin, *Three Lectures,* 5–7; Morison, *Three Centuries of Harvard,* 224–27.

26. Morison, *Three Centuries of Harvard,* 224–27; Quincy, *History of Harvard University,* 2:312–17, Reinhold, *Classica Americana,* ch. 7.

27. Larrabee, *Hellas Observed,* 31.

28. Ibid., 39.

29. Everett gave a total of fifteen lectures on antiquities and ancient art in Boston in the winters of 1822–23 and 1823–24, although the precise dates are unknown (Reid, *Edward Everett,* 203).

30. Everett, "History of Grecian Art," 187.

31. Felton, *Memorial of the Rev. John Snelling Popkin,* lxxxiv; Morison, *Three Centuries of Harvard,* 227.

32. Ralph Waldo Emerson, quoted in Morison, *Three Centuries of Harvard,* 227.

33. Marchand, *Down from Olympus,* 10.

34. Everett, "History of Grecian Art," 188, 187.

35. Schlegel, *Lectures,* 17–29.

36. Stameshkin, *Town's College,* 59.

37. On Harvard and Göttingen libraries, see Reinhold, *Classica Americana,* 208; on Yale, see Kingsley, *Sketch,* 43; and on Middlebury, see Stameshkin, *Town's College,* 39.

38. Patton, *Address,* 3.

39. Stameshkin, *Town's College,* 61.

40. Wertenbaker, *Princeton,* 161.

41. James W. Alexander, quoted in ibid., 160. On Alexander's friendship with Patton, see Patton, *New Greek and English Lexicon,* v.

42. Kingsley, *Sketch,* 44.

43. Patton, *Lecture,* 19.

44. Ibid., 20.

45. MacLean, *History of the College of New Jersey,* 266–67.

46. Everett, *Greek Grammar,* v; this preface is reprinted from the 1822 edition.

47. *National Union Catalogue,* s.v. "Buttmann, Phillipp"; see also the catalogs for the years 1800–1850 for Bowdoin, Dartmouth, Dickinson, Hamilton, Harvard, Middlebury, Princeton, and Yale.

48. Patton, *New Greek and English Lexicon,* vi.

49. Everett, *Greek Reader,* vi.

50. *National Union Catalogue*, s.v. "Jacobs, Friedrich"; see also the catalog for the years 1800–1850 for Bowdoin, Dartmouth, Dickinson, Hamilton, Harvard, Michigan, Middlebury, Princeton, and Yale.

51. Newmyer, "Charles Anthon," 41–44.

52. Patton, *Lecture*, 11.

53. Cleveland, *Remarks*, iv, 2–3, 5.

54. Patton, *Lecture*, 11.

55. Adam, *Latin Grammar*, 3.

56. *Dictionary of National Biography*, s.v. "Adam, Alexander."

57. Charles Beck to Harvard Corporation, n.d., Harvard College Papers, 2d ser., vols. 4–5 (1829–33), HUA.

58. Adam, *Roman Antiquities*, 230.

59. *Questions upon Adam's Roman Antiquities*, 1–3.

60. Felton, "Antiquities," 426.

61. Cornelius Conway Felton to Harvard Corporation, n.d., Harvard College Papers, 2d ser., vols. 4–5 (1829–33), HUA.

62. Ibid.

63. Felton to Josiah Quincy, 21 November 1832, ibid.

64. Fisher, "On the Priority of Greek Studies," 213.

65. Patton, *Lecture*, 17.

66. Cheever, "Study of Greek Literature," 281.

67. Woolsey, "Eulogy," 110.

68. Felton, "Antiquities," 426.

69. Lewis, "Classical Criticism," 255. On the deficiences of Scottish and English scholarship, see Felton, "Bode's *History*," 466; Felton, "Classical Learning in England," 270; Bancroft, "Jacobs' Greek Reader," 281; Felton, "Alcestis of Euripides," 373.

70. Bancroft, "Buttmann's Greek Grammar," 104–5.

71. "Character of Medea," 392.

72. Crosby, "Classical Study," 246.

73. Stuart, *On the Classical Tongues*, 15–16.

74. Crosby, "Classical Study," 246.

75. Felton, *Lecture on Classical Learning*, 12.

76. Stuart, *On the Classical Tongues*, 8.

77. Felton, *An Address Delivered before the Association of the Alumni of Harvard College*, 34.

78. Guyot, *Earth and Man*, 325.

79. Everett, "Circumstances," 77.

80. Coleridge, *Introduction*, 35.

81. Poe, "To Helen."

82. Horsman, *Race and Manifest Destiny*.

83. Carrott, *Egyptian Revival*.

84. Davis, *Landscape of Belief*.

85. Larrabee, *Hellas Observed,* 113.

86. Ibid., 44.

87. *Grecian Wreath of Victory;* Drisler, *Charles Anthon, L.L.D.,* 16–17.

88. Larrabee, *Hellas Observed,* 70.

89. Willard, *Advancement of Female Education;* Larrabee, *Hellas Observed,* 199–200.

90. Larrabee, *Hellas Observed,* 18; McNeal, *Nicholas Biddle in Greece.*

91. Cornelius Conway Felton, for example, delivered forty-nine lectures on ancient and modern Greece between 1852 and 1859 at the Lowell Institute in Boston. These were published posthumously as Felton, *Greece: Ancient and Modern.*

92. "Greek Revolution," 100.

93. Matthiessen, *American Renaissance.*

94. Faust, *Mothers of Invention,* 168–78.

95. Howe, *Making the American Self,* 189–211, 217–19.

96. Emerson, "Plato; Or, the Philosopher," 388.

97. Dall, *Margaret and Her Friends;* Howe, *Making the American Self,* 215 ("stern composure"). On Fuller's education, see Capper, *Margaret Fuller,* 29–38.

98. *Description of the View of Athens,* 3.

99. Edward Everett to Harvard Corporation, 13 February 1823, Harvard College Papers, vols. 9–10 (1819–24), HUA.

100. Everett to Quincy, 11 May 1837, Harvard College Papers, 2d ser., vols 6–8 (1833–38), HUA.

101. Everett to Harvard Corporation, 13 February 1823.

102. John Vanderlyn, quoted in Schoonmaker, *John Vanderlyn,* 37–38.

103. Reid, *Edward Everett,* 203.

104. Mondello, *Private Papers of John Vanderlyn,* 66.

105. *Description of the View of Athens,* 3.

106. Harvard Corporation Records, vols. 6 and 8, HUA.

107. Everett, "History of Grecian Art," 184.

108. Felton, *Lecture on Classical Learning,* 17–18.

109. Cheever, "Study of Greek Literature," 39.

110. Patton, *Lecture,* 5–6.

111. Cheever, "Study of Greek Literature," 39.

112. J.W.M., "Danger and Safety of the Republic," 151–52.

113. Felton, *Address Pronounced August 15, 1828,* 13, 16.

114. Daniel Webster, quoted in Howe, *Political Culture,* 218.

115. Miles, "Whig Party."

116. Brown, *Strength of a People,* 155; Scott, "Popular Lecture."

117. Cmiel, *Democratic Eloquence,* 58.

118. Donald, *Lincoln,* 29–31, 47; Oates, *With Malice toward None,* 10–12, 20–22.

119. Cmiel, *Democratic Eloquence,* 60; Wills, *Lincoln at Gettysburg,* 41–62.

120. Mike Walsh, quoted in Miles, "Young American Nation," 266.

121. McCardell, *Idea of a Southern Nation.*

122. Felton, *Address Pronounced August 15, 1828*, 20.

123. H, "Athenian Orators," 386, 357.

124. Gray, "Demosthenes," 48.

125. H, "Athenian Orators," 353.

126. "Ancient and Modern Eloquence," 185, 183.

127. Gray, "Demosthenes," 36.

128. Cheever, "Study of Greek Literature," 277.

129. Carter, "Pinkney's Eloquence"; Cassady, "Eloquence," 360; Felton, *Address Delivered at the Dedication of the New Building of Bristol Academy*, 16.

130. O'Brien, *Character of Hugh Legaré*, 97. For further comparisons between Cicero and Demosthenes in the antebellum South, see Lounsbury, *"Ludibria Rerum Mortalium."*

131. Howe, *Political Culture*, 219–21.

132. Cmiel, *Democratic Eloquence*, 61.

133. D.S.G.C., "Modern Oratory," 371; see also H, "Athenian Orators," 377.

134. "Ancient and Modern Eloquence," 181.

135. Felton, *Lecture on Classical Learning*, 26.

136. Champlin, *Oration of Demosthenes*, interlined copy at the Joseph Regenstein Library, University of Chicago.

137. Felton, *Lecture on Classical Learning*, 28.

138. Felton, "Greek Language and Literature," 115.

139. Felton, *Lecture on Classical Learning*, 28.

140. McCardell, *Idea of a Southern Nation*; Faust, *Ideology of Slavery*; Harrington, "Classical Antiquity."

141. Miles, "Old South."

142. Wish, "Aristotle, Plato, and the Mason-Dixon Line."

143. Holmes, "Observations," 193.

144. Josiah Priest, quoted in Wiesen, "Herodotus," 12.

145. On the North as Sparta, see Miles, "Old South," 271; on the South as Sparta, see Gildersleeve, "A Southerner in the Peloponnesian War," in Briggs, *Soldier and Scholar*, 398; on Macedonia, see Durrill, "Power of Ancient Words," 497.

146. Durrill, "Power of Ancient Words"; McCardell, *Idea of a Southern Nation*, ch. 5; Cremin, *American Education: The National Experience*, 507–11.

CHAPTER 3. FROM WORDS TO WORLDS

1. This view is explicitly stated in Laurence Veysey's justifiably influential *Emergence of the American University*: "Above all else, believers in mental discipline firmly identified themselves with a prescribed four-year course of study emphasizing the traditional subjects: Greek, Latin, mathematics, and to a lesser extent moral philosophy. In contrast, the primary demand of all academic reformers was for the transformation of the curriculum. On this front the issue between the defenders of piety and their critics was wholly joined. The protracted debate extended from before the Civil War to a culmination in 1884–85,

when the forces of orthodoxy made their last notable effort to stem the tide of change" (36). A useful critique of the earlier literature on the antebellum colleges appears in McLachlan, "American College."

2. Shelley, "Hellas," 8.

3. Patton, *Address,* 5.

4. Patton, *Lecture,* 12.

5. Felton, *Lecture on Classical Learning,* 16.

6. Holmes, "Four New Addresses," 283.

7. Felton, *Discourse Pronounced at the Inauguration,* 8.

8. Crosby, "Classical Study," 240.

9. Felton, "Bode's History," 462.

10. Persons, "Cyclical Theory," 163.

11. Crosby, "Classical Study," 247.

12. Felton, *Lecture on Classical Learning,* 16–17.

13. Ibid., 18.

14. Ibid., 32, 17.

15. Crosby, "Homer," 373.

16. Howe, *Making the American Self,* 122, 136–37. For the larger context of the idea of self-formation, see Taylor, *Sources of the Self.*

17. Marchand, *Down from Olympus,* 16.

18. Felton, *Lecture on Classical Learning,* 28.

19. "Felton's *Memorial of Dr. Popkin,*" 476.

20. Williams, *Culture and Society,* 84.

21. Felton, *Address Delivered at the Dedication of the New Building of Bristol Academy,* 13.

22. Channing, *Self-Culture,* 15, 14, 21.

23. Felton, *Address Pronounced August 15, 1828,* 11, 8.

24. "Acquisition of the Greek Language," 250–51.

25. Only fifty-five Americans studied in German universities (mostly Göttingen and Berlin) between 1810 and 1840, and this antebellum group studied largely humanistic subjects and theology, not science (Diehl, *Americans and German Scholarship,* 55, 60). Everett, Patton, Bancroft, and Beck were those in the antebellum group with a Ph.D.

26. This mid-century academic landscape is laid out in Stevenson, *Scholarly Means to Evangelical Ends.*

27. For a description of the seminary, see Storr, *Beginnings of Graduate Education.*

28. Everett, *Addresses at the Inauguration,* 34; Storr, *Beginnings of Graduate Education,* 49–50; Chittenden, *History of the Sheffield Scientific School.*

29. "Sketch of the Life of Homer," 54.

30. Ibid., 55, for example, refers to Homer's "writings."

31. Lamberton, *Homer the Theologian.*

32. Knox, introduction to *The Odyssey,* 3–11.

33. Levine, *Battle of the Books,* 122–25.

34. Turner, *Greek Heritage*, 135–36, 138.

35. Grafton, *Defenders of the Text*, 214–43.

36. "Homeric Question," 388–89.

37. Grafton, *Defenders of the Text*, 223–24.

38. For the debate in England, see Turner, *Greek Heritage*, 135–86.

39. See the Bowdoin College catalogs for 1837 and 1847.

40. Hadley, *Diary of James Hadley*, 120.

41. Coleridge, *Introduction*, 6, 8.

42. Smith, *History of Greece*, 38–44.

43. Crosby, "Homer," 343; Felton, *Iliad* (1848), v; "Homeric Poems," 308.

44. Felton, *Iliad* (1848), xi.

45. "Homeric Poems," 308.

46. Coleridge, *Introduction*, 129.

47. Felton, *Iliad* (1833), iii–iv.

48. "Ancient Greece," 132.

49. Felton, *Iliad* (1848), xi–xii.

50. Ibid., xii, xi, vii.

51. Turner, *Greek Heritage*, 141, 146, 154.

52. Coleridge, *Introduction*, 70–73.

53. Tyler, *Theology of the Greek Poets*, 135–36.

54. Coleridge, *Introduction*, 70.

55. "Homeric Question," 387.

56. Tyler, *Theology of the Greek Poets*, 97.

57. Hammond, *Remembrance of Amherst*, 13.

58. Tyler, *Theology of the Greek Poets*, 111.

59. Ibid., 73–74.

60. Hadley, *Diary of James Hadley*, 65.

61. Dover, "Expurgation of Greek Literature."

62. Vance, *America's Rome*, esp. ch. 5.

63. Felton, "Classic Mythology," 331–32.

64. James Logan, quoted in Reinhold, *Classick Pages*, 143.

65. Felton prepared *Clouds of Aristophanes* (1841), *Agamemnon of Aeschylus* (1847), and *Birds of Aristophanes* (1849); Stuart, *Oedipus Tyrannus of Sophocles* (1837); and Woolsey, *Alcestis of Euripides* (1834), *Antigone of Sophocles* (1835), *Electra of Sophocles* (1837), and *Prometheus Bound of Aeschylus* (1837).

66. Felton, "Alcestis of Euripides," 371; Woolsey, *Antigone of Sophocles*, iv.

67. Brasse, *Plays*.

68. Felton, *Lecture on Classical Learning*, 19.

69. "Recent Editions of the Antigone of Sophocles," 103.

70. "Antigone of Sophocles," 66.

71. Everett, "Circumstances," 77–78.

72. Turner, *Greek Heritage*, 213–34.

73. "Antigone of Sophocles," 64–65.

74. "Beauties of the Grecian Drama," 58.

75. "Recent Editions of the Antigone of Sophocles," 103–4.

76. Aristotle, *Poetics*, 25.

77. "Antigone of Sophocles," 66.

78. Felton, "Alcestis of Euripides," 371, 376.

79. Aristotle, *Poetics*, 49.

80. Woolsey, *Antigone of Sophocles*, iv–v.

81. "Antigone of Sophocles," 68.

82. Woolsey, *Antigone of Sophocles*, iv.

83. Felton, "Alcestis of Euripides," 375.

84. For more on Antigone as a nineteenth-century American heroine, see Winterer, "Victorian Antigone."

85. "Character of Medea," 385. See also Goodwin, "Medea," 326–27; Besant, "By Celia's Arbor," 503; and Davis, "Fine Arts in the South," 657.

86. Stuart, *On the Classical Tongues*, 13.

87. Felton, "Alcestis of Euripides," 382.

88. Schlegel, *Lectures*, 97.

89. Ibid., 98. See also Felton, *Discourse Pronounced at the Inauguration*, 22–23.

90. Felton, *Lecture on Classical Learning*, 20.

CHAPTER 4. CLASSICAL CIVILIZATION CONSECRATED

1. Adams, *Education of Henry Adams*, 53.

2. Solomon, *In the Company of Educated Women*, 62.

3. Anderson, *Education of Blacks in the South*, ch. 6.

4. Burke, *American Collegiate Populations*, ch. 5; Snyder, *One Hundred Twenty Years of American Education*, 64; Solomon, *In the Company of Educated Women*, 62.

5. Broome, "College Admission Requirements," 243.

6. *Circular of the Trustees and Faculty of the North Western University*, 7; *Catalogue of the Northwestern University*, 23–24.

7. Morison, *Development of Harvard University*, 57. These figures represent declining numbers amid overall rising enrollments. For Greek, 165 freshmen enrolled in 1884 (64 percent of the 258 freshmen), compared with just 86 students in 1900 (16 percent of 537 freshmen). For Latin, 199 freshmen enrolled in 1884 (77 percent of 258), compared with just 161 students in 1900 (30 percent of 537).

8. Pierson, *Yale Book of Numbers*, 267–69. Pierson defines a man-year-hour as "a scale for measuring student interest" that rests on the presumption that "one full-year, three-hour course in a given subject normally represented 5 percent of a student's total study time in college."

9. Smalley, "Status of Classical Studies."

10. Snyder, *One Hundred Twenty Years of American Education*, 30.

11. Kelsey, *Latin and Greek in American Education*, 3. In 1890, 100,144 students, or 33.62 percent, enrolled in Latin; in 1910, 405,504, or 49.59 percent, did.

12. Latimer, *What's Happened to Our High Schools?* 26–27. Latimer's tables list only total enrollments and the percentage of students taking Latin. I have estimated absolute numbers from his figures.

13. Atkinson, *Classical and Scientific Studies*, 11; Farrar, *Essays on a Liberal Education*; Stray, *Classics Transformed*.

14. Taylor, *Classical Study*.

15. Veysey, *Emergence of the American University*, 61.

16. Grafton and Jardine, *From Humanism to the Humanities*, xii–xiii.

17. Adams, *College Fetich*, 5.

18. Youmans, *Culture Demanded by Modern Life*, vi.

19. Youmans, "College Fetich Once More," 704.

20. Bigelow, *Modern Inquiries*, 39–40.

21. Eliot, "What Is a Liberal Education?" 208.

22. Coulter, *Work of a University*, 4.

23. Veysey, *Emergence of the American University*, 13.

24. Rudolph, *Curriculum*, 191–96.

25. Shorey, "Are the Degrees to Be Merged?" 50; Hadley et al., "Are the Degrees to Be Preserved or to Be Merged?" 71, 74, 78.

26. Wright, "Foreign-Language Requirements," 323–37.

27. Ross, *Origins of American Social Science*, chs. 1–3; Ross, "Liberal Tradition"; Pocock, *Machiavellian Moment*.

28. John Bates Clark, quoted in Ross, *Origins of American Social Science*, 119.

29. David Hollinger, "Inquiry and Uplift: Late Nineteenth-Century American Academics and the Moral Efficacy of Scientific Practice," and Dorothy Ross, "American Social Science and the Idea of Progress," in Haskell, *Authority of Experts*, 142–56 and 157–75, respectively.

30. Roberts and Turner, *Sacred and the Secular University*, 24–27.

31. Ross, "American Social Science," 162.

32. Westbrook, *John Dewey and American Democracy*, 75–76.

33. Ibid., 98.

34. Mavrogenes, "Teaching of Greek and Latin."

35. R. M. Wenley, "The Nature of Culture Studies," in Kelsey, *Latin and Greek in American Education*, 57; W. Y. Sellar, "Theories of Classical Teaching," in Taylor, *Classical Study*, 267; James Loeb, "The Value of Humanistic, Particularly Classical, Studies as a Training for Men of Affairs," in Kelsey, *Latin and Greek in American Education*, 171; James Jarves, quoted in Vance, *America's Rome*, 370.

36. See, e.g., the use in Porter, "Greek and a Liberal Education," 198.

37. Porter, "Greek and a Liberal Education," 211–12.

38. Examples of those books still in use today are Goodwin's *Syntax of the Moods and Tenses of the Greek Verb* (1860); Gildersleeve, *Pindar. The Olympian and Pythian Odes*

(1885); and Smyth, *Greek Melic Poets* (1900) (see Briggs, *Biographical Dictionary of North American Classicists*, s.v. "Goodwin, William Watson," "Gildersleeve, Basil Lanneau," and "Smyth, Herbert Weir").

39. On the wider Gilded Age critique of the industrial age, see Sproat, *Best Men*. On the New York circle of critics of high culture, see Bender, *New York Intellect*, ch. 5.

40. Paul Shorey, "National Culture and Classical Education," in Shorey, *Roosevelt Lectures*; West, *Value of the Classics*; Kelsey, *Latin and Greek in American Education*.

41. Hoeveler, *New Humanism*.

42. Turner, *Greek Heritage*, 17–36.

43. Raleigh, *Matthew Arnold and American Culture*. Frieze, for example, quoted Arnold at length when he addressed the regents and faculty as interim president.

44. Arnold, *Culture and Anarchy*, 204, 206, 209, 274–76, 278.

45. Basil Lanneau Gildersleeve, "Classics and Colleges," in *Essays and Studies*, 56, 60.

46. Basil Lanneau Gildersleeve, "Limits of Culture," in ibid., 16.

47. Wright, *College in the University*, 22.

48. Norton, "Work of the Archaeological Institute of America," 15.

49. Tomlinson, "Progress in Means of Teaching the Classics," 400, 408.

50. Veysey, *Emergence of the American University*, 44.

51. Humphreys, "Common-Sense in Classics," 295.

52. Turner, *Liberal Education of Charles Eliot Norton*, 386.

53. Gildersleeve, "Limits of Culture," in *Essays and Studies*, 5.

54. Lane, "German Universities," 452.

55. Frieze, "Art Museums," 435–37.

56. Benjamin Rush, quoted in Richard, *Founders and the Classics*, 202.

57. Gildersleeve, "Classics and Colleges," in *Essays and Studies*, 45.

58. Porter, "Greek and a Liberal Education," 218.

59. Shorey, "Philology and Classical Philology," 182.

60. Shorey, "National Culture and Classical Education," in Shorey, *Roosevelt Lectures*, 361.

61. Shorey, *Assault on Humanism*, 51–63.

62. Veysey, "The Plural Organized Worlds of the Humanities," in Oleson and Voss, *Organization of Knowledge*, 51–106; Kuklick, "Emergence of the Humanities"; Kimball, *Orators and Philosophers*; Graff, *Professing Literature*; Turner, "Secularization and Sacralization."

63. Roberts and Turner, *Sacred and the Secular University*, 75.

64. Charles B. Lamborn, "Lectures on Roman History and Literature before Junior Class by Prof. H. S. Frieze," March 1858, HSFP.

65. Wright, *College in the University*, 17.

66. See, e.g., Benedict, "Anthropology and the Humanities"; and Redfield, "Social Science among the Humanities."

67. Tolley, "Science Education of American Girls," 352.

68. Rogers, *Why American Marriages Fail*, 56.

69. Solomon, *In the Company of Educated Women,* 62.

70. Horowitz, *Power and the Passion of M. Carey Thomas,* 69, 152.

71. Tolley, "Science Education of American Girls," 350. Nonetheless, women at the turn of the century found the field of professional archaeology easier to enter than philology; women were believed to be less capable of linguistic mastery and more adept at the object-centered study of material remains.

72. Zimmerman, "Daughters of Main Street," 157.

73. Tolley, "Science Education of American Girls," 350, statistic from 349.

74. Shteir, *Cultivating Women.*

75. Tolley, "Science Education of American Girls," 345–56.

76. Ibid., 352.

77. On the relationship between secularization and the rise of the humanities, see Turner, "Secularization and Sacralization"; Marsden, *Soul of the American University;* Reuben, *Making of the Modern University,* esp. ch. 3; and Roberts and Turner, *Sacred and the Secular University.*

78. Marsden, *Soul of the American University,* 158.

79. Thomas, *Culture and Service,* 9.

80. *Nation,* 2 January 1890, 8.

81. Angell, *Reminiscences of James Burrill Angell,* 23–24.

82. White, *Autobiography of Andrew Dickson White,* 1:41.

83. Angell, *Memorial Discourse,* 18–19.

84. Felton, "Boston Public Schools," 446; Cornelius Felton to Charles Eliot Norton, 21 November 1852, Charles Eliot Norton Papers, bMS Am 1088 (2072), by permission of the Houghton Library, Harvard University.

85. Allison, *Historical Sketch of Hamilton College,* 31–33.

86. Tyler, *History of Amherst College,* 427.

87. Hammond, *Remembrance of Amherst,* 13.

88. On idealism versus rationalism and positivism in British thought in the nineteenth century, see Turner, "Triumph of Idealism."

89. Reuben, *Making of the Modern University,* 88–95; see also Kuklick, *Rise of American Philosophy,* 140–58.

90. *Calendar of the University of Michigan,* 51–52; John Dewey, "Inventory of Philosophy Taught in American Colleges" (1886), in *John Dewey,* 116–21; idem, "Philosophy in American Universities: The University of Michigan" (1890), in ibid., 3:90–92.

91. *Catalogue of Yale College,* 77.

92. Gerould, "What, Then, Is Culture?" 546–47.

93. Jane Croly, quoted in Martin, *Sound of Our Own Voices,* 85–86.

94. Benjamin Jowett, quoted in Jenkyns, *Victorians and Ancient Greece,* 250. See also Glucker, "Two Platos in Victorian Britain."

95. Lewis, "Jowett's Plato," 154.

96. Courtney, "Socrates, Buddha, and Christ," 73. See also "Plato in History."

97. *Catalogue of Yale College,* 74.

98. Norman, *Harvard Greek Play*, 27.

99. Lucien Price, quoted in Morison, *Development of Harvard University*, 63–64.

100. The penciled "Amen" appears in an interlined copy of Woolsey, *Antigone of Sophocles*, 57, at the Joseph Regenstein Library, University of Chicago.

101. Goodwin, *Report of the Director*, 11.

102. Proceedings of the Board of Regents, 29 March 1855.

103. The others were Professor James Fishburn, of Washington College, Virginia (Andrew Dixon White to James Burrill Angell, 24 December 1889, JBAP), and Charles Morris Smith.

104. White, *Autobiography of Andrew Dickson White*, 1:41.

105. Henry Simmons Frieze, "Diaries of Henry Simmons Frieze," typed by Francis Willey Kelsey, 182–327 (13 March–17 June 1856), HSFP; White, *Diaries of Andrew D. White*, 103–28.

106. Charles Morris Smith to Angell, 4 January 1890, HSFP.

107. Vance, *America's Rome*, 1–42.

108. Ibid., 5.

109. Ibid., 31.

110. Frieze, "Diaries of Henry Simmons Frieze," 189 (c. 13 March 1856), HSFP.

111. Ibid., 246 (29 April 1856), HSFP.

112. Turner, *Greek Heritage*, 63.

113. Frieze, "Diaries of Henry Simmons Frieze," 383 (29 July 1856), HSFP.

114. Angell, *Memorial Discourse*, 17–18.

115. Frieze, *Descriptive Catalogue*; Frieze, *Catalogue of the Museum of Art*; D'Ooge, *Catalogue of the Gallery*; Faberman, *Illustrated Catalogue*, 1–5.

116. Frieze, *Catalogue of the Museum of Art*, 1.

117. Proceedings of the Board of Regents, 30 September 1857, 30 September 1863.

118. Frieze, *Descriptive Catalogue*, 24.

119. Smith, *Study of the History of Art*, v.

120. "1890–91. Fine Arts 3. Mid-Year Examination, 7 February, 1891," "1890–91. Fine Arts 3. Final Examination, June 4, 1891," HUA.

121. Allan Marquand, "The History of Art as a University Study" (July 1891), Allan Marquand Papers, published with permission of the Princeton University Library. For more on the early days of art history at Princeton, see Lavin, *Eye of the Tiger*.

122. Frieze, *Catalogue of the Museum of Art*, "Introductory Notice."

123. Angell, *Memorial Discourse*, 23.

124. Edwin C. Goddard, student notebook, HSFP; Frieze, *Catalogue of the Museum of Art*, "Introductory Notice."

125. *Catalogue of Dartmouth College*, 46.

126. Tyler, *History of Amherst College*, 428.

127. Kuzniewski, *Thy Honored Name*, 174.

128. Wright, "Preface to the English Translation," in Collignon, *Manual of Greek Archaeology*, x.

129. Wright, *College in the University,* 20.

130. Basil Lanneau Gildersleeve, "Grammar and Aesthetics," in *Essays and Studies,* 151; Gildersleeve, "Classics and Colleges," in ibid., 52.

131. Gildersleeve, "Limits of Culture," in ibid., 18–19.

132. Gildersleeve, "Classics and Colleges," in ibid., 59.

133. Ibid., 58; this theme is also pursued in Gildersleeve, "Classical Study."

134. Gildersleeve, "Grammar and Aesthetics," in *Essays and Studies,* 157.

135. See Olender, *Languages of Paradise,* ch. 1.

136. William Dwight Whitney, "Philology," in *Encyclopaedia Britannica,* 11th ed. See also Alter, "William Dwight Whitney."

137. Hale, *Aims and Methods,* 42.

138. Frieze to Angell, 7 December 1871, JBAP.

139. Kelsey, "Is There a Science of Classical Philology?" 384, 373.

140. On the origins of the idea of "Western civilization," see Turner, *Liberal Education of Charles Eliot Norton,* 384–88; and Allardyce, "Rise and Fall."

141. Bryson, *Man and Society;* Stocking, *Victorian Anthropology;* Stocking, *Race, Culture, and Evolution.*

142. Clapp, "Study of the Classics," 97.

143. Wright, "Preface to the English Translation," in Collignon, *Manual of Greek Archaeology,* ix.

144. Norton, "Work of the Archaeological Institute of America," 15.

145. Harris, "On the Function of the Study of Latin and Greek," 7.

146. Nicholas Murray Butler, quoted in leaflet for the third annual meeting of American Classical League, 3 July 1922, Kelsey Museum Papers.

147. Norton, "Work of the Archaeological Institute of America," 15.

148. Angell, *Memorial Discourse,* 23–24.

149. Wenley, "Nature of Culture Studies," in Kelsey, *Latin and Greek in American Education,* 53, 56.

150. Noah Porter, "The American Colleges," in Taylor, *Classical Study,* 148–49.

151. Norlin, "Paul Shorey the Teacher," 189; Putnam, "Paul Shorey," 797.

152. Cook, "The Province of English Philology," 99.

153. *Catalogue of the University of South Carolina,* 52, 56.

154. Hamlin, "Attitude of the Christian Teacher," 3.

155. Felton, *Lecture on Classical Learning,* 16–17.

156. The classical world was described as "different" in Frost, "Greek among Required Studies," 345; as "distant" in Fisher, "Study of Greek," 121; as "vanished," "remote," and "alien" in Wright, *College in the University,* 18, 21; and as "unlike" by J. S. Mill, quoted in Taylor, *Classical Study,* 129.

157. Adams, *College Fetich,* 8–9.

158. Wright, *College in the University,* 21.

159. Trautmann, "Revolution in Ethnological Time"; Trautmann, *Lewis Henry Morgan,* 220–22.

160. Manatt and Tsountas, *Mycenaean Age*, xxi–xxii.

161. On Harrison, see Beard, *Invention of Jane Harrison*, and Peacock, *Jane Ellen Harrison*; on Frazer, see Ackerman, *J. G. Frazer*; on Morgan, see Trautmann, *Lewis Henry Morgan*; and on the Cambridge Ritualists, see Ackerman, *Myth and Ritual School*, and Calder, *Cambridge Ritualists Reconsidered*.

162. Harrison, *Prolegomena*, x, 4, 7; Harrison, *Religion of Ancient Greece*, 8–10.

163. Fustel de Coulanges, *Ancient City*, 9–10.

164. G. R. Elliott, "The Pride of Modernity," in Foerster, *Humanism and America*, 77.

165. Whitehill, *Museum of Fine Arts Boston*; DiMaggio, "Cultural Entrepreneurship in Nineteenth-Century Boston: The Creation" and "Cultural Entrepreneurship in Nineteenth-Century Boston, Part II"; Harris, "Gilded Age Revisited"; Tomkins, *Merchants and Masterpieces*; Rydell, *All the World's a Fair*; Horowitz, *Culture and the City*; Levine, *Highbrow/Lowbrow*.

166. Vance, *America's Rome*, 372–75; Yegül, *Gentlemen of Instinct and Breeding*; Valentine and Valentine, *American Academy in Rome*.

167. Vance, *America's Rome*, 374–75; Lears, *No Place of Grace*.

168. Adams, *Education of Henry Adams*, 367.

169. Bushman, *Refinement of America*, 409–11.

170. Jenkyns, *Dignity and Decadence*, ch. 7.

171. Stevenson, *Victorian Homefront*, esp. ch. 1; Kasson, *Rudeness and Civility*, 175; Howe, *Antiques from the Victorian Home*, 46.

172. Wright, *Complete Home*, 512.

173. Banner, *American Beauty*, 110–11; Newton, *Health, Art, and Reason*, 37–58.

174. Case and Case, *We Called It Culture*.

175. Church, *Callias*.

176. Erskine, *Private Life of Helen of Troy*, 42.

177. Rubin, *Making of Middlebrow Culture*, 179.

178. Martin, *Sound of Our Own Voices*, 12, 17–18, 25, 68, 78, 89, 91, 97.

179. Trachtenberg, *Incorporation of America*, 149.

180. Addams, *Twenty Years at Hull-House*, 388–89.

181. Bender, *Intellect and Public Life*, 30–46.

182. Kelly, *In the New England Fashion*, 249.

183. The quotation appears in Veysey, *Emergence of the American University*, 278. See also Stevenson, "Preparing for Public Life," 150–77; and Horowitz, *Campus Life*, 36–49.

184. William Watson Goodwin, quoted in Norman, *Harvard Greek Play*, 12.

185. Norman, *Harvard Greek Play*, 35–36.

186. Peter Arnott, "North America," in Walton, *Living Greek Theatre*, 355.

187. Norman, *Harvard Greek Play*, 49–50.

188. Ibid., 51–52.

189. Ibid., 47.

190. Ibid., 31.

191. Brown, *History of the New York Stage*, passim.

192. The program is reproduced in Norman, *Harvard Greek Play*, 122–23. I thank my colleague Jonathan Roth for translating the Greek in the program.

193. Norman, *Harvard Greek Play*, 105.

CHAPTER 5. SCHOLARSHIP VERSUS CULTURE

1. The quotation appears in John Higham, "The Matrix of Specialization," in Oleson and Voss, *Organization of Knowledge*, 7.

2. Burke, *American Collegiate Populations*, 217; Snyder, *One Hundred Twenty Years of American Education*, 75, table 23.

3. Bledstein, *Culture of Professionalism*, 271.

4. Waldstein, *Essays on the Art of Pheidias*, 26.

5. Briggs and Benario, *Basil Lanneau Gildersleeve*; Gildersleeve, *Letters*; Briggs, *Soldier and Scholar*.

6. Gildersleeve to Houghton Mifflin Company, 8 September 1886, in Gildersleeve, *Letters*, 169.

7. Gildersleeve, "Classics and Colleges," in *Essays and Studies*, 76.

8. Goodwin, "Growth of the Graduate School," 177.

9. Kelsey, "Is There a Science of Classical Philology?" 373.

10. Wright, *College in the University*, 19.

11. Kelsey, "Is There a Science of Classical Philology?" 372.

12. Goodwin, "Growth of the Graduate School," 177.

13. Gildersleeve, "Classics and Colleges," in *Essays and Studies*, 74–75; Gildersleeve "Grammar and Aesthetics," in ibid., 131.

14. For the history of the APA see Moore, "History of the American Philological Association."

15. Kelsey, "Is There a Science of Classical Philology?" 384.

16. Gildersleeve, "Grammar and Aesthetics," in *Essays and Studies*, 133–34.

17. Ibid., 131.

18. Gildersleeve to Daniel Coit Gilman, 8 August 1880, in Gildersleeve, *Letters*, 120.

19. T.E.W., "American Classicism," 93.

20. Kelsey, "Is There a Science of Classical Philology?" 385.

21. Archaeological Institute of America (hereafter AIA), *First Annual Report of the Executive Committee, 1879–1880*, 6, 8. More on the history of the early AIA can be found in Dyson, *Ancient Marbles to American Shores*; Turner, *Liberal Education of Charles Eliot Norton*; and Sheftel, "Archaeological Institute of America."

22. AIA, *First Annual Report of the Executive Committee, 1879–1880*, 5; Whitehill, *Museum of Fine Arts Boston*, 1:9; DiMaggio, "Cultural Entrepreneurship in Nineteenth-Century Boston: The Creation," 41.

23. AIA, *First Annual Report of the Executive Committee, 1879–1880*, 9–11.

24. AIA, *Seventeenth Annual Report of the Executive Committee, 1895–1896*, 1–36.

25. AIA, *First Annual Report of the Executive Committee, 1879–1880*, 21–23.

26. AIA, *Fifth Annual Report of the Executive Committee, 1883–1884*, 27–28.

27. The long tradition of private, unsystematic collecting is summarized in Dinsmoor, "Early American Studies of Mediterranean Archaeology."

28. Whitehill, *Museum of Fine Arts Boston*, 1:5–9.

29. John Taylor Johnson, "The Cesnola Collection," in Cesnola, *Cyprus*, 455. See also McFadden, *Glitter and the Gold*; and *Guide to the Cesnola Collection*.

30. Basil Lanneau Gildersleeve, "University Work in America in Classical Philology," in *Essays and Studies*, 108.

31. Kuklick, *Puritans in Babylon*, 28.

32. Marchand, *Down from Olympus*, 75–76.

33. On Schliemann, see Traill, *Schliemann of Troy*; and Marchand, *Down from Olympus*, 118–24.

34. The results of the Austrian, French, and England excavations are summarized in Fowler and Wheeler, *Handbook of Greek Archaeology*; and Marchand, *Down from Olympus*, ch. 3.

35. Education Minister Falk (1879), quoted in Marchand, *Down from Olympus*, 95.

36. Gildersleeve, "Classics and Colleges," in *Essays and Studies*, 75.

37. Martin Brimmer, in *American Architect and Building News*, 30 October 1880, quoted in Whitehill, *Museum of Fine Arts Boston*, 1:13.

38. Charles Eliot Norton to John H. Haynes, 7 March 1881, AIAP.

39. Francis Parkman and the other, anonymous member are quoted in Dort, "Archaeological Institute of America," 197.

40. Bandelier, "Archaeological Chronology," 133.

41. Norton to Thomas Carlyle, 26 July 1880, in Norton, *Letters of Charles Eliot Norton*, 2:111–12.

42. Thomas Day Seymour to Norton, 17 October 1895, AIAP.

43. "Relation of the Journal," 259–61.

44. Russell Sturgis to Seth Low, 24 February 1892, AIAP.

45. The phrase "exact science" is quoted in AIA, *Fifth Annual Report of the Executive Committee, 1883–1884*, 30.

46. AIA, *First Annual Report of the Executive Committee, 1879–1880*, 23–24.

47. Martin Brimmer to Norton, 20 November 1881, AIAP.

48. The description in this and the following three paragraphs is compiled largely from Clarke, *Report on the Investigations at Assos, 1881*; and Stillwell, *Princeton Encyclopedia of Classical Sites*, s.v. "Assos."

49. Clarke, *Report on the Investigations at Assos, 1881*, 105.

50. Ibid., 115, 114; see also plates 14 and 15.

51. Ibid., 119.

52. Clarke, *Report on the Investigations at Assos, 1882, 1883*, 14.

53. AIA, *Second Annual Report of the Executive Committee, 1880–1881*, 26–27.

54. Turner, *Liberal Education of Charles Eliot Norton*, 299.

55. J. W. Ludlow to Norton, 16 April 1883, AIAP.

56. Nathaniel Hawthorne, quoted in Vance, *America's Rome,* 371.

57. Congdon, "Assos Journals of Francis H. Bacon," 84.

58. William R. Ware to Norton, 10 September 1880, AIAP.

59. Marchand, *Down from Olympus,* 77–80.

60. W. S. Kennedy to Norton, 23 September 1880, AIAP.

61. AIA, *Second Annual Report of the Executive Committee, 1880–1881,* 29.

62. Norton to J. R. Lowell, 11 February 1881, in Norton, *Letters of Charles Eliot Norton,* 2:115.

63. G. H. Heap to James G. Blaine, 11 May 1881, AIAP.

64. Clarke, *Report on the Investigations at Assos, 1881,* 16.

65. AIA, *Fifth Annual Report of the Executive Committee, 1883–1884,* 21–25.

66. William C. Lawton to Norton, 1 November 1881; Edward Robinson to Norton, 14 November 1881; Charles Bradley to Norton, 15 December 1881; Charles Howard Walker to Norton, 18 December 1881; William James Stillman to Norton, 24 January 1882; Haynes to Stillman, 26 January 1882; Stillman to Norton, 25 March 1882; Lawton to Norton, 31 June 1882, all in AIAP.

67. Clarke, *Report on the Investigations at Assos, 1881,* 23–24.

68. Congdon, "Assos Journals of Francis H. Bacon," 88.

69. Clarke, *Report on the Investigations at Assos, 1882, 1883,* 26–30.

70. "Extract from a Tour in the Troad by Professor R. C. Jebb" (1883), in AIA, *Fourth Annual Report of the Executive Committee, 1882–1883,* 44.

71. G. Perrot to Norton, 6 December 1881, AIAP.

72. Stark, quoted in Alfred Emerson, "Recent Progress in Classical Archaeology," in AIA, *Tenth Annual Report of the Executive Committee, 1888–1889,* 62.

73. Edward Clarke Cabot, quoted in AIA, *Fifth Annual Report of the Executive Committee, 1883–1884,* 27.

74. AIA, *First Annual Report of the Executive Committee, 1879–1880,* 23.

75. Histories of the school include Lord, *History;* and Meritt, *History.*

76. AIA, *First Annual Report of the Committee on the American School of Classical Studies, 1881–82,* 54.

77. Seymour to Norton, [1895?], AIAP.

78. AIA, *Third Annual Report of the Committee on the American School of Classical Studies at Athens, 1883–84,* 11.

79. AIA, *First, Second, and Third Annual Reports of the Managing Committee,* 10.

80. Dyson, *Ancient Marbles to American Shores,* 53–54.

81. *Le cinquantenaire de L'École française d'Athènes,* frontispiece.

82. Goodwin, *Report of the Director,* 7, 12, 13.

83. Haskell, *History and Its Images,* 4.

84. Seymour, *Bulletin of the School of Classical Studies,* 15.

85. Goodwin, *Report of the Director,* 9–10.

86. AIA, *Bulletin of the School of Classical Studies,* 19.

87. These statistics are derived from Seymour, *Bulletin of the School of Classical Studies,*

NOTES TO PAGES 173–183 / 207

57–69. Of the 128 students at the school, 41 either entered with a Ph.D. in hand or earned one after their year(s) at Athens. Of these 41, 30 obtained their degrees from American universities (chiefly Johns Hopkins, Yale, and Harvard), and 11 from foreign universities, all but 1 of these from German universities.

88. AIA, *Bulletin of the School of Classical Studies,* 19–20.

89. Charles Edwin Bennett, quoted in Dyson, *Ancient Marbles to American Shores,* 55.

90. AIA, *Ninth Annual Report of the Committee on the American School of Classical Studies at Athens, 1889–90,* 31.

91. AIA, *Fifteenth Annual Report of the Committee on the American School of Classical Studies at Athens, 1895–96,* 50–51.

92. These statistics are derived from Seymour, *Bulletin of the School of Classical Studies,* 57–69.

93. See Veysey, *Emergence of the American University,* ch. 5.

94. Snyder, *One Hundred Twenty Years of American Education,* table 28 and fig. 28.

95. For information on the University of Michigan School of Political Science and early ideals of graduate education, see Turner and Bernard, "Prussian Road to University?" Quotations are from 31–32.

96. Goodwin, "Growth of the Graduate School," 175.

97. Ibid.

98. Hoeveler, *New Humanism,* 8, 11, 19, 116–17, 117 n. 18, 121.

99. Wright, *Address on the Place of Original Research,* 14.

EPILOGUE

1. Kernan, *What's Happened to the Humanities?* 4, 203, 213.

2. West, *Value of the Classics,* 359.

3. Kopff, introduction, and Shorey, "American Scholarship," in Shorey, *Roosevelt Lectures,* xix and 383–403, respectively.

4. LaFleur, "Latina Resurgens," 126.

5. Hansen and Heath, *Who Killed Homer?* 3.

6. Rudolph, *Curriculum,* 246.

7. Ibid.

8. Allardyce, "Rise and Fall"; Segal, "'Western Civ' and the Staging of History."

9. Allardyce, "Rise and Fall," 707.

10. *General Education in a Free Society,* 53.

11. Kernan, *What's Happened to the Humanities?* 5–6.

12. Bloom, *Closing of the American Mind;* Levine, *Opening of the American Mind;* and Hirsch, *Cultural Literacy,* are just three of many contributions to this debate.

13. Bernal, *Black Athena;* Lefkowitz and Rogers, *Black Athena Revisited;* Lefkowitz, *Not Out of Africa.*

14. Culham and Edmunds, *Classics.*

15. Hansen and Heath, *Who Killed Homer?* Kernan, *What's Happened to the Humanities?*

WORKS CITED

MANUSCRIPT COLLECTIONS

Bentley Historical Library. University of Michigan.
    James Burrill Angell Papers.
    Henry Simmons Frieze Papers.
    Kelsey Museum Papers.
    Proceedings of the Board of Regents.
Boston University.
    Archaeological Institute of America Papers.
Harvard University Archives.
Houghton Library. Harvard University.
    Charles Eliot Norton Papers.
Princeton University.
    Allan Marquand Papers.

PUBLISHED SOURCES

Ackerman, Robert. *J. G. Frazer: His Life and Work.* Cambridge: Cambridge Univ. Press, 1987.

———. *The Myth and Ritual School: J. G. Frazer and the Cambridge Ritualists.* New York: Garland, 1991.

"Acquisition of the Greek Language." *Knickerbocker* 8 (September 1836): 249–56.

Adam, Alexander. *Latin Grammar, with Some Improvements, and the Following Additions: Rules for the Right Pronunciation of the Latin Language; a Metrical Key to the Odes of Horace; a List of Latin Authors Arranged According to the Different Ages of Roman Literature; Tables, Showing the Value of the Various Coins, Weights, and Measures, Used among the Romans.* Edited by Benjamin A. Gould. Boston: Hilliard, Gray, 1832.

———. *Roman Antiquities: Or, an Account of the Manners and Customs of the Romans; Reflecting Their Government, Magistracy, Laws, Judicial Proceedings, Religion, Games, Military and Naval Affairs, Dress, Exercise, Baths, Marriages, Divorces, Funerals,*

Weights and Measures, Coins, Method of Writing, Houses, Gardens, Agriculture, Carriages, Public Buildings, &c. &c. Designed Chiefly to Illustrate the Latin Classics, by Explaining Words and Phrases, from the Rites and Customs to Which They Refer. Philadelphia: Mathew Carey, 1807.

Adams, Charles Francis. *A College Fetich. An Address Delivered before the Harvard Chapter of the Fraternity of the Phi Beta Kappa, in Sanders Theatre, Cambridge, June 28, 1883.* Boston: Lee & Shepard, 1883.

Adams, Charles Kendall. *Historical Sketch of the University of Michigan.* Ann Arbor, 1876.

Adams, Henry. *The Education of Henry Adams: An Autobiography.* 1918. Reprint. Boston: Houghton Mifflin, 1971.

Adams, John. *Papers of John Adams.* Edited by Robert Taylor. Vol. 1, *September 1755–October 1773.* Cambridge: Harvard Univ. Press, Belknap Press, 1977.

———. *The Works of John Adams, Second President of the United States: With a Life of the Author, Notes and Illustrations, by His Grandson Charles Francis Adams.* 10 vols. Boston: Charles C. Little and James Brown, 1850–56.

Addams, Jane. *Twenty Years at Hull-House, with Autobiographical Notes.* New York: Macmillan, 1910.

Allardyce, Gilbert. "The Rise and Fall of the Western Civilization Course." *American Historical Review* 87 (June 1982): 695–725.

Allison, Charles Elmer. *A Historical Sketch of Hamilton College, Clinton, New York.* Yonkers, N.Y.: Hubley, 1889.

Allmendiger, David F., Jr. *Paupers and Scholars: The Transformation of Student Life in Nineteenth-Century New England.* New York: St. Martin's, 1975.

Alter, Stephen G. "William Dwight Whitney and the Science of Language." Ph.D. diss., University of Michigan, 1993.

"Ancient and Modern Eloquence." *Southern Literary Messenger* 8 (March 1842): 169–85.

"Ancient Greece: Her History and Literature." *Southern Literary Messenger* 14 (March 1848): 129–39.

Anderson, James D. *The Education of Blacks in the South, 1860–1935.* Chapel Hill: Univ. of North Carolina Press, 1988.

Angell, James Burrill. *A Memorial Discourse on the Life and Services of Henry Simmons Frieze, L.L.D., Professor of Latin Language and Literature in the University from 1854 to 1889.* Ann Arbor: The University, 1890.

———. *The Reminiscences of James Burrill Angell.* New York: Longmans, Green, 1912.

"The Antigone of Sophocles." *Christian Review* 16 (January 1851): 64–77.

Archaeological Institute of America. *Bulletin of the School of Classical Studies at Athens. Report of William W. Goodwin.* Boston: Cupples, Upham, 1883.

———. *First Annual Report of the Committee on the American School of Classical Studies at Athens, 1881–82.* Cambridge, Mass.: John Wilson & Son, 1882.

———. *Third Annual Report of the Committee on the American School of Classical Studies at Athens, 1883–84.* Cambridge, Mass.: John Wilson & Son, 1884.

——. *Ninth Annual Report of the Committee on the American School of Classical Studies at Athens, 1889–90.* Cambridge, Mass.: John Wilson & Son, 1890.

——. *Fifteenth Annual Report of the Committee on the American School of Classical Studies at Athens, 1895–96.* Cambridge, Mass.: John Wilson & Son, 1896.

——. *First Annual Report of the Executive Committee, 1879–1880.* Cambridge, Mass.: John Wilson & Son, 1880.

——. *Second Annual Report of the Executive Committee, 1880–1881.* Cambridge, Mass.: John Wilson & Son, 1881.

——. *Fourth Annual Report of the Executive Committee, 1882–1883.* Cambridge, Mass.: John Wilson & Son, 1883.

——. *Fifth Annual Report of the Executive Committee, 1883–1884.* Cambridge, Mass.: John Wilson & Son, 1884.

——. *Tenth Annual Report of the Executive Committee, 1888–1889.* Cambridge, Mass.: John Wilson & Son, 1889.

——. *Seventeenth Annual Report of the Executive Committee, 1895–1896.* Cambridge, Mass.: John Wilson & Son, 1896.

——. *First, Second, and Third Annual Reports of the Managing Committee of the American School of Classical Studies at Athens.* Cambridge, Mass.: John Wilson & Son, 1886.

Aristotle. *The Poetics.* Translated by W. Hamilton Fyfe. Cambridge: Harvard Univ. Press, 1946.

Arnold, Matthew. *Culture and Anarchy.* 1869. In *Arnold: Selected Prose,* edited by P. J. Keating, 202–300. London: Penguin Books, 1987.

Aronson, Sidney H. *Status and Kinship in the Higher Civil Service: Standards of Selection in the Administrations of John Adams, Thomas Jefferson, and Andrew Jackson.* Cambridge: Harvard Univ. Press, 1964.

Atkinson, William Parsons. *Classical and Scientific Studies, and the Great Schools of England: A Lecture Read before the Society of Arts of the Massachusetts Institute of Technology, April 6, 1865.* Cambridge, Mass.: Sever & Francis, 1865.

Axtell, James. "The Death of the Liberal Arts College." *History of Education Quarterly* 11 (1971): 339–52.

Bailyn, Bernard. *The Ideological Origins of the American Revolution.* Cambridge: Harvard Univ. Press, 1967.

Bancroft, George. "Buttmann's Greek Grammar." *North American Review* 18 (1824): 99–106.

——. "Jacobs' Greek Reader." *North American Review* 18 (1824): 280–84.

Bandelier, Adolph. "Archaeological Chronology." *Nation,* 12 August 1886, 132–33.

Banner, Lois. *American Beauty.* New York: Knopf, 1983.

Banning, Lance. *The Jeffersonian Persuasion: Evolution of a Party Ideology.* Ithaca: Cornell Univ. Press, 1978.

Barnard, Henry. "Cornelius Conway Felton." *American Journal of Education* 10 (March–June 1861): 265–96.

Baym, Nina. *American Women Writers and the Work of History, 1790–1860*. New Brunswick: Rutgers Univ. Press, 1995.

——. *Feminism and American Literary History: Essays*. New Brunswick: Rutgers Univ. Press, 1992.

Beard, Mary. *The Invention of Jane Harrison*. Cambridge: Harvard Univ. Press, 2000.

"Beauties of the Grecian Drama." *Southern Literary Messenger* 24 (January 1857): 58–67.

Bender, Thomas. *Intellect and Public Life: Essays on the Social History of Academic Intellectuals in the United States*. Baltimore: Johns Hopkins Univ. Press, 1993.

——. *New York Intellect: A History of Intellectual Life in New York City, from 1750 to the Beginnings of Our Own Time*. Baltimore: Johns Hopkins Univ. Press, 1987.

Benedict, Ruth. "Anthropology and the Humanities." *American Anthropologist*, n.s., 50 (October–December 1948): 585–94.

Bernal, Martin. *Black Athena: The Afrosasiatic Roots of Classical Civilization*. Vol. 1, *The Fabrication of Ancient Greece, 1785–1985*. New Brunswick: Rutgers Univ. Press, 1987.

Besant, Helen W. "By Celia's Arbor." *Appleton's Journal* 3 (December 1877): 491–504.

Bigelow, Jacob. *Elements of Technology, Taken Chiefly from a Course of Lectures Delivered at Cambridge, on the Application of the Sciences to the Useful Arts*. Boston: Hilliard, Gray, Little, & Wilkins, 1829.

——. *Modern Inquiries: Classical, Professional, and Miscellaneous*. Boston: Little, Brown, 1867.

Bisbee, Martin Davis. *General Catalogue of Dartmouth College and the Associated Schools, 1769–1900*. Hanover: The College, 1900.

Bledstein, Burton. *The Culture of Professionalism: The Middle Class and the Development of Higher Education in America*. New York: Norton, 1976.

Bloom, Allan. *The Closing of the American Mind: How Higher Education Has Failed Democracy and Impoverished the Souls of Today's Students*. New York: Simon & Schuster, 1987.

Bolingbroke, Henry St. John, Viscount. *Letters on the Study and Use of History*. 2 vols. 1752. Reprint. New York: Garland, 1970.

Bozeman, Theodore Dwight. *Protestants in an Age of Science: The Baconian Ideal and Antebellum American Religious Thought*. Chapel Hill: Univ. of North Carolina Press, 1977.

Brasse, John. *Plays, with Original Explanatory English Notes*. London: Longman, 1838.

Bridenbaugh, Carl. *Myths and Realities: Societies of the Colonial South*. Baton Rouge: Louisiana State Univ. Press, 1963.

Briggs, Ward W., Jr., ed. *Biographical Dictionary of North American Classicists*. Westport, Conn.: Greenwood, 1994.

——. *Soldier and Scholar: Basil Lanneau Gildersleeve and the Civil War*. Charlottesville: Univ. Press of Virginia, 1998.

Briggs, Ward W., Jr., and Herbert W. Benario, eds. *Basil Lanneau Gildersleeve: An American Classicist*. Baltimore: Johns Hopkins Univ. Press, 1986.

Brink, Jean R. *Female Scholars: A Tradition of Learned Women before 1800.* Montreal: Eden, 1980.

Broderick, Francis L. "Pulpit, Physics, and Politics: The Curriculum of the College of New Jersey, 1746–1794." *William and Mary Quarterly* 6 (January 1949): 42–68.

Broome, Edwin C. "A Historical and Critical Discussion of College Admission Requirements." *Columbia University Contributions to Philosophy, Psychology and Education* 11 (1903): 175–323.

Brown, Jerry Wayne. *The Rise of Biblical Criticism in America, 1800–1870: The New England Scholars.* Middletown, Conn.: Wesleyan Univ. Press, 1969.

Brown, Richard D. *Knowledge Is Power: The Diffusion of Information in Early America, 1700–1865.* New York: Oxford Univ. Press, 1989.

———. *The Strength of a People: The Idea of an Informed Citizenry in America, 1650–1870.* Chapel Hill: Univ. of North Carolina Press, 1996.

Brown, Robert Perkins, ed. *Memories of Brown: Traditions and Recollections Gathered from Many Sources.* Providence: Brown Alumni Magazine, 1909.

Brown, T. Allston. *A History of the New York Stage, from the First Performance in 1732 to 1901.* 3 vols. New York: Dodd, Mead, 1903.

Bryson, Gladys. *Man and Society: The Scottish Inquiry of the Eighteenth Century.* Princeton: Princeton Univ. Press, 1945.

Buckminster, Joseph S. "On the Dangers and Duties of Men of Letters." *Monthly Anthology* 7 (1809): 145–58.

Burke, Colin. *American Collegiate Populations: A Test of the Traditional View.* New York: New York Univ. Press, 1982.

Bushman, Richard. *The Refinement of America: Persons, Houses, Cities.* New York: Vintage Books, 1993.

Calder, William M., ed. *The Cambridge Ritualists Reconsidered: Proceedings of the First Oldfather Conference, Held on the Campus of the University of Illinois at Urbana-Champaign, April 27–30, 1989.* Atlanta: Scholars Press, 1991.

Caldwell, Charles. *Thoughts on Physical Education, and the True Mode of Improving the Condition of Man; and on the Study of the Greek and Latin Languages.* Edinburgh: Adam & Charles Black, 1836.

Calendar of the University of Michigan, for 1886–87. Ann Arbor: The University, 1887.

Capper, Charles. *Margaret Fuller: An American Romantic Life.* Vol. 1, *The Private Years.* New York: Oxford Univ. Press, 1992.

Carey, Mathew. "The Learned Languages." *Southern Literary Messenger* 2 (August 1836): 557–61.

"Carre and Sanderson's Seminary, or Remarks on Classical and Moral Education." *Port Folio,* 4th ser., 4, no. 6 (1815): 413–20.

Carrott, Richard G. *The Egyptian Revival: Its Sources, Monuments, and Meaning, 1808–1858.* Berkeley and Los Angeles: Univ. of California Press, 1978.

Carter, St. Leger Landon. "Pinkney's Eloquence." *Southern Literary Messenger* 1 (November 1834): 94–96.

Case, Victoria, and Robert Ormond Case. *We Called It Culture: The Story of Chautauqua*. New York: Doubleday, 1948.

Cassady, F. S. "Eloquence." *Ladies' Repository* 20 (June 1860): 360–61.

Catalogue of Dartmouth College, Together with the Thayer School of Civil Engineering and the Medical College. Hanover, N.H.: The College, 1897.

Catalogue of the Northwestern University, at Evanston, Illinois, for the Academic Year, 1870–'71 with a General Description of the University. Chicago: Spalding & La Monte, 1871.

Catalogue of the Officers and Students of Yale College. New Haven: Yale University, 1901.

Catalogue of the University of South Carolina, 1890–91. Columbia, S.C.: Presbyterian Publishing House, 1891.

Cesnola, Luigi Palma di. *Cyprus: Its Ancient Cities, Tombs, and Temples: A Narrative of Researches and Excavations during Ten Years' Residence in that Island*. New York: Harper & Bros., 1878.

Champlin, J. T. *The Oration of Demosthenes on the Crown, with Notes*. Boston: William H. Dennet, 1868.

Channing, William Ellery. *Self-Culture: An Address Introductory to the Franklin Lectures, Delivered at Boston, Sept. 1838*. In *The Works of William Ellery Channing*, 12–36. New York: Burt Franklin, 1970.

"Character of Medea." *Southern Literary Messenger* 5 (June 1839): 383–92.

Cheever, G. B. "Study of Greek Literature." *American Quarterly Register* 4 (1832): 273–90; 5 (1832): 33–46; 5 (1833): 218–36.

Chittenden, Russell H. *History of the Sheffield Scientific School of Yale University, 1846–1922*. New Haven: Yale Univ. Press, 1928.

Church, Alfred J. *Callias: A Tale of the Fall of Athens*. Meadville, Pa.: Chautauqua Century, 1891.

Circular of the Trustees and Faculty of the North Western University; Evanston, Illinois. Chicago: Rounds' Premium Printing Establishment, 1856.

Clapp, Edward B. "The Study of the Classics." *Overland Monthly and Outwest Magazine* 28, no. 163 (1896): 93–103.

Clarke, James Freeman. *James Freeman Clarke: Autobiography, Diary and Correspondence*. Edited by Edward Everett Hale. Boston: Houghton Mifflin, 1899.

Clarke, John. *An Essay upon Study. Wherein Directions are given for the Due Conduct thereof, and the Collection of a Library, proper for the Purpose, consisting of the Choicest Books in all the several Parts of Learning*. London: Arthur Bettesworth, 1731.

———. *An Essay upon the Education of Youth in Grammar Schools. In Which the Vulgar Method of Teaching is Examined, and a New One Proposed, for the More Easy and Speedy Training Up of Youth to the Knowledge of the Learned Languages; Together with History, Chronology, Geography &c*. 2d. ed. London: Arthur Bettesworth, 1730.

Clarke, Joseph Thacher. *Report on the Investigations at Assos, 1881*. 2 vols. Boston: A. Williams, 1882.

――. *Report on the Investigations at Assos, 1882, 1883*. New York: Macmillan, 1898.

Clarke, Martin L. *Classical Education in Britain, 1500–1900*. Cambridge: Cambridge Univ. Press, 1959.

"Classical Learning." *North American Review* 23 (1826): 142–50.

"The Classics in Modern Higher Education." *American Catholic Quarterly Review* 10 (January 1885): 140–62.

Cleveland, Henry. *Remarks on the Classical Education of Boys*. Boston: Hilliard, Gray, 1834.

Cmiel, Kenneth. *Democratic Eloquence: The Fight over Popular Speech in Nineteenth-Century America*. Berkeley and Los Angeles: Univ. of California Press, 1990.

Cohen, Sol, comp. *Education in the United States: A Documentary History*. 5 vols. New York: Random House, 1974.

Colbourn, Trevor. *The Lamp of Experience: Whig History and the Intellectual Origins of the American Revolution*. Chapel Hill: Univ. of North Carolina Press, 1965.

――. "Thomas Jefferson's Uses of the Past." *William and Mary Quarterly* 15 (January 1958): 56–70.

Coleridge, Henry Nelson. *Introduction to the Study of the Greek Classic Poets. Designed Principally for the Use of Young Persons at School and College*. London: John Murray, 1830.

"College Book III." *Publications of the Colonial Society of Massachusetts* 15 (1925): 169–332.

Collignon, Maxime. *A Manual of Greek Archaeology*. New York: Cassell & Company, 1886.

Congdon, Lenore O., ed. "The Assos Journals of Francis H. Bacon." *Archaeology* 27 (April 1974): 83–95.

Cook, Albert S. "The Province of English Philology" (1898). In *The Origins of Literary Studies in America: A Documentary Anthology*, edited by Gerald Graff and Michael Warner, 96–102. New York: Routledge, 1989.

Cooke, Josiah Parsons. "Scientific Culture: Its Spirit, Its Aim, and Its Methods." *Popular Science Monthly* 25 (September 1884): 1–24.

Coulter, John. *The Work of a University: Inaugural Address at Lake Forest, Ill., June 15, 1893*. Madison, Wis.: Tracy, Gibbs, 1894.

Courtney, W. L. "Socrates, Buddha, and Christ." *North American Review* 140 (1885): 63–77.

Cremin, Lawrence A. *American Education: The Colonial Experience, 1607–1783*. New York: Harper & Row, 1970.

――. *American Education: The National Experience, 1783–1876*. New York: Harper & Row, 1980.

Crosby, Alpheus. "Classical Study, as a Part of a Liberal Education." *American Quarterly Observer* 1 (1833): 237–51.

――. "Homer." *North American Review* 37 (1853): 340–74.

Cruttwell, Charles Thomas. *A History of Roman Literature: From the Earliest Period to the Death of Marcus Aurelius*. New York: Charles Scribner's Sons, 1877.

Culham, Phyllis, and Lowell Edmunds, eds. *Classics: A Discipline and Profession in Crisis?* Lanham, Md.: Univ. Press of America, 1989.

"The Curious Branches of Knowledge Vindicated." *Port Folio*, 5th ser., 5, no. 1 (1816): 13–22.

Dall, Caroline W. Healey. *Margaret and Her Friends. Or, Ten Conversations with Margaret Fuller upon the Mythology of the Greeks and Its Expression in Art.* Boston: Roberts Bros., 1895.

Dalzel, Andrew, ed. *ΑΝΑΛΕΚΤΑ ʹΕΛΛΗΝΙΚΑ ΜΕΙΖΟΝΑ, sive Collectanea Graeca Majora: ad usum Academicae Juventutis Accomodata. Cum Notis Philologicis: quas Partim Collegit, Partim Scripsit Andreas Dalzel.* 2 vols. Cambridge, Mass.: G. Hilliard, 1808.

Davidson, Cathy. *Revolution and the Word: The Rise of the Novel in America.* New York: Oxford Univ. Press, 1986.

Davis, Herbert. "The Augustan Conception of History." In *Reason and the Imagination: Studies in the History of Ideas 1600–1800,* edited by J. A. Mazzeo, 213–29. New York: Columbia Univ. Press, 1962.

Davis, John. *The Landscape of Belief: Encountering the Holy Land in Nineteenth-Century American Art and Culture.* Princeton: Princeton Univ. Press, 1996.

Davis, Natalie Zemon. "Gender and Genre: Women as Historical Writers, 1400–1820." In *Beyond Their Sex: Learned Women of the European Past,* edited by Patricia LaBalme, 153–82. New York: New York Univ. Press, 1980.

Davis, Richard Beale. *A Colonial Southern Bookshelf: Reading in the Eighteenth Century.* Athens: Univ. of Georgia Press, 1979.

Davis, Samuel. "Fine Arts in the South." *Southern Literary Messenger* 34 (December 1862): 657–61.

Day, Jeremiah, and James Luce Kingsley. "Original Papers in Relation to a Course of Liberal Education." *American Journal of Science and Arts* 15 (January 1829): 297–351.

DeBow, James. "The Commercial Age." *DeBow's Review* 7 (September 1849): 225–39.

Description of the View of Athens and the Surrounding Country; With an Improved Explanation, Giving a Complete Outline of the Whole Picture, with Numbers and References. Cambridge, Mass.: Metcalf, Keith, & Nichols, 1842.

Dewey, John. *John Dewey.* Vol. 1, *The Early Works, 1882–1898.* Edited by Jo Ann Boydston et al. Carbondale: Southern Illinois Univ. Press, 1969.

Diehl, Carl. *Americans and German Scholarship, 1770–1870.* New Haven: Yale Univ. Press, 1978.

DiMaggio, Paul. "Cultural Entrepreneurship in Nineteenth-Century Boston: The Creation of an Organizational Base for High Culture in America." *Media, Culture, and Society* 4 (1982): 33–50.

———. "Cultural Entrepreneurship in Nineteenth-Century Boston, Part II: The Classification and Framing of American Art." *Media, Culture, and Society* 4 (1982): 303–22.

Dinsmoor, William B. "Early American Studies of Mediterranean Archaeology." *Proceedings of the American Philosophical Society* 87 (July 1943): 70–104.

Donald, David Herbert. *Lincoln.* New York: Simon & Schuster, 1995.

D'Ooge, Martin L. *Catalogue of the Gallery of Art and Archaeology in the University of Michigan.* Ann Arbor: The University, 1906.

Dort, Anne V. "The Archaeological Institute of America—Early Days." *Archaeology* 7 (December 1954): 195–201.

Dover, K. J. "Expurgation of Greek Literature." In *The Greeks and Their Legacy: Collected Papers.* Vol. 2, *Prose Literature, History, Society, Transmission, Influence,* 270–91. Oxford: Basil Blackwell, 1988.

Drisler, Henry. *Charles Anthon, L.L.D., Late Jay-Professor of the Greek Language and Literature in Columbia College: A Commemorative Discourse Prepared and Delivered at the Request of the Trustees and Alumni of the College.* New York: Van Nostrand, 1868.

D.S.G.C. "Modern Oratory." *Southern Literary Messenger* 18 (June 1852): 370–75.

Durrill, Wayne K. "The Power of Ancient Words: Classical Scholarship and Social Change at South Carolina College, 1804–1860." *Journal of Southern History* 65 (1999): 469–98.

Dyson, Stephen L. *Ancient Marbles to American Shores: Classical Archaeology in the United States.* Philadelphia: Univ. of Pennsylvania Press, 1998.

Eadie, John W., ed. *Classical Traditions in Early America.* Ann Arbor: Center for Coördination of Ancient and Modern Studies, 1976.

"Editorial: Enrolment in High-School Studies." *Classical Journal* 8 (1913): 317–21.

Eggert, C. A. "A Plea for Modern Languages." *North American Review* 138 (1884): 374–82.

Eisner, Robert. *Travelers to an Antique Land: The History and Literature of Travel to Greece.* Ann Arbor: Univ. of Michigan Press, 1991.

Eliot, Charles William. "The Function of Education in Democratic Society." In *Charles W. Eliot and Popular Education,* edited by Edward A. Krug, 103–16. New York: Teachers College Press, 1961.

———. "What Is a Liberal Education?" *Century* 28 (1884): 203–12.

Emerson, Edward Waldo. *The Early Years of the Saturday Club, 1855–1870.* Boston: Houghton Mifflin, 1918.

Emerson, Ralph Waldo. *Complete Works.* Vol. 1, *Nature, Addresses, and Lectures.* Cambridge, Mass.: Riverside, 1883.

———. "Plato; Or, the Philosopher." In *Essays and Representative Men,* 388–419. 1850. Reprint. London: Clear-Type, 1900.

Erskine, John. *The Private Life of Helen of Troy.* Indianapolis: Bobbs-Merrill, 1925.

Everett, Edward. *Addresses at the Inauguration of the Hon. Edward Everett, LL.D., as President of the University at Cambridge, Thursday, April 30, 1846.* Boston: Charles C. Little & James Brown, 1846.

———. "Circumstances Favorable to the Progress of Literature in America." In *American Philosophic Addresses, 1700–1900,* edited by Joseph Blau, 64–93. New York: Columbia Univ. Press, 1946.

———. *Greek Grammar, Principally Abridged from that of Buttmann, for the Use of Schools.* 1822. Reprint. Boston: Cummings, Hilliard, 1826.

——. "The History of Grecian Art." *North American Review* 12 (1821): 178–98.

——, ed. *The Greek Reader, by Frederic Jacobs, Adapted to the Translation of Buttmann's Greek Grammar.* Boston: Oliver Everett, 1823.

Exercises at the Unveiling of the Monument Erected in Memory of Henry Simmons Frieze. Ann Arbor, 1899.

Faberman, Hilarie. *Illustrated Catalogue of European and American Painting and Sculpture.* Ann Arbor: The University of Michigan Museum of Art, 1988.

Farnham, Christie Anne. *The Education of the Southern Belle: Higher Education and Student Socialization in the Antebellum South.* New York: New York Univ. Press, 1994.

Farrand, Elizabeth. *History of the University of Michigan.* Ann Arbor: Register, 1885.

Farrar, F. W. *Essays on a Liberal Education.* London: Macmillan, 1867.

Faust, Drew Gilpin, ed. *The Ideology of Slavery: Proslavery Thought in the Antebellum South, 1830–1860.* Baton Rouge: Louisiana State Univ. Press, 1981.

——. *Mothers of Invention: Women of the Slaveholding South in the American Civil War.* Chapel Hill: Univ. of North Carolina Press, 1996.

Felton, Cornelius Conway. *An Address Delivered at the Dedication of the New Building of Bristol Academy in Taunton, August 25, 1852.* Cambridge, Mass.: Metcalf, 1852.

——. *An Address Delivered before the Association of the Alumni of Harvard College, July 20, 1854.* Cambridge, Mass.: John Bartlett, 1854.

——. *An Address Pronounced August 15, 1828, at the Close of the Second Term of the Livingston County High School, Temple Hill, Geneseo, New York.* Cambridge, Mass.: Hilliard, Metcalf, 1828.

——. *An Address Pronounced on the Anniversary of the Concord Lyceum, November 4, 1829.* Cambridge, Mass.: Hilliard & Brown, 1829.

——. "The Alcestis of Euripides." *North American Review* 42 (1836): 369–88.

——. "Antiquities, Biography, and Mythology." *North American Review* 70 (1850): 424–33.

——. *The Birds of Aristophanes. With Notes, and a Metrical Table.* Cambridge, Mass.: John Bartlett, 1849.

——. "Bode's *History of Greek Poetry.*" *North American Review* 50 (1840): 461–69.

——. "Boston Public Schools." *North American Review* 66 (1848): 446–58.

——. "Classical Learning in England." *North American Review* 54 (1842): 269–83.

——. "Classic Mythology." *North American Review* 41 (1835): 327–48.

——. *A Discourse Pronounced at the Inauguration of the Author as Eliot Professor of Greek Literature in Harvard University, August 26, 1834.* Cambridge, Mass.: James Munroe, 1834.

——. *Greece: Ancient and Modern: Lectures Delivered before the Lowell Institute.* 2 vols. Boston: Ticknor & Fields, 1867.

——. "Greek Language and Literature." *North American Review* 42 (1836): 94–116.

——. *A Lecture on Classical Learning, Delivered before the Convention of Teachers, and Other Friends of Education, Assembled to Form the American Institute of Instruction, August 20, 1830.* Boston: Hilliard, Gray, Little, & Wilkins, 1831.

———. *A Memorial of the Rev. John Snelling Popkin, D.D.* Cambridge, Mass.: John Bartlett, 1852.

———, ed. *The Agamemnon of Aeschylus, with Notes.* Boston: James Munroe, 1847.

———. *The Clouds of Aristophanes. With Notes.* Cambridge, Mass.: John Owen, 1841.

———. *The Iliad of Homer, from the Text of Wolf. With English Notes.* Rev. ed. Boston: James Munroe, 1848.

———. *The Iliad of Homer, from the Text of Wolf. With English Notes and Flaxman's Illustrative Designs.* Boston: Hilliard, Gray, 1833.

"Felton's *Memorial of Dr. Popkin.*" *North American Review* 75 (1852): 473–88.

Ferguson, Adam. *Essay on the History of Civil Society.* 1767. Reprint. Edinburgh: Univ. Press of Edinburgh, 1966.

Ferguson, Robert A. *Law and Letters in American Culture.* Cambridge: Harvard Univ. Press, 1984.

Fiering, Norman. *Moral Philosophy at Seventeenth-Century Harvard: A Discipline in Transition.* Chapel Hill: Univ. of North Carolina Press, 1981.

Finkelstein, Martin. "From Tutor to Specialized Scholar." *History of Higher Education Annual* 3 (1983): 99–121.

Fisher, George Park. "The Study of Greek." *Princeton Review* 13 (January–June 1884): 111–26.

Fisher, H. M. "On the Priority of Greek Studies." *North American Review* 11 (1820): 209–18.

Fleming, E. McClung. "From Indian Princess to Greek Goddess: The American Image, 1783–1815." *Winterthur Portfolio* 3 (1966): 37–66.

Foerster, Norman. *Humanism and America: Essays on the Outlook of Modern Civilisation.* New York: Farrar & Rinehart, 1930.

Fowler, Harold North, and James Rignall Wheeler. *A Handbook of Greek Archaeology.* New York: American Book Co., 1909.

Fowler, R. "'On Not Knowing Greek': The Classics and the Woman of Letters." *Classical Journal* 78 (1983): 337–49.

Frieze, Henry Simmons. "Art Museums and Their Connection with Public Libraries." In *Public Libraries in the United States of America: Their History, Condition, and Management,* by United States Office of Education, 434–44. Washington, D.C.: Government Printing Office, 1876.

———. *Catalogue of the Museum of Art and History in the University of Michigan.* Ann Arbor: The University, 1876.

———. *Descriptive Catalogue of the Museum of Art and Antiquities in the University of Michigan.* Ann Arbor: E. B. Pond, 1858.

———. "Relations of the State University to Religion." *Commencement Annual of the University of Michigan* 7 (29 June 1887): 21–51.

Frost, William. "Greek among Required Studies." *Bibliotheca Sacra* 42 (April 1885): 327–50.

Frothingham, Paul R. *Edward Everett, Orator and Statesman.* Boston: Houghton Mifflin, 1925.

Fustel de Coulanges, Numa-Denis. *The Ancient City: A Study on the Religion, Laws, and Institutions of Greece and Rome.* Translated by Willard Small. Boston: Lothrop, Lee & Shepard, 1873.

Geiger, Roger L., and Julie Ann Bubolz. "College as It Was in the Mid-Nineteenth Century." *History of Higher Education Annual* 16 (1996): 105–15.

Gelles, Edith Belle. *Portia: The World of Abigail Adams.* Bloomington: Indiana Univ. Press, 1992.

General Education in a Free Society: Report of the Harvard Committee. Cambridge: Harvard Univ. Press, 1945.

Gerould, Katherine Fullerton. "What, Then, Is Culture?" In *Essays of the Past and Present,* edited by Warner Taylor, 537–47. New York: Harper & Bros., 1927.

Gildersleeve, Basil Lanneau. "Classical Study." *New Eclectic Magazine,* October 1869, 385–94.

———. *Essays and Studies Educational and Literary.* 1890. New York: Johnson Reprint Corp., 1960.

———. *The Letters of Basil Lanneau Gildersleeve.* Edited by Ward W. Briggs Jr. Baltimore: Johns Hopkins Univ. Press, 1987.

———, ed. *Pindar. The Olympian and Pythian Odes, with an Introductory Essay, Notes, and Indexes.* New York: Harper & Bros., 1885.

Glucker, John. "The Two Platos in Victorian Britain." In *Polyhistor: Studies in the History and Historiography of Ancient Philosophy,* edited by Keimpe A. Algra, Pieter W. van der Horst, and David T. Runia, 385–406. Leiden: E. J. Brill, 1996.

Goldgar, Anne. *Impolite Learning: Conduct and Community in the Republic of Letters, 1680–1750.* New Haven: Yale Univ. Press, 1995.

Goodwin, Pamela Helen. "Medea." *Ladies Repository* 1 (April 1875): 326–34.

———. "Shakespeare's Cordelia." *Ladies Repository* 2 (September 1875): 193–203.

Goodwin, William Watson. "The Growth of the Graduate School." *Harvard Graduates' Magazine* 9 (December 1900): 169–79.

———. *Report of the Director of the American School of Classical Studies at Athens for the Year 1882–'83.* Washington, D.C.: Government Printing Office, 1884.

———. *Syntax of the Moods and Tenses of the Greek Verb.* Cambridge, Mass.: Sever & Francis, 1860.

Goring, Elizabeth. *A Mischievous Pastime: Digging in Cyprus in the Nineteenth Century.* Edinburgh: National Museums of Scotland, 1988.

Graff, Gerald. *Professing Literature: An Institutional History.* Chicago: Univ. of Chicago Press, 1987.

Grafton, Anthony. *Defenders of the Text: The Traditions of Scholarship in an Age of Science, 1450–1800.* Cambridge: Harvard Univ. Press, 1991.

Grafton, Anthony, and Lisa Jardine. *From Humanism to the Humanities: Education and the Liberal Arts in Fifteenth- and Sixteenth-Century Europe.* Cambridge: Harvard Univ. Press, 1986.

Grasso, Christopher. *A Speaking Aristocracy: Transforming Public Discourse in Eighteenth-Century Connecticut.* Chapel Hill: Univ. of North Carolina Press, 1999.

Gray, J. C. "Demosthenes." *North American Review* 22 (1826): 34–52.

The Grecian Wreath of Victory. New York: W. E. Dean, 1824.

"Greek Revolution." *American Quarterly Review* 5 (March 1829): 99–117.

Greven, Philip. *The Protestant Temperament: Patterns of Child-Rearing, Religious Experience, and the Self in Early America.* Chicago: Univ. of Chicago Press, 1977.

Gribbin, William. "Rollin's Histories and American Republicanism." *William and Mary Quarterly* 29 (October 1972): 611–22.

Grimké, Thomas Smith. *Reflections on the Character and Objects of All Science and Literature, and on the Relative Excellence and Value of Religious and Secular Education, and of Sacred and Classical Literature in Two Addresses and an Oration with Additions and Improvements.* New Haven: Hezekiah Howe, 1831.

Guide to the Cesnola Collection. New York: Willard Felt, 1875.

Gummere, Richard. *The American Colonial Mind and the Classical Tradition: Essays in Comparative Culture.* Cambridge: Harvard Univ. Press, 1963.

Guyot, Arnold. *The Earth and Man. Lectures on Comparative Physical Geography, In Its Relation to the History of Mankind.* Translated by Cornelius Conway Felton. 1849. Reprint. New York: Scribner, Armstrong, 1874.

H. "The Athenian Orators." *Southern Quarterly Review* 4 (October 1851): 352–89.

Hadley, James. *Diary of James Hadley, 1843–1872, Tutor and Professor of Greek in Yale College, 1845–1872.* Edited by Laura Hadley Moseley. New Haven: Yale Univ. Press, 1951.

Hadley, James, et al. "Discussion of, Are the Degrees of Bachelor of Science, Bachelor of Philosophy, and Bachelor of Letters to be Preserved or to Be Merged in the Degree of Bachelor of Arts?" *Association of American Universities, Journal of Proceedings of the Annual Conferences, Fifth Annual Conference,* 1903–4, 74–82.

Hale, William Gardner. *Aims and Methods of Classical Study.* Boston: Ginn, 1887.

Hall, Benjamin Homer. *A Collection of College Words and Customs.* Cambridge, Mass.: John Bartlett, 1856.

Hamlin, Charles E. "The Attitude of the Christian Teacher in Respect to Science." *Baptist Quarterly* 6 (1872): 1–29.

Hammond, William Gardiner. *Remembrance of Amherst: An Undergraduate's Diary, 1846–1848.* Edited by George F. Whicher. New York: Columbia Univ. Press, 1946.

Hansen, Victor David, and John Heath. *Who Killed Homer? The Demise of Classical Education and the Recovery of Greek Wisdom.* New York: Free Press, 1998.

Harding, Thomas S. *College Literary Societies: Their Contribution to Higher Education in the United States, 1815–1876.* New York: Pageant Press International, 1971.

Harrington, J. Drew. "Classical Antiquity and the Proslavery Argument." *Slavery and Abolition* 10 (May 1989): 60–72.

Harris, Neil. "The Gilded Age Revisited: Boston and the Museum Movement." *American Quarterly* 14 (winter 1962): 545–66.

Harris, William Torrey. "On the Function of the Study of Latin and Greek in American Education." *Journal of Social Science* 20 (1885): 1–13.

Harrison, Jane Ellen. *Prolegomena to the Study of Greek Religion*. 3d ed. Cambridge: Cambridge Univ. Press, 1922.

———. *The Religion of Ancient Greece*. London: Archibald Constable, 1905.

Haskell, Francis. *History and Its Images: Art and the Interpretation of the Past*. New Haven: Yale Univ. Press, 1993.

Haskell, Francis, and Nicholas Penny. *Taste and the Antique: The Lure of Classical Sculpture, 1500–1900*. New Haven: Yale Univ. Press, 1981.

Haskell, Thomas, ed. *The Authority of Experts: Studies in History and Theory*. Bloomington: Indiana Univ. Press, 1984.

Herbst, Jürgen. *The German Historical School in American Scholarship: A Study in the Transfer of Culture*. Ithaca: Cornell Univ. Press, 1965.

Hicks, Edward L. *A Manual of Greek Historical Inscriptions*. Oxford: Clarendon, 1882.

Higginson, Thomas Wentworth. "A Plea for Culture." *Atlantic Monthly* 19 (January 1867): 29–37.

Hillard, George S. "Memoir of Cornelius Conway Felton, L.L.D." *Proceedings of the Massachusetts Historical Society* 10 (1868): 352–68.

Hinsdale, Burke A. *History of the University of Michigan*. Edited by Isaac N. Demmon. Ann Arbor: The University, 1906.

Hirsch, E. D. *Cultural Literacy: What Every American Needs to Know*. Boston: Houghton Mifflin, 1987.

A History of Columbia University, 1754–1894. New York: Columbia Univ. Press, 1904.

Hoeveler, J. David, Jr. *The New Humanism: A Critique of Modern America, 1900–1940*. Charlottesville: Univ. Press of Virginia, 1977.

Hofstadter, Richard. *Anti-Intellectualism in American Life*. New York: Knopf, 1963.

Hofstadter, Richard, and Walter Metzger. *The Development of Academic Freedom in the United States*. New York: Columbia Univ. Press, 1955.

Hofstadter, Richard, and Wilson Smith, eds. *American Higher Education: A Documentary History*. 2 vols. Chicago: Univ. of Chicago Press, 1961.

Holmes, George Frederick. "Four New Addresses." *Southern Literary Messenger* 15 (May 1849): 280–89.

———. "Observations on a Passage in the Politics of Aristotle Relative to Slavery." *Southern Literary Messenger* 16 (April 1850): 193–205.

"Homeric Poems." *American Quarterly Review* 4 (December 1827): 307–37.

"The Homeric Question." *North American Review* 70 (1850): 387–407.

Hopkinson, Francis. "A New Plan of Education" (1775). In *Comical Spirit of Seventy-Six: The Humor of Francis Hopkinson*, edited by Paul M. Zall, 59–63. San Marino, Calif.: Huntington Library, 1976.

Horowitz, Helen Lefkowitz. *Campus Life: Undergraduate Cultures from the End of the Eighteenth Century to the Present*. New York: Knopf, 1987.

———. *Culture and the City: Cultural Philanthropy in Chicago from the 1880s to 1917*. Lexington: Univ. Press of Kentucky, 1976.

———. *The Power and Passion of M. Carey Thomas*. New York: Knopf, 1994.

Horsman, Reginald. *Race and Manifest Destiny: The Origins of American Racial Anglo-Saxonism.* Cambridge: Harvard Univ. Press, 1981.

Hovencamp, Herbert. *Science and Religion in America, 1800–1860.* Philadelphia: University of Pennsylvania Press, 1978.

Howe, Bea. *Antiques from the Victorian Home.* New York: Charles Scribner's Sons, 1973.

Howe, Daniel Walker. *Making the American Self: Jonathan Edwards to Abraham Lincoln.* Cambridge: Harvard Univ. Press, 1997.

———. *The Political Culture of the American Whigs.* Chicago: Univ. of Chicago Press, 1979.

———. *The Unitarian Conscience: Harvard Moral Philosophy, 1805–1861.* 2d ed. Middletown, Conn.: Wesleyan Univ. Press, 1988.

Humphreys, E. R. "Common-Sense in Classics." *Education,* January 1881, 444–51

Hutcheson, Maud Macdonald. "Mercy Warren, 1728–1814." *William and Mary Quarterly* 10 (July 1953): 378–402.

Ibbotson, Joseph D., ed. *Documentary History of Hamilton College.* Clinton, N.Y.: Hamilton College, 1922.

Jaeger, Werner. *Paideia: The Ideals of Greek Culture.* Translated by Gilbert Highet. 3 vols. Oxford: Basil Blackwell, 1939.

Jay, Eric G. *New Testament Greek: An Introductory Grammar.* London: S.P.C.K., 1987.

Jenkyns, Richard. *Dignity and Decadence: Victorian Art and the Classical Inheritance.* Cambridge: Harvard Univ. Press, 1992.

———. *The Victorians and Ancient Greece.* Oxford: Basil Blackwell, 1980.

J.W.M. "The Danger and Safety of the Republic." *Southern Quarterly Review* 14 (July 1848): 150–69.

Kammen, Michael. "From Liberty to Prosperity: Reflections upon the Role of Revolutionary Iconography in National Tradition." *Proceedings of the American Antiquarian Society* 86, pt. 2 (1976): 237–72.

Kane, Joseph Nathan, and Gerald L. Alexander. *Nicknames and Sobriquets of U.S. Cities and States.* Metuchen, N.J.: Scarecrow, 1970.

Kasson, John F. *Rudeness and Civility: Manners in Nineteenth-Century America.* New York: Hill & Wang, 1990.

Kelley, Brooks M. *Yale: A History.* New Haven: Yale Univ. Press, 1974.

Kelley, Mary. "Reading Women/Women Reading: The Making of Learned Women in Antebellum America." *Journal of American History* 83 (1996): 401–24.

Kelly, Catherine. *In the New England Fashion: Reshaping Women's Lives in the Nineteenth Century.* Ithaca: Cornell Univ. Press, 1999.

Kelsey, Francis Willey. "Is There a Science of Classical Philology?" *Classical Philology* 3 (October 1908): 369–85.

———, ed. *Latin and Greek in American Education: With Symposia on the Value of Humanistic Studies.* New York: Macmillan, 1927.

Kennon, Donald R., ed. *A Republic for the Ages: The United States Capitol and the Political Culture of the Early Republic.* Charlottesville: Univ. Press of Virginia, 1999.

Kerber, Linda. *Federalists in Dissent: Imagery and Ideology in Jeffersonian America.* Ithaca: Cornell Univ. Press, 1970.

———. *Women of the Republic: Intellect and Ideology in Revolutionary America.* Chapel Hill: Univ. of North Carolina Press, 1980.

Kernan, Alvin, ed. *What's Happened to the Humanities?* Princeton: Princeton Univ. Press, 1997.

Kimball, Bruce. *Orators and Philosophers: A History of the Idea of Liberal Education.* New York: Teachers College, Columbia University, 1986.

———. *The "True Professional Ideal" in America: A History.* Cambridge, Mass.: Blackwell, 1992.

Kingsley, James Luce. *A Sketch of the History of Yale College.* Boston: Perkins, Marvin, 1835.

Knight, Edgar, ed. *A Documentary History of Education in the South before 1860.* 5 vols. Chapel Hill: Univ. of North Carolina Press, 1949–53.

Knox, Bernard. Introduction to *The Odyssey,* by Homer, translated by Robert Fagles. New York: Viking, 1996.

Kuklick, Bruce. "The Emergence of the Humanities." *South Atlantic Quarterly* 81 (1990): 194–206.

———. *Puritans in Babylon: The Ancient Near East and American Intellectual Life, 1880–1930.* Princeton: Princeton Univ. Press, 1996.

———. *The Rise of American Philosophy: Cambridge, Massachusetts, 1860–1930.* New Haven: Yale Univ. Press, 1977.

Kuzniewski, Anthony J. *Thy Honored Name: A History of the College of the Holy Cross, 1843–1994.* Washington, D.C.: Catholic Univ. of America Press, 1999.

LaBorde, Maximilian. *History of the South Carolina College.* Charleston, S.C.: Walker, Evans, & Cogswell, 1874.

LaFleur, Richard. *"Latina Resurgens:* Classical Language Enrollments in American Schools and Colleges." *Classical Outlook* 74 (summer 1997): 125–30.

Lamberton, Robert. *Homer the Theologian: Neoplatonist Allegorical Reading and the Growth of the Epic Tradition.* Berkeley and Los Angeles: Univ. of California Press, 1986.

Lane, George Martin. "German Universities." *North American Review* 96 (1863): 447–66.

Larrabee, Stephen. *Hellas Observed: The American Experience of Greece, 1775–1865.* New York: New York Univ. Press, 1957.

Latimer, John Francis. *What's Happened to Our High Schools?* Washington, D.C.: Public Affairs, 1929.

Lavin, Marilyn A. *The Eye of the Tiger: The Founding and Development of the Department of Art and Archaeology, 1883–1923, Princeton University.* Princeton: Department of Art and Archaeology & the Art Museum, Princeton University, 1983.

Lears, T. Jackson. *No Place of Grace: Antimodernism and the Transformation of American Culture, 1880–1920.* New York: Pantheon, 1981.

Le cinquantenaire de L'École française d'Athènes, célébré à Athènes les 16, 17, 18 avril 1898. Athens: Imprimerie Perris Frères, 1899.

Lefkowitz, Mary R. *Heroines and Hysterics.* New York: St. Martin's, 1981.

———. *Not Out of Africa: How Afrocentrism Became an Excuse to Teach Myth as History.* New York: Basic Books, 1996.

Lefkowitz, Mary R., and Guy MacLean Rogers, eds. *Black Athena Revisited.* Chapel Hill: Univ. of North Carolina Press, 1996.

Legaré, Hugh Swinton. *Writings of Hugh Swinton Legaré.* Edited by Mary Legaré. 2 vols. Charleston, S.C.: Burges & James, 1846.

Leppmann, Wolfgang. *Winckelmann.* New York: Knopf, 1970.

Levine, Joseph. *The Battle of the Books: History and Literature in the Augustan Age.* Ithaca: Cornell Univ. Press, 1991.

Levine, Lawrence. *Highbrow/Lowbrow: The Emergence of Cultural Hierarchy in America.* Cambridge: Harvard Univ. Press, 1988.

———. *The Opening of the American Mind: Canons, Culture, and History.* Boston: Beacon, 1996.

Lewis, Tayler. "Classical Criticism." *Knickerbocker* 30 (September 1847): 246–56.

———. "Jowett's Plato." *Princeton Review* 1 (January 1872): 137–59.

Litto, Frederic M. "Addison's *Cato* in the Colonies." *William and Mary Quarterly* 23 (July 1966): 431–49.

Locke, John. *Educational Writings of John Locke.* Edited by James Axtell. London: Cambridge Univ. Press, 1968.

Lord, Louis. *A History of the American School of Classical Studies at Athens, 1882–1942.* Cambridge: Harvard Univ. Press, 1947.

Lounsbury, Richard. "*Ludibria Rerum Mortalium:* Charlestonian Intellectuals and Their Classics." In *Intellectual Life in Antebellum Charleston,* edited by Michael O'Brien and David Moltke-Hansen, 325–69. Knoxville: Univ. of Tennessee Press, 1986.

MacCormack, Sabine. "Limits of Understanding: Perceptions of Greco-Roman and Amerindian Paganism in Early Modern Europe." In *America in European Consciousness, 1493–1750,* edited by Karen Ordahl Kupperman, 79–129. Chapel Hill: Univ. of North Carolina Press, 1995.

Mack, Charles R., and Lynn Robertston, eds. *The Roman Remains: John Izard Middleton's Visual Souvenirs of 1820–1823, with Additional Views in Italy, France, and Switzerland.* Charleston: Univ. of South Carolina Press, 1997.

MacLean, John. *History of the College of New Jersey, from Its Origins in 1746 to the Commencement of 1854.* Philadelphia: J. B. Lippincott, 1877.

Manatt, Irving, and Chrestos Tsountas. *The Mycenaean Age: A Study of the Monuments and Culture of Pre-Homeric Greece.* Boston: Houghton Mifflin, 1897.

Marambaud, Pierre. *William Byrd of Westover, 1674–1744.* Charlottesville: Univ. Press of Virginia, 1971.

Marchand, Suzanne. *Down from Olympus: Archaeology and Philhellenism in Germany, 1750–1970.* Princeton: Princeton Univ. Press, 1996.

Marsden, George. *The Soul of the American University: From Protestant Establishment to Established Nonbelief.* New York: Oxford Univ. Press, 1994.

Martin, Theodora Penny. *The Sound of Our Own Voices: Women's Study Clubs, 1860–1910.* Boston: Beacon, 1987.

Matthiessen, F. O. *American Renaissance: Art and Expression in the Age of Emerson and Whitman.* 1941. Reprint. New York: Oxford Univ. Press, 1968.

Mavrogenes, Nancy. "The Teaching of Greek and Latin According to Francis Parker and John Dewey." *Classical Outlook* 60 (October–November 1982): 3–6.

McCardell, John. *The Idea of a Southern Nation: Southern Nationalists and Southern Nationalism, 1830–1860.* New York: Norton, 1979.

McCaughey, Robert. "The Transformation of American Academic Life: Harvard University, 1821–1892." *Perspectives in American History* 8 (1974): 239–332.

McCoy, Drew. *The Elusive Republic: Political Economy in Jeffersonian America.* Chapel Hill: Univ. of North Carolina Press, 1980.

McFadden, Elizabeth. *The Glitter and the Gold: A Spirited Account of the Metropolitan Museum of Art's First Director, the Audacious and High-Handed Luigi Palma di Cesnola.* New York: Dial, 1971.

McLachlan, James. "The American College in the Nineteenth Century: Toward a Reappraisal." *Teachers College Record* 80 (1978): 287–306.

———. "The *Choice of Hercules:* American Student Societies in the Early Nineteenth Century." In *The University in Society,* edited by Lawrence Stone, vol. 2, *Europe, Scotland, and the United States from the Sixteenth to the Twentieth Century,* 449–94. Princeton: Princeton Univ. Press, 1974.

———. "Classical Names, American Identities: Some Notes on College Students and the Classical Tradition in the 1770s." In *Classical Traditions in Early America: Essays,* edited by John W. Eadie, 81–95. Ann Arbor: Center for Coördination of Ancient and Modern Studies, 1976.

McNeal, R. A., ed. *Nicholas Biddle in Greece: The Journals and Letters of 1806.* University Park: Pennsylvania State Univ. Press, 1993.

Meritt, Lucy Shoe. *History of the American School of Classical Studies at Athens, 1939–1980.* Princeton: American School of Classical Studies at Athens, 1984.

Middlekauff, Robert. *Ancients and Axioms: Secondary Education in Eighteenth-Century New England.* New Haven: Yale Univ. Press, 1963.

Middleton, John Izard. *Grecian Remains in Italy, a Description of Cyclopian Walls, and of Roman Antiquities. With Topographical and Picturesque Views of Ancient Latium.* London: Edward Orme, 1812.

Miles, Edwin. "The Old South and the Classical World." *North Carolina Historical Review* 48 (1971): 258–75.

——— "The Whig Party and the Menace of Caesar." *Tennessee Historical Quarterly* 27 (1968): 361–79.

———. "The Young American Nation and the Classical World." *Journal of the History of Ideas* 35 (1974): 254–74.

Miller, Perry. *The New England Mind: The Seventeenth Century.* Cambridge: Harvard Univ. Press, 1954.

Miller, Samuel. *A Brief Retrospect of the Eighteenth Century.* 2 vols. New York: Burt Frank-lin, 1803.

———. *Memoir of the Rev. Charles Nisbet, D.D., Late President of Dickinson College, Carlisle.* New York: Robert Carter, 1840.

Momigliano, Arnaldo. "Ancient History and the Antiquarian." *Journal of the Warburg and Courtauld Institutes* 13 (1950): 285–313.

Mondello, Salvatore. *The Private Papers of John Vanderlyn (1775–1852), American Portrait Painter.* Lampeter, Wales: Edwin Mellen, 1990.

Moore, F. G. "A History of the American Philological Association." *Transactions of the American Philological Association* 50 (1919): 5–32.

Morgan, Edmund S. *Virginians at Home: Family Life in the Eighteenth Century.* Williams-burg, Va.: Colonial Williamsburg, 1952.

Morison, Samuel Eliot. *The Development of Harvard University since the Inauguration of President Eliot, 1869–1929.* Cambridge: Harvard Univ. Press, 1930.

———. *The Founding of Harvard College.* Cambridge: Harvard Univ. Press, 1963.

———. *Harvard College in the Seventeenth Century.* 2 vols. Cambridge: Harvard Univ. Press, 1936.

———. *Three Centuries of Harvard, 1636–1936.* 5th ed. Cambridge: Harvard Univ. Press, 1946.

Murdock, Kenneth. "The Teaching of Latin and Greek at the Boston Latin School in 1712." *Publications of the Colonial Society of Massachusetts* 27 (March 1927): 21–29.

Murray, Judith Sargent. *The Gleaner.* Introduction by Nina Baym. Schenectady, N.Y.: Union College Press, 1992.

Newmyer, Stephen. "Charles Anthon: Knickerbocker Scholar." *Classical Outlook* 59 (De-cember 1981–January 1982): 41–44.

Newton, Stella Mary. *Health, Art, and Reason: Dress Reformers of the Nineteenth Century.* London: John Murray, 1974.

Nisbet, Charles. "Classical Learning." *Port Folio,* 2d ser., 4, no. 25 (1807), passim; 5, no. 1 (1808), passim.

Noll, Mark. *Princeton and the Republic, 1768–1822: The Search for a Christian Enlightenment in the Era of Samuel Stanhope Smith.* Princeton: Princeton Univ. Press, 1989.

Norlin, George. "Paul Shorey the Teacher." *Classical Philology* 29 (1934): 188–91.

Norman, Henry. *An Account of the Harvard Greek Play.* Boston: James R. Osgood, 1882.

Norton, Charles Eliot. "The First American Classical Archaeologist." *American Journal of Archaeology and of the History of the Fine Arts* 1 (1885): 3–9.

———. *Letters of Charles Eliot Norton.* Edited by M. A. DeWolfe Howe and Sara Norton. 2 vols. Boston: Houghton Mifflin, 1913.

———. "The Work of the Archaeological Institute of America: An Address." *American Journal of Archaeology* 4 (1900): 1–16.

Nye, Russel B. *The Cultural Life of the New Nation, 1776–1830.* New York: Harper & Row, 1960.

Oates, Stephen B. *With Malice toward None: The Life of Abraham Lincoln*. New York: Harper & Row, 1977.

O'Brien, Michael. *A Character of Hugh Legaré*. Knoxville: Univ. of Tennessee Press, 1985.

Olender, Maurice. *The Languages of Paradise: Race, Religion, and Philology in the Nineteenth Century*. Translated by Arthur Goldhammer. Cambridge: Harvard Univ. Press, 1992.

Oleson, Alexandra, and John Voss, eds. *The Organization of Knowledge in Modern America, 1860–1920*. Baltimore: Johns Hopkins Univ. Press, 1979.

"On Female Authorship." *Lady's Magazine and Repository of Entertaining Knowledge* 1 (1793): 69–72.

Ong, Walter. "Latin Language Study as a Renaissance Puberty Rite." *Studies in Philology* 56 (1959): 103–24.

"Otis's Rudiments of Latin Prosody." *Monthly Anthology* 5 (1808): 222–26.

Pangle, Lorraine S., and Thomas Pangle. *The Learning of Liberty: The Educational Ideas of the American Founders*. Lawrence: Univ. Press of Kansas, 1993.

Patton, Robert Bridges. *Address, Delivered before the Philological Society of Middlebury College*. Middlebury, Vt.: J. W. Copeland, 1823.

———. *A Lecture, on Classical and National Education; Delivered December 28, 1825, in the Chapel of Nassau Hall, before the Literary and Philosophical Society of New Jersey*. Princeton: D. A. Borrenstein, 1826.

———, ed. *A New Greek and English Lexicon*. Boston: Hilliard, Gray, 1833.

———. *The Seven before Thebes: A Tragedy of Aeschylus. Printed from the Text of Schütz, under the Care and Direction of the Senior Class of Nassau Hall*. Princeton: D. A. Borrenstein, 1826.

Peabody, Andrew P. *A Sermon Preached in the Appleton Chapel, March 9, 1862, Being the Sunday after the Funeral of Cornelius Conway Felton, L.L.D., President of Harvard University*. Cambridge, Mass.: Sever & Francis, 1862.

Peacock, Sandra. *Jane Ellen Harrison: The Mask and the Self*. New Haven: Yale Univ. Press, 1988.

Persons, Stow. "The Cyclical Theory of History in Eighteenth Century America." *American Quarterly* 6 (summer 1954): 147–63.

Pfeiffer, Rudolf. *History of Classical Scholarship from 1300 to 1850*. Oxford: Clarendon, 1976.

"Philology." *Port Folio*, 1st ser., 48, no. 48 (1801): 373.

Pierson, George Wilson. *A Yale Book of Numbers: Historical Statistics of the College and University, 1701–1976*. New Haven: Yale Univ. Press, 1983.

"Plato in History." *North American Review* 83 (1856): 67–84.

Pluggé, Domis. *History of Greek Play Production from 1881 to 1936*. New York: Teachers College, Columbia University, 1938.

Pocock, J. G. A. *The Machiavellian Moment: Florentine Political Thought and the Atlantic Republican Tradition*. Princeton: Princeton Univ. Press, 1975.

Poe, Edgar Allan. "To Helen." In *Complete Poems of Edgar Allan Poe*, edited by Louis Untermeyer, 60. New York: Heritage, 1943.

Popkin, John Snelling. "On the Art of Teaching." *Port Folio*, 5th ser., 5, no. 16 (1823): 313–21.

———. "On the Study of the Classics." *Port Folio*, 5th ser., 5, no. 16 (1823): 308–13.

———. "On the Use of Translations and Auxiliary Books." *Port Folio*, 5th ser., 5, no. 16 (1823): 455–61.

———. *Three Lectures on Liberal Education.* 1836. In *A Memorial of the Rev. John Snelling Popkin, D.D.*, edited by Cornelius Conway Felton, 5–73. Cambridge: John Bartlett, 1852.

Porter, Noah. "Greek and a Liberal Education." *Princeton Review* 14 (July–December 1884): 195–218.

Putnam, Emily James. "Paul Shorey." *Atlantic Monthly* 161 (1938): 795–804.

Questions upon Adam's Roman Antiquities. For the Use of the Students in Harvard College. Cambridge, Mass.: James Munroe, 1834.

Quincy, Josiah. *The History of Harvard University.* 2 vols. Cambridge, Mass.: John Owen, 1840.

Rahe, Paul. *Republics Ancient and Modern: Classical Republicanism and the American Revolution.* Chapel Hill: Univ. of North Carolina Press, 1992.

Raleigh, John Henry. *Matthew Arnold and American Culture.* Berkeley and Los Angeles: Univ. of California Press, 1961.

Rawson, Elizabeth. *The Spartan Tradition in European Thought.* Oxford: Clarendon, 1969.

"Recent Editions of the Antigone of Sophocles." *Methodist Quarterly Review*, January 1852, 96–118.

Redfield, Robert. "Social Science among the Humanities." *Measure* 1 (winter 1950): 60–74.

Reid, Ronald F. *Edward Everett: Unionist Orator.* New York: Greenwood, 1990.

Reinhold, Meyer. *Classica Americana: The Greek and Roman Heritage in the United States.* Detroit: Wayne State Univ. Press, 1984.

———, ed. *The Classick Pages: Classical Reading of Eighteenth-Century Americans.* University Park, Pa.: American Philological Association, 1975.

"The Relation of the Journal to American Archaeology." *American Journal of Archaeology* 4 (1888): 259–61.

Reuben, Julie. *The Making of the Modern University: Intellectual Transformation and the Marginalization of Morality.* Chicago: Univ. of Chicago Press, 1996.

Richard, Carl J. *The Founders and the Classics: Greece, Rome, and the American Enlightenment.* Cambridge: Harvard Univ. Press, 1994.

Roberts, Jon, and James Turner. *The Sacred and the Secular University.* Princeton: Princeton Univ. Press, 2000.

Robson, David. *Educating Republicans: The College in the Era of the American Revolution, 1750–1800.* Westport, Conn.: Greenwood, 1985.

Rogers, Anna A. *Why American Marriages Fail.* Boston: Houghton Mifflin, 1909.

Ross, Dorothy. "The Liberal Tradition Revisited and the Republican Tradition Addressed." In *New Directions in American Intellectual History,* edited by John Higham and Paul Conkin, 116–31. Baltimore: Johns Hopkins Univ. Press, 1979.

———. *The Origins of American Social Science.* Cambridge: Cambridge Univ. Press, 1991.

Rowland, Kate Mason. *The Life of George Mason, 1725–1792.* Vol. 1. New York: G. P. Putnam's Sons, 1892.

Rowson, Susanna. *A Present for Young Ladies; Containing Poems, Dialogues, Addresses, &c., &c. &c. as Recited by the Pupils of Mrs. Rowson's Academy, at the Annual Exhibitions.* Boston: John West, 1811.

Rubin, Joan Shelley. *The Making of Middlebrow Culture.* Chapel Hill: Univ. of North Carolina Press, 1992.

Rudolph, Frederick. *Curriculum: A History of the American Undergraduate Course of Study since 1636.* San Francisco: Jossey-Bass, 1977.

Ryan, Mary. *Women in Public: Between Banners and Ballots, 1825–1880.* Baltimore: Johns Hopkins Univ. Press, 1990.

Rydell, Robert W. *All the World's a Fair: Visions of Empire at American International Expositions, 1876–1916.* Chicago: Univ. of Chicago Press, 1984.

Sandys, John Edwin. *A History of Classical Scholarship.* Vol. 3, *The Eighteenth Century in Germany and the Nineteenth Century in Europe and the United States of America.* Cambridge: Cambridge Univ. Press, 1908.

Schlegel, August. *Lectures on Dramatic Art and Literature.* Rev. ed. London: G. Bell and Sons, 1894.

Schoonmaker, Marius. *John Vanderlyn, Artist, 1775–1852: A Biography.* Kingston, N.Y.: Senate House Association, 1950.

Scott, Donald M. "The Popular Lecture and the Creation of a Public in Mid-Nineteenth-Century America." *Journal of American History* 66 (1980): 791–809.

Segal, Daniel. "'Western Civ' and the Staging of History in American Higher Education." *American Historical Review* 105 (June 2000): 770–803.

Seymour, Thomas Day. *Bulletin of the School of Classical Studies Athens, 5: The First Twenty Years of the American School of Classical Studies at Athens.* Norwood, Mass.: Norwood, 1902.

Sheftel, Phoebe F. "The Archaeological Institute of America, 1879–1979: A Centennial Review." *American Journal of Archaeology* 83 (1979): 3–17.

Shelley, Percy Bysshe. "Hellas: A Lyrical Drama" (1821). In *The Complete Works of Percy Bysshe Shelley,* edited by Roger Ingpen and Walter E. Peck, 3:7–57. London: Ernest Benn, 1927.

Shields, David. *Civil Tongues and Polite Letters in British America.* Chapel Hill: Univ. of North Carolina Press, 1997.

Shipton, C. K. "Secondary Education in the Puritan Colonies." *New England Quarterly* 7 (1934): 646–61.

Shorey, Paul. "Are the Degrees of Bachelor of Science, Bachelor of Philosophy, and Bachelor of Letters to Be Preserved or to Be Merged in the Degree of Bachelor of Arts?"

Association of American Universities, Journal of Proceedings of the Annual Conferences, Fifth Annual Conference, 1903–4, 63–74.

———. *The Assault on Humanism.* Boston: Atlantic Monthly, 1917.

———. "Philology and Classical Philology." *Classical Journal* 1 (1906): 169–96.

———. *The Roosevelt Lectures of Paul Shorey (1913–1914).* Translated from the German into English with annotations by Edgar C. Reinke. Edited by Ward W. Briggs Jr. and E. Christian Kopff. Introduction by E. Christian Kopff. Hildesheim: Georg Olms Verlag, 1995.

Shteir, Ann B. *Cultivating Women, Cultivating Science: Flora's Daughters and Botany in England, 1760 to 1860.* Baltimore: Johns Hopkins Univ. Press, 1996.

Shuckburgh, E. S., ed. *The Antigone of Sophocles with a Commentary, Abridged from the Large Edition of Richard C. Jebb.* 1902. Reprint. Cambridge: Cambridge Univ. Press, 1984.

Skemp, Sheila. *Judith Sargent Murray: A Brief Biography with Documents.* New York: Bedford, 1998.

"Sketch of the Life of Homer." *Lady and Gentleman's Pocket Magazine of Literary and Polite Amusement* 1 (1796): 54–56.

Smalley, Frank. "Status of Classical Studies in Secondary Schools." *Classical Journal* 1 (1905–6): 111–19.

Smith, Bonnie. *The Gender of History: Men, Women, and Historical Practice.* Cambridge: Harvard Univ. Press, 1998.

Smith, E. Baldwin. *The Study of the History of Art in the Colleges and Universities of the United States.* Princeton, 1912.

Smith, William. *A History of Greece, from the Earliest Times to the Roman Conquest, with Supplementary Chapters on the History of Literature and Art, by William Smith, with Notes, and a Continuation to the Present Time, by C. C. Felton.* Boston: Hickling, Swan, & Brown, 1855.

Smith, Wilson, ed. *Theories of Education in Early America, 1655–1819.* Indianapolis: Bobbs-Merrill, 1973.

Smyth, Herbert Weir. *Greek Melic Poets.* New York: Macmillan, 1900.

Snyder, Martin D. "The Icon of Antiquity." In *The Usefulness of Classical Learning in the Eighteenth Century,* edited by Susan Ford Wiltshire, 27–52. N.p.: American Philological Assocation, 1977.

Snyder, Thomas, ed. *One Hundred Twenty Years of American Education: A Statistical Portrait.* Washington, D.C.: National Center for Education Statistics, 1993.

Solomon, Barbara. *In the Company of Educated Women: A History of Women and Higher Education in America.* New Haven: Yale Univ. Press, 1985.

Sproat, John G. *The Best Men: Liberal Reformers in the Gilded Age.* New York: Oxford Univ. Press, 1968.

Stameshkin, David M. *The Town's College: Middlebury College, 1800–1915.* Middlebury, Vt.: Middlebury College Press, 1985.

Stevenson, Louise. "Preparing for Public Life: The Collegiate Students at New York University 1832–1881." In *The University and the City: From Medieval Origins to the Present*, edited by Thomas Bender, 150–77. New York: Oxford Univ. Press, 1988.

——. *Scholarly Means to Evangelical Ends: The New Haven Scholars and the Transformation of Higher Learning in America, 1830–1860*. Baltimore: Johns Hopkins Univ. Press, 1986.

——. *The Victorian Homefront: American Thought and Culture, 1860–1880*. New York: Twayne, 1991.

Stillwell, Richard, ed. *The Princeton Encyclopedia of Classical Sites*. Princeton: Princeton Univ. Press, 1976.

Stocking, George W., Jr. *Race, Culture, and Evolution: Essays in the History of Anthropology*. 2d ed. Chicago: Univ. of Chicago Press, 1982.

——. *Victorian Anthropology*. New York: Free Press, 1987.

Storr, Richard. *The Beginnings of Graduate Education in America*. Chicago: Univ. of Chicago Press, 1953.

Stray, Christopher. *Classics Transformed: Schools, Universities, and Society in England, 1830–1960*. New York: Oxford Univ. Press, 1998.

Strong, Caleb. "Speech to the Massachusetts Legislature, Jan. 18, 1805." In *Patriotism and Piety, the Speeches of His Excellency Caleb Strong, Esq., to the Senate and House of Representatives of the Commonwealth of Massachusetts; with Their Answers, and Other Official Publick Papers of His Excellency, from 1800 to 1807*. Newburyport, Mass.: Edmund M. Blunt, 1808.

Stuart, Isaac. *The Oedipus Tyrannus of Sophocles: With Notes and a Critique on the Subject of the Play*. New York: Gould and Newman, 1837.

——. *On the Classical Tongues and the Advantages of their Study. An Inaugural Discourse, Pronounced before the Governor and Legislature of South Carolina*. Columbia, S.C.: A. S. Johnston, 1836.

Taylor, Charles. *Sources of the Self: The Making of the Modern Identity*. Cambridge: Harvard Univ. Press, 1989.

Taylor, Samuel H., ed. *Classical Study: Its Value Illustrated from the Writings of Eminent Scholars*. Andover, Mass.: Warren F. Draper, 1870.

T.C. [Thomas Cooper?]. "Classical Education." *Port Folio*, 4th ser., 1, no. 1 (1813): 567–82.

T.E.W. "American Classicism." *Classical Weekly*, 11 January 1908.

Thacher, Thomas A. "An Address Commemorative of Professor James L. Kingsley, Delivered in the Chapel of Yale College, October 29th, 1852." *New Englander* 10 (1852): 631–58.

Thomas, Calvin. *Culture and Service. An Address Delivered at the Sixtieth Annual Commencement of the University of Michigan*. N.p., 1904.

Thomson, Ian, and Louis Perraud. *Ten Latin Schooltexts of the Later Middle Ages*. Lewiston, N.Y.: E. Mellen, 1990.

Tolles, Frederick B. "Quaker Humanist: James Logan as a Classical Scholar." *Pennsylvania Magazine of History and Biography* 79 (1955): 415–38.

Tolley, Kim. "The Science Education of American Girls, 1784–1932." Ed.D. diss., University of California at Berkeley, 1996.

———. "Science for Ladies, Classics for Gentlemen: A Comparative Analysis of Scientific Subjects in the Curricula of Boys' and Girls' Secondary Schools in the United States, 1794–1850." *History of Education Quarterly* 36 (1996): 129–53.

Tomkins, Calvin. *Merchants and Masterpieces: The Story of the Metropolitan Museum of Art.* New York: E. P. Dutton, 1970.

Tomlinson, Everett Titsworth. "Progress in Means of Teaching the Classics." *Education,* March 1885, 400–409.

Trachtenberg, Alan. *The Incorporation of America: Culture and Society in the Gilded Age.* New York: Hill & Wang, 1982.

Traill, David. *Schliemann of Troy: Treasure and Deceit.* New York: St. Martin's, 1995.

Trautmann, Thomas. *Lewis Henry Morgan and the Invention of Kinship.* Berkeley and Los Angeles: Univ. of California Press, 1987.

———. "The Revolution in Ethnological Time." *Man* 27, no. 2 (1991): 379–97.

Trevelyan, Humphrey. *Goethe and the Greeks.* Cambridge: Cambridge Univ. Press, 1941.

Turner, Frank M. *The Greek Heritage in Victorian Britain.* New Haven: Yale Univ. Press, 1981.

———. "The Triumph of Idealism in Victorian Classical Studies." In *Contesting Cultural Authority: Essays in Victorian Intellectual Life,* 322–60. Cambridge: Cambridge Univ. Press, 1992.

Turner, James. *The Liberal Education of Charles Eliot Norton.* Baltimore: Johns Hopkins Univ. Press, 1999.

———. "Secularization and Sacralization: Speculations on Some Religious Origins of the Secular Humanities Curriculum, 1850–1900." In *The Secularization of the Academy,* edited by George Marsden and Bradley Longfield, 74–106. New York: Oxford Univ. Press, 1992.

Turner, James, and Paul Bernard. "The Prussian Road to University? German Models and the University of Michigan, 1837–c. 1895." *Rackham Reports* (University of Michigan), 1988–89, 6–52.

"Two Acts of Self-Devotion." *Littell's Living Age,* 14 June 1873, 643–60.

Tyler, William S. *History of Amherst College during its First Half Century, 1821–1871.* Springfield, Mass.: Clark W. Bryan, 1873.

———. *The Theology of the Greek Poets.* Boston: Draper & Halliday, 1867.

Valentine, Lucia, and Arthur Valentine. *The American Academy in Rome, 1894–1969.* Charlottesville: Univ. Press of Virginia, 1973.

Vance, William. *America's Rome.* Vol. 1, *Classical Rome.* New Haven: Yale Univ. Press, 1989.

Veysey, Laurence. *The Emergence of the American University.* Chicago: Univ. of Chicago Press, 1965.

Waldstein, Charles. *Essays on the Art of Pheidias.* Cambridge: Cambridge Univ. Press, 1885.

Waldstreicher, David. *In the Midst of Perpetual Fetes: The Making of American Nationalism, 1776–1820.* Chapel Hill: Univ. of North Carolina Press, 1997.

Walton, J. Michael. *Living Greek Theatre: A Handbook of Classical Performance and Modern Production.* New York: Greenwood, 1987.

Warner, Michael. *The Letters of the Republic: Publication and the Public Sphere in Eighteenth-Century America.* Cambridge: Harvard Univ. Press, 1990.

Webbe, Joseph. *Lectures and Exercises out of Cicero.* 1627. Reprint. Menston, England: Scolar Press, 1972.

Wertenbaker, Thomas Jefferson. *Princeton, 1746–1896.* Princeton: Princeton Univ. Press, 1946.

West, Andrew F., ed. *Value of the Classics.* Princeton: Princeton Univ. Press, 1917.

Westbrook, Robert. *John Dewey and American Democracy.* Ithaca: Cornell Univ. Press, 1991.

White, Andrew Dickson. *The Autobiography of Andrew Dickson White.* 2 vols. New York: Century, 1905.

———. *The Diaries of Andrew D. White.* Edited by Robert Morris Ogden. Ithaca: Cornell Univ. Press, 1959.

Whitehill, Walter M. *Museum of Fine Arts, Boston: A Centennial History.* 2 vols. Cambridge: Harvard Univ. Press, Belknap Press, 1970.

Wiesen, David S. "Ancient History and Early American Education." In *The Usefulness of Classical Learning in the Eighteenth Century,* edited by Susan Ford Wiltshire, 53–69. N.p.: American Philological Assocation, 1977.

———. "Herodotus and the Modern Debate over Race and Slavery." *The Ancient World* 3, no. 1 (1980): 3–16.

Wilamowitz-Möllendorff, Ulrich von. *History of Classical Scholarship.* Edited by Hugh Lloyd-Jones. Translated by Alan Harris. London: Duckworth, 1982.

Willard, Emma. *Advancement of Female Education: Or, A Series of Addresses, in Favor of Establishing at Athens, Greece, a Female Seminary, Especially Designed to Instruct Female Teachers.* Troy, N.Y.: Norman Tuttle, 1833.

Williams, Raymond. *Culture and Society, 1780–1950.* 1958. Reprint. New York: Columbia Univ. Press, 1983.

Wills, Garry. *Cincinnatus: George Washington and the Enlightenment.* Garden City, N.Y.: Doubleday, 1984.

———. *Lincoln at Gettysburg: The Words that Remade America.* New York: Simon & Schuster, 1992.

Wilson, James. "Classical Literature." *Port Folio,* 3d ser., 3, no. 7 (1812): 450–60.

Winterer, Caroline. "Victorian Antigone: Classicism and Women's Education in America, 1840–1900." *American Quarterly* 53 (March 2001): 70–93.

Wish, Harvey. "Aristotle, Plato, and the Mason-Dixon Line." *Journal of the History of Ideas* 10 (1949): 254–66.

Wolf, F. A. *Prolegomena to Homer, 1795.* Edited and translated by Anthony Grafton, Glenn W. Most, and James E. G. Zetzel. Princeton: Princeton Univ. Press, 1985.

Wood, Gordon S. *The Creation of the American Republic, 1776–1787.* Chapel Hill: Univ. of North Carolina Press, 1969.

———. *The Radicalism of the American Revolution.* New York: Knopf, 1992.

Woody, Thomas. *A History of Women's Education in the United States.* 2 vols. New York: Science, 1929.

Woolsey, Theodore Dwight. "Eulogy of Cornelius Conway Felton, L.L.D., & G., One of the Regents of the Smithsonian Institution." In *Annual Report of the Board of Regents of the Smithsonian Institution for 1861,* 109–16. Washington, D.C.: Government Printing Office, 1862.

———, ed. *The Alcestis of Euripides, with Notes, for the Use of Colleges in the United States.* Boston: J. Munroe, 1834.

———. *The Antigone of Sophocles, with Notes, for the Use of Colleges in the United States.* Boston: J. Munroe, 1835.

———. *The Electra of Sophocles, with Notes, for the Use of Colleges in the United States.* Boston: J. Munroe, 1837.

———. *The Prometheus Bound of Aeschylus, with Notes, for the Use of Colleges in the United States.* Boston: J. Munroe, 1837.

Wright, Ellsworth D. "Foreign-Language Requirements for the A.B. Degree." *Classical Journal* 7 (1912): 323–37.

Wright, John Henry. *An Address on the Place of Original Research in College Education . . . Read Before the National Educational Association, Department of Higher Instruction, July 14, 1882, at Saratoga, N.Y.* Boston: Alfred Mudge & Son, 1883.

———. *The College in the University and Classical Philology in the College. An Address at the Opening of the Eleventh Academic Year of the Johns Hopkins University, October 7, 1886.* Baltimore: Johns Hopkins University, 1886.

Wright, Julia McNair. *The Complete Home: An Encyclopaedia of Domestic Life and Affairs.* Philadelphia: J. C. McCurdy, 1879.

Wright, Louis B. *The First Gentlemen of Virginia: Intellectual Qualities of the Early Colonial Ruling Class.* San Marino, Calif.: Huntington Library, 1940.

Yegül, Fikret. *Gentlemen of Instinct and Breeding: Architecture at the American Academy in Rome, 1894–1940.* New York: Oxford Univ. Press, 1991.

Youmans, E. L. "The College Fetich Once More." *Popular Science Monthly* 25 (May–October 1884): 701–4.

———. *The Culture Demanded by Modern Life.* New York: D. Appleton, 1867.

Zagarri, Rosemarie. *A Woman's Dilemma: Mercy Otis Warren and the American Revolution.* Wheeling, Ill.: Harlan Davidson, 1995.

Zimmerman, Joan. "Daughters of Main Street: Culture and the Female Community at Grinnell, 1884–1917." In *Woman's Being, Woman's Place: Female Identity and Vocation in American History,* edited by Mary Kelley, 154–70. Boston: G. K. Hall, 1979.

INDEX